"A fascinating portrait of one of the twentieth century's most intriguing literary figures."

—*Hartford Courant*

"If the ultimate compliment one can make of an artist's biography is that it makes you want to revisit the [artist's] work, *Ignatius Rising* hits that mark. The story of Toole is a tragic and bittersweet tale, but there is great joy in reading of the early development of Ignatius, a character so vividly drawn he will doubtlessly outlive the infamy of his creator."

—*Seattle Times*

"*Ignatius Rising* amply describes the forces that caused Toole's life to unravel—among them an overbearing mother, a conflicted sexuality, and an inability to stomach literary rejection."

—*New York Times Book Review*

"Brilliantly follows the downward spiral of Toole's life from pampered, prodigious child to lost, hard-drinking, perhaps even schizophrenic adult."

—*Tampa Tribune*

"An oddly entertaining biography of a tormented writer and his unlikely legacy. . . . [An] engagingly told footnote to American literary history."

—*Kirkus Reviews*

Ignatius Rising

Ignatius Rising

The Life of
John Kennedy Toole

René Pol Nevils & Deborah George Hardy

Louisiana State University Press ✕ Baton Rouge

Louisiana Paperback Edition, 2005
First Printing

Designer: Amanda McDonald Scallan
Typeface: Granjon
Typesetter: Coghill Composition Co., Inc.
Printer and binder: Thomson-Shore, Inc.

People and sources consulted during the research of this book are acknowledged at the end of the text.

Library of Congress Cataloging-in-Publication Data

Nevils, René Pol.
    Ignatius rising : the life of John Kennedy Toole / René Pol Nevils and Deborah George Hardy.
        p.   cm.
    ISBN 0-8071-2680-2 (cloth)
        1. Toole, John Kennedy, 1937–1969.   2. Novelists, American—20th century—Biography.
    3. New Orleans (La.)—Biography.   I. Hardy, Deborah George.   II. Title.

PS3570.O54 Z79   2001
813′.54—dc21
[B]   00-063462

ISBN 0-8071-3059-1 (pbk.)

Our thanks to Louis Alvarez, Caroline Ancelet, Clelie Ancelet, Emile Ancelet, Terese Angwin, Nancy Bailey, Amy Nesbit Brassett, Lori DeFils, Re Divincenti, Malaika Favorite, Conor Fitzpatrick, Charles Fleming, Alvin George, Lakmali Gunawardena, Stokes Howell, Judy Kahn, Troy Mellon, Bob Mellon, Robin Patridge, Robbie Rubin, and Van Wade-Day.
    Special thanks to our families—especially Nana, Robin, Miles, Chris, and Sarah—to Maureen Hewitt, and to the excellent and good-natured midwife of this book, Nicola Mason, editor at LSU Press.

To John and Rick

But he lives on, and the wonder of him still lingers
in the world, and will continue to live!

—*Thelma Toole*

Ignatius Rising

Introduction

The old woman had read in the *Times-Picayune* that the famous writer was teaching at Loyola University for only one semester. After dogging him for weeks with letters and phone calls, she managed to trap the author in his office and begged him to read her son's manuscript. Having been pursued before by would-be authors, the writer was skillful at avoiding such situations, but Walker Percy had never encountered a force like Thelma Ducoing Toole. He could not know that she had been hurt by too many people too many times for any small slight to dampen her determination. She had always been shameless in promoting her son and felt no reservation about forcing herself on a stranger on his behalf. At seventy-five, Thelma was alone in the world with no money and little future—and she was long past using tact and patience to get what she wanted. The infirmities of old age had forced her to creep behind a walker, but her purpose remained strong and steady.

Percy complained to his wife, "This little woman is about to drive me crazy" with her talk of an undiscovered "masterpiece." When Thelma had offered to bring Percy the "great novel" written by her "genius" son, the writer asked why, if her son were such a genius, did he not come himself? When Percy received the news that Mrs. Toole's son was dead seven years and his novel had been written in the early sixties, the situation changed from annoying to creepy. As Percy later wrote, "If there was something I didn't want to do, this was surely it: to deal with the mother of a dead novelist and, worst of all, to have to deal with a manuscript that she said was 'great.'"

Late in the semester the mother appeared at Percy's office declaring that she would hang around for as long as it took to be admitted. The writer might have eluded her once more, but he decided to speak to her because Thelma's appearance "intrigued" him. Thelma looked as if she had managed to ignore an entire generation. Her appearance was one familiar to Percy from his days in Faulkner country as well as the Garden District of New Orleans. Her navy blue suit and the small purse dangling from her gloved arm denied the existence of fast-food restaurants, southern Republicans, and Valium. But it was the small, perky hat with its wisp of veil perched on Thelma's bravely blonded curls that snared him by demanding an attention that a consummate gentleman was unable to refuse. Percy found that he could not be rude to a crippled widow with a bad perm and a dead son.

On her visit to Loyola's English department, Thelma was accompanied by a small, skinny, toothless man costumed in a rough approximation of a chauffeur's getup. She did not introduce this person to Percy, referring to him only as her driver and speaking to him somewhat sternly. Told by Thelma to stay put, the elderly driver (who was, in fact, much more than that) obeyed, standing silent and anonymous near the door while she moved slowly toward Percy. She fixed very blue eyes on the writer as she balanced the heavy manuscript box on the rim of her walker.

Handing the box to Percy, she told him again what a great book it contained and assured him that upon reading it he could not help but agree with her. No doubt Percy was as intrigued with her voice as with her outfit. Thelma spoke in a theatrical manner, with rounded vowels that obscured the defining accents of New Orleans, uptown or down. Her gloved hands made graceful patterns in the air as she extracted from Percy a promise to read the book immediately and contact her with what she hoped would be good news. Then Thelma limped out of the office, trailed by her silent companion with his short-billed hat firmly pressed on thinning gray hair.

As he watched them leave, Walker Percy, prestigious man of letters and dodger of unsolicited manuscripts, probably realized that he was trussed up and oven ready. Later, no doubt recalling that moment when the smell of cooked goose hovered in the air, Percy wrote, "There was no getting out of it; only one hope remained—that I could read a few pages and that they would be bad enough for me, in good conscience, to read no farther."

The manuscript sat on his desk all day and rode home with Percy that night. Like the woman who delivered it, the book refused to be ignored. Dreading what lay ahead of him, Percy brought the manuscript into his study, and removing the smeared and stained onionskin papers from their box, he began to read *A Confederacy of Dunces* by John Kennedy Toole. Percy said at first he read "with a sinking feeling that it was not bad enough to quit, then with a prickle of interest, then a growing excitement, and finally an incredulity: surely it was not possible that it was so good." And as he read, he began to laugh, then to laugh harder, and finally to appreciate that the author's mother was right to think this a great novel. Percy later wrote that it blindsided him with its "gargantuan tumultuous human tragicomedy."

After that first reading, Percy was convinced that the novel was "a fine book." The tone, the speech, and the sense of place were so right that he asked his wife, Bunt, to read it and give him her opinion. He said nothing to give away his thoughts. This was a long-standing practice between them. He wanted his wife to come at the novel with no preconceptions and respond honestly, without worrying whether they were in agreement.

Bunt Percy went out onto the front porch and read the book straight through. When she came in, Walker could tell from her expression that she had loved it. He looked at her intently and asked, "But does it hold?" She replied that she thought it did. Walker described the novel as "pure New Orleans," and Bunt also felt that it was "an absolutely accurate picture of the city." She had not yet seen Mrs. Toole and did not know that both the author of *Confederacy* and his mother were as "pure New Orleans" as the novel.

The Tooles' story begins in that most lunatic of American cities, where a new king is crowned every year and the dead are buried aboveground. For the mother there was no finer place on earth than the Crescent City of her birth. For the son, there was no escaping New Orleans or the family he both loved and despised. After his suicide, the family dragged him back to lie in one of the famous *cities des mortes*. The living city that surrounds him adores dark humor and mystery, and Toole's vision of New Orleans thrives long after his death.

One

Gen. Jackson had a few cannon but only one mortar at the Battle of New Orleans. A sharpshooter named Jean Ducoing handled it, but good.

—*New Orleans Item*

JOHN KENNEDY is a great name for a Boston politician, but it was a star-crossed choice for Toole. The name was unlucky in that it reflected the two halves of his heritage—one of which he would be taught to disparage.

Toole's very beginning was a confusing state of affairs. He was a December baby, one of those poorly timed midwinter children born at the end and the beginning of a year. Added to that initial misfortune was the confusion over what to call the baby. The "John" he shared with his father, whose own father had also been a John. Kennedy was the name of Thelma's grandmother. At first the child was called "Kenny," then the more grown-up "Ken." In his last sad months Toole rejected both of these and reclaimed his father's name, refusing to be called by the Kennedy that was his mother's choice. It seems odd that Thelma

Toole did not include her maiden name when considering a name for her first child. The name Ducoing (pronounced *Dewcoin*) was the proudest part of Thelma's heritage. Perhaps she was saving it for a daughter, but given that Thelma was already in her late thirties when Kenny was born, a second child was, at that time, an unlikely prospect.

Attaining status in New Orleans has never had much to do with the getting of money but rather with the getting of ancestry. The best way to achieve social stature is to be born into an "old" family and to stick the ancient name somewhere on your birth certificate. Those with top billing can claim an ancestor who was hanging around the site of St. Louis Cathedral between 1718 and 1768, when the city was being settled, or at the very least one who bore arms in the swamps near Chalmette on or about January 8, 1815, during the Battle of New Orleans. This is enough to initially qualify a person as refined and cultured, though it helps to have carried on a few traditions supposedly possessed by these well-armed European forebears.

These traditions include playing any musical instrument short of a tissue-paper comb and lacing one's conversation with French. For the latter requirement a few endearments, some swear words, and half the Hail Mary will suffice. Having remained Roman Catholic for two hundred years in this most Catholic of American cities is a plus for a family. Fallen-away Catholics remain in the fold if they can visit a relative buried in one of the two St. Louis Cemeteries.

The Ducoings had the credentials to qualify them as "old" New Orleans. They were Creole, a term whose meaning has been the subject of debate since before Napoleon Bonaparte sold the Louisiana Territory to Thomas Jefferson's United States in 1803. According to New Orleans historian Gwendolyn Midlo Hall, the word may come from the Portuguese *crioulo,* a term used by early settlers when referring to people of African descent born in the New World. There are white Creoles and Creoles of color. The black Creoles are descendants of Africans whose ancestors lived in the French and Spanish settlements of the Caribbean before coming to North America. White Creoles are those New Orleanians descended from colonists of French or Spanish Louisiana. Both races of Creoles believe their heritage sets them apart from and above the late-coming Americans. Thelma Ducoing Toole took her Creole lineage seriously enough to include a reference to it in her son's baby book, which is preserved in Tulane University's Howard-Tilton Memorial Library.

The first Ducoing in New Orleans, Jean François, was born in Bordeaux, France, in 1776 before coming to colonial Louisiana in the early years of the nineteenth century. By the time Louisiana joined the Union in 1812, Ducoing was a tin smith on what is present-day Iberville Street in the French Quarter. That same year war broke out with England over maritime issues and the American westward expansion. As a businessman Ducoing had a vested interest in defending the city against the invading British. On New Year's Day, 1815, Ducoing took charge of the single heavy mortar possessed by the outgunned and outmanned United States Army.

Ducoing was wounded in the ensuing artillery duels that saw General Andrew Jackson rout the Redcoats through the swamps and out to sea. The combatants would not learn until later that a peace treaty had been signed two weeks before the fighting began.

For his part in the victory, Ducoing received the honor of a life pension from the state of Louisiana. Following the war his business thrived as the city entered a golden era of expansion and affluence. In 1837 Ducoing and his wife, Catherine Verrett (sometimes rendered *Burrett*), received a legacy of land in the newly created Faubourg Marigny. A century later, Ducoings were living on this same property, and Thelma was born in the house her great-grandfather built.

Even before the Battle of New Orleans the city had begun to outgrow the neat blocks of the Vieux Carré laid out by French engineer Adrien de Pauger in 1722 and improved by four decades of Spanish rule. By 1816, with the assurance of peace and a stable government, newcomers crowded into a city already trebled in population since its purchase from France. Many of the Tennessee volunteers who fought with Jackson settled land along the river, and new arrivals abandoned their westward plans, opting to remain in New Orleans. The colonial Caribbean ambience that the original settlers treasured was in danger of being lost, and the Creoles resented the influx of strangers who did not seem to appreciate speaking, singing, and praying only *en Français*. The French Quarter was not large enough to contain both the haughty Creoles and the swaggering English-speaking Americans. The latter group moved on the far side of Canal Street along St. Charles Avenue. The Creole population, feeling outnumbered and resentful of northern influence, settled in newly created faubourgs, or "false towns," carved from large plantations. The first of these faubourgs was a French Creole area developed by Bernard Xavier Phillippe de Marigny de Mandeville. Marigny named the main street Elysian Fields Avenue after its Parisian counterpart, the Champs-Elysées. It was a lovely, exclusive area of wide shady streets and closely set houses perfectly suited to its clannish residents.

The Faubourg Marigny is presently experiencing a renaissance, but it was in decline at the time of Thelma's birth in 1901. At the turn of the twentieth century, the French Creoles had managed to absorb the waves of Irish and German immigrants who moved into the area. By the time Thelma Ducoing became a Toole, however, the Creoles were in the minority. They had been pushed out by an even larger group of Italian immigrants and by the natural shifts of a city.

The Ducoing property had been subdivided and parts of it sold off in the nineteenth century. The residential lots, like most in the faubourg, were long and narrow, about fifty feet across the front and a hundred feet deep. The lots were cluttered with outbuildings, stables, and servants' quarters. The main houses were shuttered Creole cottages one room wide, each room opening into the other. In these "shotgun" houses, large extended families lived side by side, in each other's pockets. It was not unusual to find widows, married couples, grown siblings, little children, and visitors sharing the same household. The 1910 census lists a cousin from New York named Margaret Reilly living with the Ducoings and employed as a saleswoman in a local department store.

This sort of communal living was de rigueur for the Ducoings even before a second wave of Irish immigrants moved into the faubourg in the 1880s. Thelma's grandmother and mother came from Ireland, but Creole connections elevated their station in New Orleans. The Tooles were not so fortunate. Their family came to America from Ireland after the potato famines of the late 1840s. By that point longtime New Orleans Irish had separated themselves from the less successful newcomers— branding the latter group with the scornful term "channel Irish."

The Irish Channel section of New Orleans runs along the Mississippi

River near Tchoupitoulas (pronounced *Chop-a-tool-us*) Street. Many Irish immigrants were laborers who helped to dig the New Basin Canal. It was perilous work because of the dangers of cholera and yellow fever. Black freedmen wouldn't go near the place, and slaves were much too valuable to be subjected to disease. Irishmen, on the other hand, were considered tough and expendable. Enticed by brochures promising good pay, Irish came by boatloads to dig the canal. Many settled between the docks and warehouses along waterfront streets. This area was infamous for gang warfare and excessive drinking, and was considered a place where only the strong could thrive. Even Irish who had never lived in the Channel were greeted with suspicion when they moved into other neighborhoods.

John Kennedy Toole's paternal grandparents moved into the Faubourg Marigny following their marriage in 1890. Like the Ducoings, they were working-class people. Mary Orfila Toole was a second-generation American whose large Spanish family lived throughout the Vieux Carré. Her husband, John, made enough as a boilermaker to afford a German servant girl to help out with the housework. The Irish Tooles were full of Celtic charm and a great love of storytelling. They lived down the block from the Ducoings, and so John Kennedy Toole's parents grew up together, as neighbors but not as equals.

Thelma's father, Paul Apollonius Ducoing, had charge of the succession docket for the New Orleans city clerk of court. It was a political position secured by his father, Frank Ducoing, whose former commander in the Confederate army was the civil sheriff of the city. Paul Ducoing was not privately educated like his own father, but he had the traits of a consummate Creole. His word was law in the household, though his wife was the one charged with carrying out his orders. He believed that what money he had was for spending and left it to Mrs. Ducoing to worry about how to pay mundane home expenses. He preferred to spend time with his own friends in cafés and private clubs. Although he was a very successful man, it was well known in Ducoing's social circle that he was shifty in business affairs.

To perpetuate this system, rigid social training was required. When a son reached adolescence, he would be expected to accompany his father on outings with the local *bon vivants*. Daughters were encouraged to learn the skills that would keep a home running smoothly. They must also be instructed in the cultural arts that would make them desirable wives and mothers. This training included lessons in music, drawing, elocution, and dance.

Thelma Agnes, the youngest daughter, was born in 1901 and by everyone's account was a natural actress. She reveled in these refined accomplishments. Throughout her life she spoke with a rolled "r," and her often-gloved fingers gestured with dainty flourishes. She had received, as she said, "grace training for the hands." As a child, Thelma took both violin and piano lessons. She dreamed of going on the concert stage, but she never worked at the classics required for that career. Instead, Thelma preferred playing parlor ditties of the gay nineties for the amusement of her family.

Throughout her life, Thelma Toole gave the impression that she had been denied higher education because of her gender, but this was not exactly so. There were all-female colleges in New Orleans at this time, such as H. Sophie Newcomb and St. Mary's Dominican College. A girl of Thelma's talent and intelligence would certainly have qualified for either, but her family did not encourage university education, even had their finances allowed it. Thelma chose instead to attend Soulé College, a commercial training school situated in a large, rambling antebellum home in the Garden District. Although it was not a normal school or teachers' college, Soulé provided the certification necessary for Thelma to be hired as a third-grade teacher in the New Orleans public school system. She was pretty, perky, and never shy when it came to displaying her musical and dramatic talent. Thelma made herself popular and indispensable when it came to putting on school programs.

John Dewey Toole Jr. was a handsome, charming neighbor three years older than Thelma. At Warren Easton High School he was the 1917 state debate champion. With this honor came a full scholarship to Louisiana State University in Baton Rouge. Bright though he was, Toole chose not to pursue higher education, deciding instead to join the army. Although many soldiers from New Orleans, including Thelma's brother, were serving in France, Toole's company was not sent abroad. After his discharge in 1919, John went to work for the Pontchartrain Motor Car Company, which was the largest dealership in the city. He was a hard worker and well liked. By the time he was twenty-one, John was making a good salary as the manager of the repair parts shop. He was saving his money by living at home on St. Claude Street with his widowed mother and three brothers.

John and Thelma walked out together for five years in a typical courtship of the time. New Orleans has always been famous for fun, and there was no shortage of that in the roaring twenties, regardless of one's finances or pedigree. The Catholic Holy Days had been turned into city holidays. From Twelfth Night (January 6) until Ash Wednesday there were King cake parties and Carnival balls. Tea dances were a popular summer diversion. The mild winters of New Orleans allowed a variety of year-round picnics and excursions to the beaches along Lake Pontchartrain. Concerts, theatricals, opera and movie palaces provided entertainment no matter what the weather or the season. Thelma and John took advantage of all of these.

Thelma adored the attention and excitement of courtship. A studio photograph of her at age twenty-one shows her to have been a very pretty girl with a slim figure and dark hair. She often said of this picture, "I was mad about clothes. I used to spend all my salary as a schoolteacher on clothes. I had this blue velvet dress made especially for this photograph." It must have matched her eyes.

The courtship ended with a wedding at the Catholic Church of Saints Peter and Paul on December 27, 1926. The honeymoon was brief, and the marriage didn't fare as well as the engagement. At first the couple lived with John's brother James and his family, but that uncomfortable arrangement didn't last, for various reasons. The Victorian tradition of separate families occupying the same house was on the way out, and the two Toole families did not get along. A plumber who had also taught himself to read three languages, James Toole had a reputation for being eccentric. Thelma later reported that he often bathed in hot milk. No doubt Thelma's grand ambitions and Creole air of superiority were already well known to her down-to-earth Irish in-laws. It is enough to say that after growing up on Elysian Fields, Thelma had had enough of familial close quarters. She also wanted to move to the better side of the tracks. James and the rest of the family did not beg her to stay. This began a lifelong pattern of problems between the two groups of relatives.

In New Orleans it was not a railroad track but Canal Street that
divided the city's society. At the beginning of the nineteenth century,
property was cleared for a waterway to connect with the Mississippi
River. The canal was never built, but because of this design, the street is
wide enough to accommodate the many Mardi Gras parades that roll
through the city. North of this broad thoroughfare is the Creole past.
The city's jewel, the Vieux Carré, is there, and next to it are arranged
the old French faubourgs like Marigny, St. John, and Pontchartrain. In
this area known as "downtown" is also the Faubourg Tremé, which was
settled by free Creoles of color following the uprising in Santo Domingo
in the late 1700s.

The Tooles' search for a new home took them south of Canal Street
heading upriver to what is known in New Orleans as "uptown." The
very sound of it indicated high aspirations of class and material achievement. When the couple moved away from Elysian Fields, they took with
them big plans and fresh hopes for getting a piece of the American
dream. In the booming economy of the twenties, the odds were in their
favor.

John Toole left his salaried job at the parts shop and took a new
position as a salesman for Pontchartrain Motors. This was a bold move
since the job paid commission only, but with his ready wit and winning
personality, John was a natural. The Oldsmobile was a popular car, and
John's 10 percent commission would have been around a hundred dollars
per sale.

Things were looking good for the couple, and they moved to a small
rental apartment in the Carrollton section of the city. This was a quiet,
small community at the end of the streetcar line that ran across New
Orleans. They lived near Palmer Park, with its art deco arch flanked by
palm trees. It was far from the busy melting pot of the Marigny, but it
wasn't quite the Garden District with its historic grand mansions and
famous gardens. This move to the fringes of uptown defined the Tooles'
life and their future.

The move and John's commission-only salary required that the couple work hard to stay financially sound. Things were complicated by the
fact that Thelma's teaching position at Lakeview School had been taken
away when she married, a common practice around the country. This

was due in part to an all-male school board that thought if a woman were married to a wage earner, there was no reason for her to occupy a job that someone else needed. In the archives of the New Orleans public schools, there are packets of letters from married women begging to be rehired. Even if their husbands were disabled or the women had been abandoned, their pleas were refused. It took the filing of a class-action lawsuit against the school board in 1937 to persuade that body to allow these women to return to the classroom.

Denied a steady teaching position, Thelma gave lessons in music and dramatic expression. Her specialty was elocution. Since some accents in New Orleans are strong, similar to those in the Bronx section of New York City, it was important to some parents that their children practice a more standard form of speech. Although Thelma could slip in and out of the New Orleans accent, she taught her students to sound the ending consonants and use precise pronunciation. When her charges walked through the door of her class, she would slap them in the lower abdomen, under the bust, and finally under the chin, ordering, "Stomach in, chest out, chin up."

Thelma hired out as a pianist for private parties, displaying a vast repertoire of show tunes and novelty numbers. She was known in local theatrical circles for arranging minor cultural performances like children's music recitals and variety revues. It certainly wasn't the Tooles' fault that the Great Depression came along at precisely the moment they should have been making their fortune. Thelma Toole remarked often enough that they stayed poor because her husband was not much of a salesman. That his commissions could not support the couple was certainly true, but in the grim 1930s a thousand-dollar car was a luxury few could afford.

Still, the two of them made their share of foolish mistakes. John Toole had been a salaried manager of the parts shop, but there is no evidence that he tried to get his old job back. Although Thelma's family had influence with the city government, she never used those political connections in an attempt to gain steady employment. Neither did she try to receive training in another profession. She preferred to remain a private tutor, a provider of her own brand of culture to anyone who would pay for it. She spent her days crisscrossing the city on the bus or the streetcar, seeking students to keep herself in business. She was diligent and sincere about her work. It was her sad luck that in 1930, with milk selling for twelve cents a gallon and bread at a nickel a loaf, people had precious little cash to spend on the kind of tutelage Thelma could offer. That she had any students at all shows how devoted New Orleanians were to the idea of culture.

Two

At 3 yrs. old, he asked me why I wanted a boy. I told him I liked boys. Then he replied, "But girls are much sweeter!"

One night when I extinguished the light he said: "This darkness is darker than garden soil."

Upon returning from a party when he was five years old, this observation delighted me: "Jean Ruth has a voice like silver clanging!"

—*Little Sayings from the baby book of John Kennedy Toole, recorded by his mother*

FOR THE FIRST TEN YEARS of their marriage, hard times and worse luck dogged every effort John and Thelma made to get ahead financially. It seems they also found little fulfillment or happiness in one another. In the deep sea of matrimony, they were merely treading water. She was disappointed in what she perceived to be John's failure to give her the sort of high life she craved. John plodded along, stubbornly resisting any change that might have helped him. In the spring of 1937, just as the Depression was winding down and the economy looking up, the couple turned a corner in their personal life. At age thirty-six a surprised Thelma found herself pregnant for the first time and expecting a special delivery for Christmas. The couple got ready for the change in their life by moving to a new apartment on Webster Street, just a block off St. Charles Avenue in a huge white frame Victorian home. The neighborhood was neat, and there was a public elementary school on the corner.

The Tooles' baby was born on December 17, late on a Friday evening at Touro Infirmary, the city's largest and best lying-in hospital. In her later years Thelma would rave about how special and wonderful Kenny was in the nursery. Even if this is discounted as a severe case of mother love, his baby pictures do show Ken to be an exceptionally beautiful child. He was fine and fair with large brown eyes. His dark hair dipped in a single wave over a high forehead. Even as a toddler he posed for photos with a confident smile, clearly enjoying the limelight.

As the only child of older parents, Kenny did not lack for attention. His parents doted on him to distraction and vied for his affection, but there was never any doubt that Thelma was the dominant parent. From the beginning she claimed Kenny as hers exclusively, and he became her raison d'être. The Tooles' social life suffered as friends and even family were discarded as Kenny became the focus of his mother's existence. From his birth Thelma placed an extraordinary importance on her child, identifying with his successes and bemoaning his failures, stamping his life with the force of her powerful personality.

Thelma was still quite beautiful, slim and dark-haired. She claimed that all Kenny's attributes came from her side of the family, but it was his father whom the baby favored in looks. Though John was balding and overweight at forty, the resemblance is clear in the few pictures that exist of father and son. They shared dark eyes, a round face, and the same square way of standing head-on to face the camera.

Father and son shared much of the same temperament as well, with Kenny as loving and giving as a Friday's child is supposed to be. They were both overwhelmed by Thelma's aggressive, quixotic nature, and allowed themselves to be dominated by her fierce love and protection.

On January 16, a month-old Kenny was baptized into the Roman Catholic faith at the Church of the Most Holy Name of Jesus on St. Charles Avenue. A landmark building on the Loyola University campus and built in the Gothic style, Holy Name was at the time the largest and most prestigious of the New Orleans parish churches. It was an uptown church and a long way from the old Irish parish of Saints Peter and

Paul, where the Tooles had been married. Already Kenny was being taught to participate in the social rites of uptown New Orleans.

Thelma's influence in the family is shown by her choice of his godparents. His godfather, Arthur Ducoing, was Thelma's bachelor brother. His godmother, Margaret "Dollie" Garvey, was Thelma's spinster half-sister and "Nandy" to her new godson. Having no children of their own, these two took their duties very seriously. They remained devoted to Kenny throughout his life. This favoring of Thelma's family over John's surely offended the Tooles and may have furthered the antipathy between the families.

Kenny's baby album is the best-preserved article of his early life. It is pink moiré silk with a pink bow that raises the question, Why pink and not blue? Gender color-coding for babies was taken very seriously in the South at the time of Kenny's birth, and it is doubtful that Thelma bought the book after the baby was born. It is more likely that she or a friend bought the book during the pregnancy in the superstitious hope of influencing the baby's sex, only to find that the plan hadn't worked and the album was unreturnable. In any case, as with most first babies' albums, the pages of the book have been filled completely.

Among the baby gifts listed are some which show that Kenny was well received into the world of southern gentility. There are monogrammed sterling silver cups with matching flatware, handmade baby clothes, a Madeira embroidered pillowcase, and a silk quilt. From the Catholics on both sides of the family he received four silver medals. These would have been pinned to his bed sheet, undershirts, and baby clothes to provide the maximum spiritual protection.

In 1938 John Toole was working very hard at the car dealership, where sales were picking up as the South pulled out of the Depression. Kenny's first trip as an infant was to a car convention in Lansing, Michigan. He traveled with his parents on the train and stayed a week, being taken to all the activities. The trip was pleasant (and rare) enough for his mother to keep a record of it in Kenny's baby book. It was one of only a very few trips the family took together.

At age two Kenny was healthy and precocious. Because his father was in the business of selling cars, Kenny learned early to identify eleven different models. He spoke clearly enough to say such names as Packard,

LaSalle, and Studebaker. All his life Kenny loved wheeled vehicles, from the shiny tricycle he rode on Webster Street to the 1950 Oldsmobile he painted for a friend.

The neighborhood on Webster Street was a fine and quiet place to raise a child. The houses were mostly rambling Victorian structures that had been divided into apartments with garages converted from stables. The Tooles had the entire ground floor to themselves. There was a large shady yard with plenty of trees to climb. In the back was a small play-house, and porches around the main house to sit on. The garden furni-ture was made of stripped willow branches that were curved and twisted into comfortable chairs and swings. The old LaSalle elementary school across the street had been built before the turn of the century, when the neighborhood was new. As a toddler Ken played in his own yard and watched the children during their recess while he waited for his older friends to come home. There was a large unfenced playground at the school with swings and jungle gyms open to all the local children.

Thelma continued her tutoring; with another mouth to feed, the money was welcome. When she was working, Kenny stayed home with a black woman named Beulah Mathews who had worked for the Du-coing family. In a photo of the two of them, Beulah is shown nuzzling a dreamy-eyed baby who appears supremely contented. She loved and enjoyed the baby in her care. Pictures of him taken at this time show Kenny playing barefoot in the dusty yard, as ordinary as any toddler in the sultry weather of New Orleans—but ordinary did not fit the picture Kenny's mother had of him. She had bigger plans for her son than for him to stay at home with a nursemaid. When he was three Thelma decided that Kenny was ready for nursery school, and off he went.

The private kindergarten he attended was run by three sisters. Miss Stella Mercadel ran the preschool in the morning. Dancing lessons were given in the afternoon. The school, famous throughout the Garden Dis-trict, suited Kenny's ambitious parents. Daily from nine to noon at the rate of six dollars a month, Kenny learned from the exclusive and "Fa-mous Calvert System." According to the school's brochure, this method of teaching started in Boston. It was a basic small-group kindergarten that stressed individual attention and many learning activities.

Because Miss Stella's school was private and not bound by state regulations, Kenny's mother was welcome to participate in the ways she knew best. Even working a busy schedule, Thelma had often slipped home to spend time with Kenny. Now that he was in school she could take part by playing the piano and helping to direct the class programs. These activities also brought her into contact with parents whose children were potential students of her own kind of dramatic education.

It must be remembered that Kenny's birth coincided with the golden age of child star Shirley Temple, the hottest name in Hollywood. Children all over America were subjected to every sort of lesson to make them attractive to the talent scouts, legitimate or otherwise, who scoured the country seeking another Deanna Durbin or Freddie Bartholomew. "Let's put on a show" was a line heard in every town as well as in the *Our Gang* comedies. Thelma Toole had spent more than a decade building a reputation in this field, and now fate had presented her with an opportunity to have a little star of her own.

When Kenny was two, he and his mother were watching the children entering the LaSalle schoolyard across the street. Turning to his mother, the little boy said, "I'm going to be good to my teacher." When questioned as to what that entailed, he replied, "I'm going to serenade her, then dance, do tricks and make signs." For the next ten years he practiced doing just that.

From the time Kenny could talk he was encourged to perform. Alert, intelligent, and verbally precocious, he came alive in front of an audience, whether they were family, friends, or a group of complete strangers. Like his father, who had a repertoire of hysterically funny voices, Kenny was a natural mimic. They were both rare individuals who could reproduce at will any accent or variety of sound effects. Add to that Kenny's natural acting ability and the encouragement of a trained live-in coach, and one can understand why at an early age he seemed headed for a life on the stage.

Kenny was also studying to be a southern gentleman. In New Orleans this can be a career in itself. Uptown gentlemen pride themselves on their manners and refinement. Kenny had little calling cards engraved with his full name. These would be included in replies to invitations and with gifts. He almost certainly included one in a gift sent to his teacher. Miss Mercadel's reply thanks Kenny for the "dainty comb" she would tuck into her purse. All the traditions were observed in the Toole household. John was a charming and gracious man who expected no less from his son. Thelma knew all the nuances of society. The two of them trained their little man in the social graces, and he retained that instruction all through his life.

Longtime friend and fellow writer Emilie Dietrich Griffin recalled that Ken had wonderful manners and could get along with anyone anywhere. According to Griffin, "He never felt out of place no matter where he was." He was "lots of fun" to go out with on a date or with a crowd. She said, "Ken was very honorable with women," as any southern gentleman was expected to be.

By age three Kenny was ready to enter into the cultural life of New Orleans. This meant that he was ready for Mardi Gras, which has always been the most important event on the city calendar. Along with every other breathing child, he had watched the parades during the Carnival season. No doubt one of his first complete sentences was "Throw me something, mister!" a plea shouted by onlookers hoping to catch beads tossed from a float. As a toddler his first Mardi Gras costume was a white satin drum-major getup. It sported braid and buttons and was topped off with a fez bristling with ostrich feathers. Like many uptown children, Kenny had a studio picture taken in this first of many Carnival costumes.

Kenny also went to his first Mardi Gras ball, quite a coup for Thelma. The Children's Carnival Club of New Orleans was organized in 1925 to ape the adult balls and introduce children to the highly structured event. Even when youngsters are involved, there is no deviation from set routine. Invitations are highly prized and very thrilling to parents who have thrown a lot of social weight into obtaining one for their child. Such an event surely has more meaning for a parent than a toddler, but Kenny was always delighted with a big performance.

Even today only a small percentage of revelers get to attend an old-line ball held by elite krewes (or clubs) in New Orleans. Some guests who do attend find that once is enough. Based on European tradition, these balls are a serious mimicry of royalty. They can be a costly and sometimes boring ritual with a rigid and unvarying format. The evening begins quietly, with an elegant promenade of last year's king

and queen, who bid farewell to their reign. A tableau or musical program follows, after which a new royal couple is presented in a fanfare
of trumpets. These royals then perform the "Grand March," strolling
elegantly amongst the crowd before settling on their thrones to receive a
champagne toast and the homage of their subjects. After this, there are
special call-out dances where small favors are given to the fortunate female guests whose names appear on a dance card. Because there is much
sitting and watching, the formal festivities are tiring enough to put even
the brightest child to sleep. It is only later, at the Queen's Supper, when
the band strikes up and the real revelry begins.

Following two years of private nursery school, Kenny began attending regular kindergarten in the New Orleans Parish public schools. That
choice of public over private or parochial school is an interesting one.
Because of the predominantly Catholic population of the city, public
schooling in New Orleans had gotten off to a slow start in the nineteenth
century. Parochial education had had the edge ever since the Ursuline
Sisters opened their convent school in the Vieux Carré in 1727. Even
today at three o'clock on a school day, the uptown area more than other
parts of the city abounds with young people wearing the monogrammed
blazers of private and parochial school uniforms. Until the public schools
adopted a uniform policy in the 1990s, a child in street clothes was often
marked as a second-tier student. As upwardly mobile as the Tooles
wished to be, it was unusual that they chose to send their only child to
public school.

It surely wasn't the money involved, since the tuition was less than
the Tooles had been paying at Miss Mercadel's school, and the uniforms
required were less expensive than regular school clothes. It certainly
wasn't a matter of faultfinding with the subject matter and the system
that delivered it, since parochial systems have always catered to the best
and brightest. Their reason for choosing the public system may have
been more complex. The Tooles were themselves products of the public
school system. Though they were practicing Catholics, they never entered into the life of their parish church and felt no special need to
support the system. Later in life Thelma became suspicious of the Vatican's influence on the Church. Whenever she made a donation, she made

sure it went to a specific priest or project. She did not want her money to end up in a general fund that would benefit Rome.

As a former teacher Thelma had definite ideas about education and most definite plans concerning the education of her own child. One imagines that for her, one drawback of the parochial system might have been the nuns who ran it. They were not easily influenced by any parent, not even one as strong-willed as Kenny's mother. Sending Kenny to Catholic school meant doing it the sisters' way or not at all. It's likely that Thelma was smart enough to see that a clash, with her as the loser, would have been inevitable. She would have a better chance to make her presence felt in the public system.

Kenny entered kindergarten at McDonogh #14 Elementary School in the fall of 1942. His friend and neighbor John Geiser III started with him in the same class. Geiser lived down the block, and the two were playmates and friends who had attended Miss Mercadel's school together. Although LaSalle school was close to their homes, the Misses Mercadel preferred the kindergarten teacher at McDonogh. The boys' parents petitioned the school board for permission to attend the larger and more imposing McDonogh school. John Geiser was some weeks younger than Kenny, but because Kenny was born after December 1, the school board rules put them in the same class.

It was their good fortune to be placed with Imelda Bourgeois Ruhlman, a first-year teacher and recent graduate of Tulane. She would later recall that Kenny was "very bright all the time, very bright . . . and he spoke beautifully." He rarely made a mistake or an omission in his work. He had already mastered every skill the curriculum demanded. His report card for that year shows only E's (for excellent) and satisfactory progress in Citizenship (a patriotic euphemism for conduct). There is only one check mark missing. The first six weeks of grading he didn't work and play well with the other children. This is hardly surprising given the fact that he was an only child who was considered to be an *enfant prodige* at home.

Mrs. Ruhlman remembered that particular class of children (her first) as being one of the brightest she ever taught. There was a piano in the room, and Ruhlman, who played by ear, selected a few children to come to her house on Saturdays and take beginning lessons from her.

Children who banged on the keyboard were not invited. Kenny and a few others would try to finger the keys. Although Kenny's mother taught piano, he did not want to take lessons from her. Ruhlman did not know why that was so, but she was happy to have him as a student. Kenny liked the lessons so much that after a year with Mrs. Ruhlman he continued musical instruction with his mother.

John and Kenny walked the six blocks to school together every day. At first one mother would take them and the other would pick them up, but soon the boys began to go on their own. It was a safe residential section, and the walk was pleasant. Their mothers were always waiting when they got to their front doors. John's mother was a housewife, and Kenny's mother taught elocution lessons at home.

The boys were in and out of each other's houses, and as an adult John Geiser retains strong memories of that time. John recalled that most fathers of the era remained somewhat aloof from the family and let the mothers rear the children. He remembered thinking his own father was very special because he spent time playing with his son. John remembered noticing that the Tooles were older than most other parents and that Mr. Toole was never without a tie. He said that while the boys and Mrs. Toole played in the front part of the house, Mr. Toole would go through to the back room and read. Mrs. Toole was always up to interesting things and found all sorts of games to play that involved learning in some way. Geiser said that he was stimulated by being around them.

Child prodigy or not, Kenny at the end of kindergarten ran afoul of the public school rules. He knew the work, had made himself popular with the other children and endeared himself to the teacher, but that wasn't enough to get him promoted to the first grade. According to the parish rules adopted in 1930, Kenny was not the right age to be promoted. He would have had to turn six by December 1 of his first-grade year. John Geiser was in a similar predicament. In order to gain permission for the boys to skip a second session of kindergarten, their parents appealed to the school authorities.

In cases like these the school board's procedure was to administer a test of general knowledge rather than a formal IQ examination. Geiser remembered them both being promised a treat if they passed the test.

Since the two children were both so bright, the carrot was probably to keep them on their best behavior. Kenny, however, became bored and refused to answer all the questions, but both boys did well enough to obtain admission to the first grade.

John and Kenny received the promised but very different treats— John a requested brown leather bomber jacket that he wore until it fell apart, Kenny a set of the textbooks for first grade so that he could get a head start. Geiser was not sure that choice originated with Kenny, but would not be surprised if it had, because "Kenny really wanted to excel."

Geiser remembered that once when walking to school Kenny said, "You know after the war we are going to have television." When Geiser asked what "television" was, Kenny said, "It is like a radio and movie combined." "He must have read it or been told by his mother," recalled Geiser. "They were a pretty good team." There was much intellectual interaction between mother and son. Sometimes Geiser got tired of all that bookish activity in the Toole house and just wanted to go out to play.

"After the war" was a phrase Americans were familiar with in 1943 when Kenny started first grade. Residents of New Orleans felt especially vulnerable because of the city's position near the mouth of the Mississippi River. More than once German submarines captured at sea contained fresh bread and vegetables that could have been purchased only in the New Orleans area. The city practiced air-raid drills and installed blackout shades. The block captains kept sandbags, shovels, and a wheelbarrow in their yards just in case the drill turned out to be the real thing. The war had a positive effect on the Toole household in that Thelma earned extra income providing musical accompaniment for lavish patriotic celebrations staged by the parks department.

Shortly after Kenny was ensconced in first grade, his mother started a parishwide ruckus. She said her concern began with Kenny throwing an unusual tantrum, declaring that he wasn't learning anything in school. Boredom in school is quite usual with bright children, but an aware teacher and supportive parents can keep the students stimulated and happy in class. Thelma took a different and more disruptive tack. She decided that Kenny should skip straight to the second grade. This was possible because at that time the New Orleans public schools had a single-semester promotion policy. If the teacher and the principal felt that after the fall semester a child had learned all he needed for the year, the child could advance to the next grade after Christmas.

Mrs. Ruhlman had known Mrs. Toole over the years and remembered her as a nice lady who now and then "would get a little fiery." Miss Langtry, the first-grade teacher, and Mrs. Toole did not see eye to eye on teaching style or on discipline. On the other hand, Miss Mary "May" Byrne, the very genteel lady who taught second grade, was quite taken with sweet little Kenny. This proposal to transfer Kenny to Miss Byrne's class in the spring of 1944 fell on deaf ears at McDonogh Elementary. A determined Thelma went back to the school board to have Kenny evaluated for promotion. This time he was given a Stanford-Binet IQ test by Miss Claire Charlaron, the psychologist employed by the school board. As few records were kept during World War II due to a paper shortage and because Kenny's cumulative folder did not survive water damage to the storage room at Fortier High School, there is no verification of the test results. A score of 130 would be enough today to have a child classified as "gifted," but it isn't extremely high and not at all on a genius level, though Thelma returned to McDonogh waving a paper stating that her child had a "genius" score of 133. In later years Thelma would defend the fact that her son's score wasn't higher by saying he refused to cooperate with the tester, and she reported that she, Principal Elizabeth Danner, and Kenny's first-grade teacher had a class-A shouting match right in the hall of the school. Mrs. Ruhlman said there was indeed some sort of argument about Kenny leaving Miss Langtry's class, but despite this unpleasant incident, Kenny did skip into second grade.

A childhood friend of John Kennedy Toole's, Emilie Dietrich Griffin, recalled that one similarity between her and Kenny concerned their mothers, who were "alike in their expectations for us." They thought that Emilie and Kenny could and must accomplish something out of the ordinary. The children felt this and pushed themselves accordingly. "We were expected to do something great," said Griffin, who lives a calm and ordered life as a successful writer of books on religion and Catholic spirituality.

An older Thelma would brag that her son jumped ahead two grades. This wasn't exactly so, but he did start out younger and smaller than his peers and with a label as well. The arbitrary title of "genius" can be a heavy burden for six-year-old shoulders, even when it is validly applied, but there is no way to be sure that Kenny was a true child prodigy or if he felt equal to the title.

Although she was very fond of Kenny, Miss Byrne would complain that Mrs. Toole was a "professional mother" endlessly bragging on her sole offspring. It would irritate the teacher when Mrs. Toole would rave about Kenny's brilliance to the exclusion of other excellent students at McDonogh school. For years afterward, whenever Miss Byrne would run into Ken's mother, she would tell her nephew Robert Byrne, "I saw Thelma Toole, and she's still Thelma Toole." In a lengthy interview with Carmine Palumbo in 1995 Robert Byrne further related that he had shared this story with Ken. When Byrne recalled how Mrs. Toole had referred to her son as a genius, Ken seemed surprised.

Stories abound of young Kenny intellectually running roughshod over his classmates in primary school. His vocabulary was prodigious, and his language mystified many of his peers. He used his wit and verbal precocity in negative ways. In a classroom essay later reprinted in "Odyssey among the Dunces," an article by Dalt Wonk that appeared in the Dixie magazine section of the *Times-Picayune,* Kenny demonstrates insufferable juvenile hubris:

> To my dear reader.
> This intellectual volume of learning I proudly present. It helps those who are too dumb to go to school. I find myself very highly learned and smart. I have been praised so many times in my 10 years of life that this epic should speak for itself. So the intellectual beings and highly cultured prodigies that read this great tome will feel that they may speak freely to another highly intellectual friend.

Even Kenny's doting mother realized that this attitude would poison his relations with other children. In her interview with Wonk she reports admonishing her son, "Poor darling. You won't have any friends if you talk like that." It may never have occurred to Thelma to wonder if Kenny were experimenting with self-parody.

Three

I knew the way people in town thought about things. . . . If you were different from anybody in town, you had to get out. That's why everybody was so much alike. The way they talked, what they did, what they liked, what they hated. . . . They used to tell us in school to think for yourself, but you couldn't do that in the town.

—*The Neon Bible*

WHAT KENNY'S FATHER THOUGHT of these goings on is not known. Mr. Toole was a pleasant man, but was not ambitious enough to meet his wife's high expectations. He had not turned out to be Thelma's notion of the proper father for her son, so a disappointed Thelma bypassed her husband and took Kenny all to herself. While John Toole complained to his own family that he had little influence in raising his son, he did not assert his paternal authority. Mrs. Ruhlman remembered him as being a "quiet man, gentle and rather genteel." He was smart but shy, preferring to stay in the background, where he contented himself with just being there, loving his child and watching him grow. With his forceful wife's obsessive love for their son to contend with, this quiet approach was as much as he either could manage or was allowed.

Baseball and cars were a bond between the two Toole males. They played catch together, and Ken was on a neighborhood team. As an adult Ken described himself to some friends as a "pretty good ballplayer." He loved cars, especially convertibles. The Tooles were unusual in that they had a car during the war, when most people had to walk or use public transport. Even the Geisers, who were better off financially, didn't have a family car. John's father, a painting contractor, only had a truck.

From the beginning Thelma steered her son toward her interests, and Kenny was delighted with them. Music was important to both of them. As an adult one of Ken's secret lives revolved around music, but not the kind his mother would have enjoyed. In kindergarten he went to his first opera, a marvelous New Orleans production of *Carmen*. Kenny himself had a pleasant voice and often sang in public. Although he could play the piano, Kenny found the theater to be the better outlet for his creative instincts.

During the 1930s the New Orleans Recreation Department had organized a traveling theater troupe. This offshoot of the federal WPA consisted of talented boys and girls who put on plays and holiday pageants. Sometimes Thelma Toole was hired to play piano for these performances, a job that brought in welcome income. This work also brought her some private students for voice and drama coaching. Above all, Thelma was a persistent stage mother for actor, singer, dancer, and comic impressionist "Kennedy Toole."

Kenny had always been a performer and had worked up a number of routines even before he started Miss Mercadel's nursery school. As his mother's best student and her little bit of Hollywood, he was available for every party and family get-together for a song, a dance, or a bit of comic dialogue. By the time he was ten, Kenny and his mother were ready to move into leading roles.

In 1948 Thelma formed her own troupe of players, the Junior Variety Performers. This was a group of about fifty boys and girls of all ages and talents. Depending on what was needed, Thelma would choose who would perform where. Singers, acrobats, tappers, and toe dancers executed routines purely for Miss Thelma's approbation, and for every conceivable audience: the Protestant Bethany Home for the Aged, St. Vincent's Hospital for the Incurables, Charity Hospital's convalescent ward—plus every Moose, Elk, and Rotary member was treated to some part of the JVP and its star, Kennedy Toole.

Norma Palumbo was one of the charter members of that group and a classmate of Kenny's at McDonogh. The two of them had a special connection because their mothers were so strict with them. She recalled Kenny's mother making him write thank-you notes for even the most trivial things and never wanting him out of her sight.

When Kenny did elude his mother, he became a real clown, acting silly and making everyone laugh. Palumbo said that the troupe was well received everywhere, and that Kenny seemed to love the limelight. She was surprised to learn years later that Kenny's father survived him. She had always thought that Mrs. Toole was a widow or divorced, because there was never any mention or evidence of a Mr. Toole in all the years she knew the family. He never came to any school functions or to see Kenny perform. She knew that his mother loved him, and that "all the teachers loved him. The kids all loved him. I didn't know a father existed."

Kenny had so much going on that year that he began to keep a scrapbook. Hand-drawn in crayon and subtitled "The Play's the Thing," it chronicles a busy time for the young actor. He was performing at least once a week on the stage, radio, or with his mother's troupe. He had the lead in three plays produced by the Children's Workshop Theatre of New Orleans. He was MC of a local radio show called "Telekids" and modeled for newspaper ads. He kept the scripts marked with actor's notes and the playbills, underlining his name. He had worked up a one-man show of comic impressions titled *Great Lovers of the World*. Obviously proud of his accomplishments, he saved many mementos of this period.

Among his mother's things at the Tulane Library is a studio photograph taken of Kenny that shows a child on the verge of puberty. His dark neat hair still dips in that baby wave, and his features are even in a face that is a bit too full. A childhood case of chicken pox left him with three small pockmarks across the bridge of his nose that add more interest than blemish. If his mien is serious, it is because his life was very serious. An A-plus student with a burgeoning theatrical career doesn't have much time to waste. He divided his mind as well as his time seeking perfection in his various roles as son, scholar, and rising star. Appearances on local radio and television shows extended his résumé, and for the first time Ken had a part in the adult New Orleans community theater.

Ken's entrance into high school brought many changes to the Toole household. Kenny the actor cut back on his stage appearances and became Ken the scholar. The family moved to an unattractive duplex on Cambronne Street, but stayed there only a year. In order to be closer to Fortier High, they moved to an apartment on Audubon Street, where they were to live for many years. John Toole was still selling automobiles, but not as successfully as before. Ken earned his own pocket money in various ways. Before school he had a paper route, and he sold magazines door to door in the afternoon. In addition to her traveling troupe, Thelma served as director of an entity called the Lakeview School of Speech and the Dramatic Arts, founded by Ottoline la Biche, whom Thelma referred to as "a beacon of culture and enlightenment to children, youths, and adults." The Tooles were the busiest of families, scratching their way through life.

Ken's new school, Alcee Fortier High, was entering a period of change at the time he began the ninth grade. It would soon become coed, but the first two years Ken attended, it was an all-boys public school of about six hundred students. Fortier remains a huge imposing brick structure built up high above Freret Street in order to accommodate a basement. Since New Orleans is below sea level, basements are of necessity aboveground. Constructed long before air conditioning, Fortier had high ceilings and tall sash windows for better air circulation. It must have been a sweatbox most of the time, but academically it was excellent, with such famous alumni as Senator Russell Long, son of Governor Huey "Kingfish" Long; journalist Howard K. Smith; and Louisiana governor David Treen.

Although one of the youngest students at Fortier, Ken did well there from the very beginning. He made and stayed on the A honor roll, joined clubs, and made a few new friends. He continued studying Spanish, which would serve him well later in life. Ken continued to perform the first and last dramatic readings in his mother's recitals, but in pictures taken at those performances, he looks less comfortable on stage.

Ken had physically matured at the beginning of adolescence. By thirteen he was shaving daily and had already reached his full height of 5′10″. He looked so grown-up that no one questioned him driving his own car at that young age. Reciting poems on stage along with little girls lisping abbreviated versions of Longfellow's "Evangeline" would have been agony to any high-school boy. Pat Holmes Guizerix, an elocution student of Mrs. Toole's, had a strong recollection of Ken's unwilling participation in those events. After forty years she still remembered "a vivid sense of pity for him. His mother would force him to be overly dramatic in his recitations, and it was embarrassing, but what could he do? It was his mother, after all, and she completely dominated him. He didn't have any say in the matter." She said he was overweight and out of place, "just hanging around in the background waiting for his mother to call on him." He was no longer Kenny, the cute little child actor. He needed a new outlet for his creative mind, away from his mother's overbearing presence.

Ken had entered high school without a set group of friends. One reason for this was that the majority of his free time had been spent in theatrical pursuits, where he met young people from many schools. Another reason was that his home was off limits to other kids. Mrs. Toole was never easy about Ken associating with ordinary children. She demanded that he be in every way superior to others his age—better, smarter, more adult—and she reserved the right to approve his friends, fearing that contact with average people would somehow rub off on her son.

Larry McGee was one of the few boys on Thelma's approved list. Ken met Larry, an extremely kind and gentle person who would eventually become a psychologist, when they entered high school, and shortly thereafter Ken Toole became Larry's first unofficial client. Ken was having a rough time in gym class. The open locker room intimidated him. He had been raised to be modest and fully clothed in front of other people, and the boys ribbed Ken about his reluctance to undress around them. Larry McGee stepped in and helped Ken work through this problem. By talking and joking with him, Larry got Ken to ignore the teasing until it finally stopped, and the two became best friends during their years at Fortier.

Maurice duQuesnay, who attended Fortier at this time, agreed that Ken would have had great trouble with a physical education class, which at Fortier could be brutal, with a lot of body contact. The communal showers were a shock to all the boys, but especially to one as sheltered as Ken, who was not proud of his pudgy physique. Several acquaintances agreed that sexuality in general was a distasteful subject to Ken, and it would remain so throughout this life. Once, on a Newman Club overnight outing, he was quite repelled by what he perceived as promiscuous goings on by some of the students, and he took a lot of teasing for his prudishness.

It is possible that there was another reason for Ken's difficulties with the gym classes at Fortier. There is some indication that, by the time he was in high school, Ken was struggling with his sexual identity. Later in life Ken would tell a couple of friends that he was sexually active during his teen years. He claimed to have been physically involved with a handsome older schoolmate. Purportedly giddy over the young man, Ken was thrilled to find his affection reciprocated. It is impossible to know if the story is true or if Ken adjusted his memory to impress his friends.

Although reticent in his social life, Ken found a new passion in writing. In the ninth grade he began entering and winning essay contests. Some of the papers were on mundane topics like "Progress in the Deep South," or "The Louisiana Purchase," and one had the cumbersome title "What the American Merchant Marine Means to My Country," but all were well researched and nicely crafted. Aided by his mother's proofing, the grammar and spelling were perfect. He joined the staff of the school newspaper, *Silver and Blue,* and worked on the Fortier yearbook, *The Tarpon.* Ken followed his father's earlier example by learning to debate and was invited to speak at gatherings of civic organizations like Kiwanis and Rotary Clubs.

These activities—so safe, suitable, and designed to please the audience—were hallmarks of those early Eisenhower years of the Cold War, when students were seldom inclined to call undue attention to themselves and it would take something out of the ordinary to stir them up.

That "something" arrived at Fortier in the fall of 1952, when the all-boys Fortier High merged with the all-girls Eleanor McMain High, and the school went coed, doubling in size. Single-gender high schools have always been a deeply held tradition in New Orleans, a holdover from the Catholic parochial system begun before the public schools were created, and few were excited about the changes. Young New Orleans men in the 1950s were instructed to treat girls with great care and to watch what they did and said around young ladies. Being around them all day would be an inhibiting factor on male adolescent behavior.

According to Karen Damonte Pickren (Fortier '55), the girls at Mc-Main felt the same way about merging schools. "We liked having our own school away from the boys," she said. "We didn't have to worry about wearing makeup and dressing up every day." There had always been interaction between McMain and Fortier. McMain, for instance, supplied cheerleaders for the Tarpons, and there were joint school outings and social activities—but the schools were separate, and the students preferred it that way, but they were powerless to stop the gender desegregation.

The boys at Fortier started a protest movement when the school board announced the merger. Pickren said that it was quite a flap. "This was the fifties, you know. Kids just didn't speak up as they do today. A group of boys made big signs and paraded in front of the school board office." It didn't last very long, but "it made big fuss, I can tell you, although it didn't do any good." The school board's decision was irrevocable, and the change was effected immediately.

When the girls came in Ken's junior year, he was putting on weight and steering clear of organized sports, preferring to focus on the sedentary pastimes of journalism and club work. Gym class had never been a comfortable place for Ken, and he spent only compulsory time there. Being overweight became a vicious cycle and was tough on his teen confidence, especially around girls, who always seemed to notice he was not in shape.

"He was a fat boy," said Pickren, who took a journalism class with Ken in her junior year. Although she sat by him the entire year, she doesn't remember any significant conversation with him. He seemed "consumed with newspaper activities and was always busy with the teacher." She would have remembered if he were unfriendly, but "he just kept to himself and did his work." It did not occur to her that this busyness on Ken's part may have been compensation for the loneliness and a sense of rejection he felt throughout high school. The school was so huge, she admitted, that "you couldn't know everyone." She had talked to many of her friends and her husband, Roy (Fortier '53), but none of them remembered Ken. "Everyone knew who the athletes and the cheerleaders were," she said, but "the rest of us just fell into different cliques." Ken belonged to no clique at all.

Larry's sister, Jane McGee Kingsmill, dated Ken in high school. She said, "There were four of us all the time." Jane, Ken, Larry, and his girlfriend, Helen "Buzzy" Pond, went everywhere together, and Ken became a kid for the first time. "When he was with us he became years younger than he appeared to be in school," Kingsmill remembered. In public he was always very proper, very meticulous in appearance and behavior, but "he really let his hair down with us," Kingsmill said. "He was always thinking of fun things to do and didn't mind getting into silly situations. It was the only time he was allowed to be silly. We did not talk about ambitions or the future." They didn't know he was interested in writing. They were just happy to be young together.

Ken was beginning a pattern of compartmentalizing his life and personality. He tried to keep his mother ignorant of his close and constant contact with the McGee family, and his love of pranks and practical jokes was never expressed in front of any adult. He began to develop secrets that later worked against him, but in high school the McGees served as a relief from the controlling atmosphere of his own home.

The families had been friends since Mr. McGee bought an Oldsmobile from John Toole in 1934. They were social acquaintances until Ken was born. Mrs. McGee did not care for Thelma Toole, but was fond of Mr. Toole, though she found him to be "long-suffering." She was very fond of Ken and welcomed him into their family activities.

Ken and Larry were partners in a morning paper route, delivering the now-defunct *New Orleans States-Item* and the Sunday *Times-Picayune.* The route wound through uptown New Orleans. Ken's first car, which he got when he was thirteen, was a green 1936 Oldsmobile. This was two years before he could legally get a driver's license, but the paper never questioned his age or asked for any documentation. He drove the Olds for two years and then sold it to the McGee children when he got a newer model. Sometimes, if they were behind schedule

on the job, the two boys would roust Jane Kingsmill at three or four in
the morning. Of course, she was too young to have a license, but she
would idle the engine and steer the car down the dark streets. Ken and
Larry would stand on the running boards and toss out the papers along
Napoleon Avenue.

Just as Ken and Larry were best friends, so were Jane and Buzzy.
The two couples always double-dated since Ken had his own car. Although they saw each other for two years, Kingsmill does not remember
being any more intimate with Ken than just holding hands and the
occasional kiss. "We were more like good friends," she said, "just out to
have fun. Ken was always coming up with some goofy kid stuff." Ken
also had the ability to surprise Kingsmill with his sophistication. Often
the four would hang around the area on Magazine Street where the
International Trade Mart is located. Foreign visitors and merchants did
business there. In the duty-free shops and restaurants there was always
something exciting to see, and late one afternoon Ken called Kingsmill's
attention to a tall, handsome, well-dressed man coming out of the trade
mart. When the man passed them, Kingsmill noticed that he had very
long nails and the middle finger on his right hand was painted a dark
cherry-red. Ken remarked to Kingsmill, "That man is queer." The
man's name was Clay Shaw. In later years he would be named as a major
player in one of the many assassination theories surrounding the death
of President John Kennedy.

Kingsmill was surprised and impressed that a fourteen-year-old boy
would know about a grown man's sexual habits. It made her think that
Ken was quite "a man of the world." At the time it didn't occur to her
to ask how Ken knew this man or about his sexual habits. She said that
it was a time of such innocence, homosexuality was only a vague notion
to the young people she knew, and the particulars of that life were a
mystery. Men like Shaw were just different and set apart from everyday
reality. Neither Kingsmill nor any of her friends ever supposed that
anyone they knew might be other than heterosexual.

Ken was always thinking of some prank and was usually successful
at getting someone to help him create mischief. There was an old black
man named Momo who dressed in a white robe and carried a cross made
of driftwood from the river. Ken and Larry walked up on the levee near

St. Charles Avenue and teased him about his evangelical teachings. The old man began to chase them, swinging his cross, shouting for them to stop and "Come to be saved." The boys were afraid that Momo would throw them in the Mississippi if they refused salvation. Laughing and sweaty, they ran back to the McGee house to hide.

The golf course at Audubon Park was a make-out haven for teens at night, and groups of kids would sit in cars to talk and listen to the radio. A mildly retarded man who lived near the park often came around to peek into the car windows. Ken called him "Jojo the dog-faced boy" and scared the girls with wild stories about him. Sometimes Ken and Larry would bring flashlights and make the rounds. After surprising the love-birds at the golf course, they'd head over to lovers' lane on the lakefront and continue their antics. They would shine the torches into the cars, shouting, "God sees you!" at the couples who were snuggled down in the backseats of their four-wheeled bedrooms.

There was a teacher at Fortier well known for her strict scholastic demands, and she was unpopular with some students. Miss Fortunata Collins was a spinster teaching college prep English literature, and a few pupils spread nasty rumors about her. Ken especially disliked her. Once for an end-of-school celebration, Ken bought some cherry bombs, a par-ticularly powerful firecracker now banned from import. "It was Ken's idea," said Jane Kingsmill, for four of them to participate in a drive-by bombing at Miss Collins's house. Ken said he knew where the teacher lived and drove to a green Creole cottage near St. Rita's Catholic Church. The cottage garden was filled with cactus plants and the four hoydens proceeded to launch one cherry bomb after another at the innocent cacti. Jane remembers that "we just blew them up and drove off. We loved it and we laughed ourselves sick." What the quartet didn't know was that this was not Miss Collins's house. She lived with her brother and his family in another section of New Orleans. Kingsmill wasn't surprised when, decades later, she learned that they had bombed the wrong house. She remembered in those days teachers preferred to stay quite aloof from their students. She said she never thought of them as real people with lives outside the classroom and added, "I had the vague notion that my teachers lived together in some part of the school and were let out just to teach their classes."

Jane remembered Ken as being very handsome. She remarked on his beautiful complexion, saying he "never had a pimple, but it was his personality that really made him so attractive." Fun and laughter just bubbled out of him when he was with the McGees, and he was always reluctant to end the fun and return home.

The four friends spent much of the summertime swimming at the Audubon Park pool. Because the McGees lived on Pine Street right off St. Charles Avenue, they could walk to the pool, but as is usual with teenagers, they would much rather ride in a car. Ken liked to drive and would pick the group up at their homes. If he forgot his suit, Ken would drive a couple of blocks past his house and park, leaving the others in the car, and walk back home to get his swimming things before rejoining them. The others did not refer to this strange behavior. They knew it was because he did not want his mother to see whom he was with and possibly stop him from going. He also didn't want his friends to fall into Thelma's sphere of influence.

The young people would stay until the pool closed and then drive to an ice-cream parlor called the Spinning Wheel, which boasted thirty-two flavors of ice cream. Ken and Larry would go in and get hand-packed cartons of frozen treats to take back to the McGees'. Their house was an old two-story with porches upstairs and down. This was long before air conditioning came to New Orleans. Mrs. McGee fixed up a porch off the kitchen for the kids. She found an old gateleg table that the veneer had buckled on. She made a tablecloth for it and put a rattan shade over the light bulb and dropped it down. This became their game table. The four of them played poker, canasta, monopoly, hangman, and all sorts of games.

Mrs. McGee would make sodas with the ice cream and bake cookies for the foursome. In the long muggy nights they would stay up until two or three in the morning, when the wind from the lake had cooled the city. Buzzy lived next to the McGees, so the only one who had any distance to go was Ken, but he would keep the games going until everyone was too sleepy and cross to continue. Then he would drive the few blocks to his house. "Ken never wanted to go home," said Jane Kingsmill. He did not talk about his family, but the McGees knew he was miserable at home because he never wanted to be there and he never took his friends there.

Even after they stopped dating, Jane and Ken remained good friends. He and Larry were always going in and out of the McGee house. One time Larry bought an obscene comic book from one of the newsstand vendors. He and Ken hurried upstairs to Larry's room to read it. They locked Jane out, but she could hear them laughing and joking about it.

Larry seldom went to the Tooles' house because Ken discouraged such visits. As the natural child-parent separation began with the onset of Ken's adulthood, his mother tightened her grip on him. Thelma dominated the easygoing Ken, who was more like his father in temperament. Teenagers prefer their parents to go deaf, mute, blind, and invisible when other kids are around, but Ken's mother could never be anything but herself. She would make his guests sit and listen to her recitals of outdated piano music, and her loud, dramatic way of speaking embarrassed Ken, who loved her so much but could do nothing to moderate her behavior. It was easier to keep everyone away.

Kingsmill's fondest memory of Ken is their great adventure trip to Baton Rouge when Robert Kennon was inaugurated governor of Louisiana in January 1953. Skipping school for the first time in his life, Ken rode with Mrs. McGee and her children to the festivities at the state capitol. It was the kind of bright winter day in the Deep South that could pass for spring. The visitors toured the grounds and watched the ceremony from way back in the crowd. Mrs. McGee had packed a picnic lunch, and they feasted on sandwiches and fried chicken on the green lawn beneath the huge bronze statue of Huey Long. They stayed all day before driving back to New Orleans along the old Airline Highway. Kingsmill said it remains one of the favorite days of her life.

Ken continued to excel in school. He was news editor of the school paper. As one of the two New Orleanians voted outstanding citizen at the Pelican Boys' State convention, he was invited back to serve the following year as a counselor. He won more essay contests and did public speaking for the Key Club while maintaining an A average. Ken kept up with his religious education by attending the Newman Club, a Catholic organization for teens that met one evening a week. He won an award for outstanding student in the group and got his picture in the city paper.

Ken had found a way to get into the limelight other than appearing on the stage.

Any student's senior year can be a golden time, and Ken's was outstanding. Because Fortier was so close to Tulane and Newcomb, the students were invited to many college functions. The Greek system on those campuses was a thriving part of university life, and Ken attended parties, dances, and Mardi Gras balls just as his parents had twenty years before. In the society section of the school paper, Ken is among those listed as being seen "doing the town." In New Orleans that covers a lot of ground, and Ken began to learn every inch of it.

Now as senior editor of the school paper, he retrieved his old stage name of Kennedy Toole and splashed it on the masthead. As a perk the editor got to write the Fish Tales column. This whimsical, gossipy section, published under a pseudonym, provided Ken with an outlet for his humor. During his junior year there had been a reference in that column to a "Princess Von Mylondonck." That may have been Ken's contribution, because he created a character named Humphrey J. Mylondonck to author his Fish Tales. He knew quite well that it was the one section everyone read, and he used it to his advantage. For the December issue Mylondonck invented and published a student wish list that included Ken as wanting a girlfriend. Using the paper to flirt with a girl or ridicule someone who hurt his feelings, Ken was discovering the power of written words.

Four

Ken lived all his life uptown, but his people were downtown people, and downtown people are all a little mad. Some of them are really "downtown mad."

—*Robert Byrne, 1995 interview*

THE SPRING of 1954 found everything going Ken's way. His grades were the best they had ever been. He was chosen for the National Honor Society and won a National Merit Scholarship. The student body picked him as Most Intelligent Senior Boy. In the school paper he was referred to as an "outstanding student," and in the same article Ken declared his intention to study engineering at a university that was noted for its engineering program. Ken's father had been pushing him in this direction, knowing that this vocation would provide a steady income, something not always available to those with degrees in liberal arts.

Tulane University today is a fine and respected school that draws students from all over the world. In the 1950s Tulane was smaller, and 70 percent of its student body came from a thin rank of white males. To be from New Orleans and go to Tulane had a certain social cachet. This is what the Tooles had been working toward since Ken was born. It was the reason Thelma and John had moved uptown and sent their son to the right schools. There is a saying in uptown New Orleans that one must live there for twenty years before being considered a true resident. Now that span had passed, and the Tooles were certified as "uptown" with the Faubourg Marigny far behind them.

Until the end of her life, Mrs. Toole made sure that if everyone she met learned only one thing about her Ken, it was that he had won a full scholarship to Tulane University. Unlike his father, who turned down a scholarship to LSU, Ken did not waste his opportunity. Six months shy of his seventeenth birthday, Ken was college bound, but first there was high school to finish.

Fortier had received a Freedoms Foundation Award for demonstrating democratic practices in high-school life, and as a result thirty-one students would take a train-and-bus trip to the Northeast. Ken was among the group. In nine days they toured New York City, Philadelphia, and Washington, D.C. In the article he wrote for the paper, Ken mentioned meeting former Fortier graduate Senator Russell Long, visiting Valley Forge, and admiring the Liberty Bell. The article was a straightforward account of the trip and its purpose, but Ken's scrapbook is a more personal chronicle of his first encounter with New York. He saved everything from ticket stubs to playbills to the placemats from a Howard Johnson restaurant. His training on the yearbook staff is evident in the precise arrangement of souvenirs and photographs. The pictures show Ken posed in front of, beside, and beneath every national monument and tourist stop he ran across. This would be standard stuff but for what the photos reveal about Ken himself. In each picture he has his hands jammed into his pockets. He confronts the camera head on and always alone. There is not a single shot of him horsing around with the other students on the trip. Even his slight smile is more serious than the average sixteen-year-old's.

The trip was the beginning of a love/hate affair between Ken and the city of New York. Ken would attend school there, work there, and visit many times. He found the city both exciting and upsetting, providing him many pleasures and his greatest disappointment. He was fascinated with New Yorkers, but infuriated by them as well. Perhaps it was on this first trip that Ken planned to try making it in New York as he had done in New Orleans. He would learn that the rules were very different and the game wasn't fair.

Despite his hectic senior schedule, Ken found time to write *The Neon Bible,* a dark, short novel patterned after the southern Gothic fiction of Flannery O'Connor, an author he greatly admired. Though not a literary success, the novel is an admirable accomplishment for a sixteen-year-old boy. Set in 1940s Mississippi, the story follows a child growing up in a backwoods Baptist community. It is a place like one where Ken had once spent a short vacation with a high-school friend. In the summer following graduation, Ken entered this first novel in a contest, and when it did not win, he apparently then sent it to a publishing house or two. When nothing came of these efforts, Ken put the work aside and never submitted it again. Years later the rights to this work would be the prize in a bitter legal battle over Thelma Toole's estate.

For many uptown young men, Tulane seemed like an extension of high school, and Ken's undergraduate years were not much different from his time at Fortier. All plans for engineering were dropped immediately. Ken's natural major was English, and he consistently scored high enough to stay on the dean's list. The stylistic gifts he later displayed, however, are not evident in his papers, now archived in the Tulane library. His honors thesis on the English writer John Lyly is well researched but dry, and his short stories reflect the same amateurish introspection found in *The Neon Bible.* There is little evidence of the levity Ken wielded in his Fish Tales. This is not surprising since Ken needed to please his teachers in order to make top grades, and humor—though it is what Ken did best—is not considered substantive enough for many academicians.

It was his work for the Tulane student newspaper, *Hullabaloo,* that showed wit and promise. In addition to writing book reviews and articles, Ken was listed on the editorial staff as a cartoonist. His flair for drawing must have established itself early, for in his high-school yearbook Ken sketched a palette beside his signature. The cartoons for the Tulane paper were quite subtle and sophisticated for such a protected adolescent. One series featured Marilyn Monroe beset by jealous coeds on the Newcomb campus. Ken idolized Monroe as the perfect woman, beautiful, sensual, and vulnerable. The year after he graduated from high school, Ken wrote a letter to Bosley Crowther of the *New York Times,* praising him for an article he had written about Monroe. Crowther responded with a short but pleasant note, which Ken took the trouble to save. The other cartoons for *Hullabaloo* tended to be satiric and pointed out the hypocrisies and foibles of students and faculty. In the midst of the staid fifties, Ken was challenging the status quo with the tools he had at hand. It is also possible that this was the best stab he could make at teenage rebellion, useless as it was for him to buck maternal authority on Audubon Street.

"There was a brittle quality to all his humor," recalled Dave Prescott, a friend and Tulane classmate. He and Ken often met for coffee in the commons. Prescott said that "Ken had a wonderful wit, and he was a very good raconteur." Over the years Prescott heard many people repeating anecdotes that Ken had told him. This showed Prescott that Ken "polished his material." Some of these stories would appear in his writing. Although Prescott said that he did not know Ken well, they did correspond after undergraduate school.

Prescott told two revealing stories about Ken. At one point Ken had been interviewed by the dean of Newcomb for an award. The panel asked if he knew any medieval music, and Ken answered that he knew "Greensleeves." The fact that this bit of arcane knowledge impressed the panel amazed Ken, who assumed that everyone would know that song. Another time Ken said that May Byrne, his second-grade teacher, who lived near the elementary school, had been so delighted with Ken's talent that she invited him over after school for snacks and chats. To Prescott these two anecdotes show that "Ken was a person who had to feel special, and at the same time there was a dismissive quality about him. The stories Ken told tended to build him up, or by his condescension show how much more perceptive and knowledgeable he was relative to the situation." Even so, said Prescott, "Ken was very, very funny."

Prescott's cousin Emilie Griffin got to know Ken quite well at Tulane. They traveled in "adjacent social circles. In college we hung around together. Things like going to the cafeteria together, and mostly in groups. We were very good friends." She related that Ken was fun to be around, saying, "He could do wonderful impersonations and was extremely funny." She remembered that he was handsome with a very Irish face. Griffin was a theater major, and her best college memory of Ken was when she was "playing the part of St. Joan in *The Lark*. I went to a Mardi Gras dance dressed in my St. Joan costume. I remember dancing with Ken. He was not my date, but we danced. He was a wonderful dancer. Not many people know that about him. He really was a wonderful dancer." It would not be the last time they danced together.

Free time was at a premium when Ken became an upperclassman. He was working toward a degree in the honors program. When he was invited to join Phi Beta Kappa, Ken began to think about what kind of graduate program to aim for. Most of the writing he had been doing for the school paper was nonfiction, but Ken was determined to be a fiction writer, an ambition he related to very few people. Although he talked a lot, Ken said very little about himself or his literary aspirations. Friends like Dave Prescott and Emilie Griffin did not know that he was already writing fiction.

Writing wasn't easy since Ken lived at home with his biggest fan and supporter. While his mother stroked his ego, she also wanted to be included in whatever he did. This sort of controlling influence hindered the creative process, and Ken found it necessary to write MOM, PLEASE DON'T TOUCH on the covers of his notebooks to keep Thelma from disturbing his work. Still, he never made a move out the door to a place of his own. Whenever he lived in New Orleans, Ken felt bound to live with his parents. Although he made excuses like lack of money and the fact that the Tooles were getting older and needed him, more likely the truth was that leaving home was scarier and more painful than staying put.

Ken pledged the Delta Tau Delta fraternity while in his sophomore year at Tulane. It was a small fraternity with only eleven young men in the pledge class. Although Ken did not room there, the chapter house provided a place for him to spend time away from home. During the week he ate lunch at the house, and he attended the weekend parties. As this was New Orleans, there were plenty of parties, but the Delts were one of the more serious fraternities on campus. Their members tended to have higher grade point averages than other Greek groups and equally high ambitions.

Sam Rosamond was a pledge brother of Ken's who knew him as well as anyone in the group, yet Rosamond's memories of Ken are different from those of other people who knew him at the time. He does not recall Ken as being very witty or fond of jokes. Ken was a quiet member of the fraternity, though he was friendly to everyone. "I am not sure why he joined or why he quit," said Rosamond. He dropped out at the beginning of the spring semester, just before initiation. "He must not have gotten what he wanted out of fraternity life," said Rosamond, "and just decided to quit." He may also have quit due to time constraints and lack of money. He always had a part-time job to supplement his scholarship. The fraternity fees amounted to twenty dollars a month, including lunches, but this may have been a luxury he couldn't afford.

When interviewed, many people have called Ken a "loner." Even Jane McGee Kingsmill, as fond as she was of Ken, said, "that term definitely describes him." The word summons up images of serial killers and of Howard Hughes, but nothing could be further from the reality of John Kennedy Toole. He loved to be with people, all kinds of people. He was a dedicated observer of all aspects of human behavior. In his early stage experience he had learned how to be the life of the party who could send an audience into hysterics. One of his Dominican College students said she always had to make sure there was Kleenex in her purse when she came to class, because she would need it to wipe the tears she cried laughing at his jokes.

Although he had the gift of inspiring laughter in others, Ken was not a happy person, and getting a reputation as a loner was his own fault. He found it difficult to form and sustain close friendships. Ken's home life was so proscribed that he cherished the hours he spent out and about on his own. He traveled in many different circles and took care to see that none of them overlapped. For good reason, he was careful to never bring together the different people he knew. Each group would view him in a different way, and he would adjust his personality to suit the group. As an actor he had learned to play many parts, and he carried that over into his life.

In his sophomore year, on a serendipitous blind date, Ken met Ruth

Lafranz Kathmann, a Newcomb journalism major from Mississippi. They had much in common, especially their lively personalities. "We thought alike," she said, "and always laughed at the same things." Kathmann was bright, ambitious, and possessed of an extremely dry wit. An academically gifted student, her excellent grades assured her of a place in graduate school. Ken and Ruth loved to talk. Although their first date was to a dance, the two spent most of the time in conversation.

Ken and Ruth began dating each other exclusively, going to dances and movies, but it was never a true romance. They loved each other's company, but they never were in love in a serious or sexual way. Kathmann was emphatic that she "absolutely never" entertained the thought that she and Ken had a passionate attraction for each other. It never occurred to her to question why that might be. She only knew that she would not be the one for him, but they continued to see each other in New Orleans and farther north.

Kathmann met Ken's mother once in a tense, emotional visit to Audubon Street. Thelma didn't think any woman could be good enough for her son, a notion not unusual for a parent scared of losing control of a child, and she received Kathmann with the hostility one directs toward an intruder. In an interview for the *Times-Picayune* in 1980, Thelma told reporter Jeanie Blake that although women pursued her "terribly attractive" son, he "wasn't interested in them, mentally or physically." Thelma wasn't comfortable talking to Blake about other women in Ken's life, and she dismissed the possibility that anyone except her was important to him, saying "Boys and men have romantic feeling towards their mothers, you know." Later, New Orleans friend Rhoda Faust would recall that Thelma spoke of being the "only woman my son ever wanted" to be with for any length of time.

During his days at Tulane, Ken's college friends thought they were his only friends. They discussed intellectual activities and planned rosy futures over dinner in wood-paneled pubs on St. Charles Avenue. When asked if Ken would have spent much time in the French Quarter, one friend and former Tulane student sniffed, "Only tourists and people from Baton Rouge ever went into the Quarter." Actually Ken learned the Vieux Carré intimately, but not in the company of anyone from the

university. He got that sort of education from a very different set of
friends.

Sidney Snow was one who knew a very different John Kennedy
Toole from the brilliant honor student that the uptown people knew.
They met in 1957 when Snow was still in high school. Snow said, "He
just showed up one day at Metairie Junior High School when we were
loading instruments on the truck. He asked if he could help, and we put
him to work." Then and now Snow was a New Orleans musician playing a variety of instruments everywhere for money and the love of the
sounds. He still plays for tourists in and around Jackson Square, near
the Café du Monde. "They call me 'Dr. Guitar,'" he said proudly in
that peculiar Bronx accent the New Orleanians call "y'at."

Snow called Ken "Tooley," pronouncing the silent "e" on Toole. He
said he knew people who called Ken "Johnny," but "Tooley was a nickname that came from the Channel. Someone must have seen it written
and thought you had to say it that way." Snow grew up in the St.
Thomas housing projects near Clay Street. It was a rough part of town,
and he "got the impression that Toole's family wouldn't want him hanging around the Irish Channel." Ken was at least six years older than the
guys in Snow's band, but Snow always "thought he was younger than
me. He was so enthusiastic about music and bands and all. He wanted
to know all the lyrics to the blues and all the funky old songs." The
funky blues songs were the reason Ken showed up at the junior high
school. "He heard that my brother was a blues authority," said Snow,
and Ken wanted to talk to him. From that time until 1966, Ken was a
"hang out guy with the band. There was no set time for him to come
around. Ken would just turn up when he was in town and the band was
playing," Snow remembered. "He'd be off the scene for a while, but
then he'd show up again." At this time Snow was playing with the Night
Owls and a singer named Rollin' Stone. One of the other musicians in
the band, Don Stevens, who went by "Steve Cha-Cha," became a special
friend to Ken.

Stevens played guitar and loved the Beat poets. "That's what they
had in common," said Snow. "He and Tooley kept a notebook with
words for blues music and poetry in it." Some of the poetry was about
the Beats. There was a local poet named Moondog, now deceased, who
used to write the kind of poetry they liked. Asked where the notebook

is now, Snow regretted that, although he'd once had possession of it and has looked for it over the years, he is sure that the notebook, like so much else, "got lost when [Hurricane] Betsy came through New Orleans." Snow said that six feet of water in the street flooded his home and ruined all he had in 1965.

Like many musicians, Stevens had a second job. He was the hot tamale man and pushed a cart filled with New Orleans' Own Fiesta Hot Tamales around the city. Ken would take Stevens's route when Stevens needed some relief. Snow said that Ken loved to eat those hot tamales. "Steve was closer to Tooley than to anyone else in the group," recalled Snow. "Tooley had a tambourine" and would play on the street with Stevens on guitar. In the mid-sixties Stevens burned out on a bad acid trip, and Ken was with him when the ambulance came to take his friend away. Snow said that it "upset Tooley real bad because they were close." Although Stevens survived, his mind was badly damaged by drugs. Later he remembered knowing Toole, but recalled nothing about their times together.

Because it was their home turf, the musicians used to hang out in the Irish Channel at Parasol's Bar. This famous landmark is known today for its wild St. Patrick's Day party attended by thousands of people, but in the fifties it was just a neighborhood tavern. The white frame building sat on a corner smack in the middle of the Channel on a narrow curbless street. The houses surrounding it were dilapidated Victorian-era Creole cottages decorated with unpainted gingerbread trim. These long, narrow structures were set close together. Louvers on the doors and windows provided some ventilation, but ensured that there was little peace and privacy. It wasn't the part of town that the fastidious Ken was used to, but "Tooley loved it," said Snow. He would come to Parasol's, drink, and "eat two roast beef po' boys from there at one time." Since these sandwiches are a foot long and stuffed with meat, it is apparent that Ken did not leave his appetite uptown. Snow remembered that they were just kids, always looking for excitement and "some trouble to get into." They liked to play sports, baseball in particular, and "Tooley called himself a pretty good ballplayer." They used to drink beer, and some of them, Ken included, would break Benzedrex inhalers (containing an amphetamine derivative) for a quick high, though Ken had a near religious feeling for liquor. New Orleans has always been a hard-drinking town, and in those days being able to hold one's liquor was the sign of a real man.

"Pot didn't come in," said Snow, "until around the time of Sergeant Pepper"—at the end of the sixties, by which time Ken was no longer with the group.

Snow related that one night, when they were sneaking into Audubon Park to go fishing in one of the ponds, "Tooley got stuck on a fence post." He remembered that Ken was a big heavy guy and "it took four of us to pull him off the post" and out of the mud. They laughed all the time. Ken was "witty, funny, fast, fast, fast. Especially puns; we used to pun a lot." It was silly, juvenile humor. The other guys would get enough and say, "Shut up, shut up." Ken entertained them with his imitations. "He could do anyone, and he did great duck calls, too," Snow said. "Tooley would cup his hands and make a sound," then he would holler, " 'Feeding call!' He seemed like a real good brother to me." Ken helped load the band's equipment, ran errands, picked up hamburgers, and assisted in setting up for gigs. His reward was being around artistic bohemian people who never made an intellectual demand or voiced a criticism of him. Ken enjoyed the same kind of adolescent fun with them that he'd had years before with the McGee children.

When Ken graduated with honors from Tulane in 1958, he looked forward to pursuing his advanced degree there or farther afield. He took graduate courses at his alma mater that summer, but first worked for a month in Biloxi, Mississippi. Snapshots taken on the beach at that time show a relaxed and happy Ken looking trim and handsome. Around his neck hangs a silver scapular medal, which, according to the religious teachings of his childhood, offered the protection of the Sacred Heart of Jesus. In other photographs, Ken is pictured holding a cigarette. Like many of his friends, he had taken up smoking—that sophisticated habit of the 1950s.

Returning home, Ken went to work in the office of Haspel Brothers, Inc. This locally owned family business manufactured men's clothing. Ken worked part time and grossed forty dollars a week. His boss was J. B. Tonkel, who was married to one of the Haspel daughters and ran the division that made Tulane-brand shirts. The work was tedious, and Ken had a lot of opportunities to observe the world of business. Because he knew and loved New Orleans gossip, Ken watched the Haspel family's business dealings with great interest, absorbing and remembering their troubles and intrigues.

Five

I had a pair of British tan, which are really orange, pants. When it got cold I would wear those, and I had a green corduroy shirt and a red corduroy coat, and blue wool socks . . . and then I had the hat. . . . It was a little rain hat, and it had ear flaps.

—*Robert Byrne, 1995 interview*

IN 1958 JOHN KENNEDY TOOLE applied for and won a Woodrow Wilson Fellowship to study for a master's degree in English literature at Columbia University. Three years earlier, during his fall semester as a sophomore, Ken had traveled to New York with two college friends. The theater, the museums, and the city itself were as exciting as he remembered them from his high-school trip. He saved the Broadway playbills in his old scrapbook. The idea of living in New York thrilled him. Equally attractive was the prospect of moving away from home and taking on the big city on his own.

Unlike many young people who leave home for the first time, Ken remained extremely focused after uprooting to the Big Apple. It helped that his academic life provided a firm structure. Finishing a master's degree in one year is possible with a great deal of work, and Ken never shied away from that. There wasn't going to be much time for socializing, but when he put forth some effort, Ken made friends easily. Another Tulane student, Elizabeth Marshall, had won a fellowship as well, and Ruth Kathmann was also there. Their presence lent a safety net of southern sensibility when Yankee ways got too much to bear.

Like many southerners who move north, Ken at first found New York intimidating. To begin with there was so much *more* of everything there—four seasons instead of just two, and more kinds of people as well. Religion and politics played a part in the life of the city in a way Ken had never imagined. This was also the end of a staid and settled decade in postwar America. Already the cultural revolution of the sixties was happening in New York, and everything was coming unglued. Columbia itself was moving out of the midcentury doldrums and entering a period of change.

In order to complete his postgraduate work in a single year, Ken had to take a full load in school. That left no time for employment, and he was forced to use his grant money to make ends meet. Living in a dormitory like Furnald Hall was cheap, but he always needed extra cash. He couldn't count on his parents for assistance because they were doing well to take care of themselves. Often during Ken's sojourn in the city, Uncle Arthur and Aunt Nandy would send the odd check to rescue the fortunes of the grad student.

His good friend and steady date Ruth Kathmann, enrolled in the Columbia graduate program in journalism, also had very little money to spend, and everything they did was predicated on how much it would cost. The places they went and events they attended were ones that could be done cheaply. Ken was always complaining that he had no money, and the dates were usually Dutch treat, but Ken was thoughtful when it came to Ruth. If she were ill he would leave an apple and a note in her office mailbox to cheer her up.

Since Ken loved to dance, one of his favorite places was the Roseland Ballroom. Ken and Ruth would dance all night for two dollars. This was something that the couple did alone. The Big Band sound was outdated to most young people in the days when Buddy Holly was topping the charts, but Ken and Ruth loved the live orchestra at the old dance palace. As the youngest and liveliest couple on the floor, they attracted a great deal of flattering attention. They would dance until the place closed, fueled only by soft drinks since no liquor was allowed. Ken and Ruth kept steady company that year and were fond of each other.

The story of their relationship has always been a confusing one, and this is partly due to Kathmann herself. Her contemporaries said that they remember the couple being engaged. Contradicting that, Kathmann said in an interview for Dixie magazine (the Sunday magazine section of the *Times-Picayune*) that though Ken proposed, she rejected him outright. When questioned later she did not want to put a time or place to this proposal. In his 1995 interview, Robert Byrne said that they were engaged, but that Kathmann got tired of waiting around for Ken to finalize plans. For his part, Ken never discouraged any talk of his having a serious girlfriend. Tied as he was by family and financial obligations, it would have been difficult for him to contemplate marriage even if he had been seriously in love. His mother would have put a stop to any such nonsense. It may have been that talk of an engagement was a cover for a fear of physical intimacy or sexual ambivalence. What is certain is that there was more smoke than flame in his relationship with Kathmann. After Ken returned to Louisiana, they did not get together on a regular basis and she went on to marry someone else.

At Columbia, Ken was poring over the books every moment he could, trying to get everything done in one year according to his plan. His master of arts degree was granted by the Department of English and Comparative Literature following an examination and a master's essay. Ken's topic was the humor of Elizabethan poet John Lyly. Because this was the same subject as his honors thesis at Tulane, much of the research had already been done.

The only creative writing that Ken produced at Columbia was connected with his graduate work. Two short stories written then were dark with loneliness and dread. The characters were violent, pitiful, and unredeemed. The poems, like the stories, were immature and floundering. A trio of poems about New York that referenced obscure texts may have impressed the teacher, but they did not make for good verse. Ken at twenty-one had not found his voice, and there was little comedy in these pieces. He would find that voice much farther south, in a city with more than its share of colorful characters. It is interesting to note that

Ken signed his graduate-school work as John Toole, reserving Ken for use by friends in Louisiana.

Ken returned to his home state in the summer of 1959 to take a position as an assistant professor of English at Southwestern Louisiana Institute (SLI), in that part of the state known as Acadiana. Now called the University of Louisiana at Lafayette, the school then supported a student body of five thousand, mostly from the surrounding region. The Cajun patois could be heard in the corridors, and things French were greatly encouraged, especially food. Ken often said that SLI had the fattest English department in the Deep South. After a year of living on bland Yankee food, Ken fell into a culinary heaven of filé gumbo, craw-fish étouffé, and jambalaya served at a never-ending round of parties where he soon became one of the most sought-after guests. It was with-out a doubt the most wonderful year of his life. Ken reached out to people there in a way he never had before, and he developed a deep trust with the friends he made in Lafayette—a trust that continued for the rest of his life.

Ken made such an indelible mark on the lives of those who met him at SLI that years later they remembered him vividly. Wearing his new Brooks Brothers suits with his tie thrown over one shoulder, Ken brought an Ivy League air to the small campus. His intelligence was recognized and his humor appreciated. Though he was only a three-hour drive from his parents, that was far enough away for Ken to live his own life. In his role as teacher, partygoer, and jolly bachelor, Ken found Lafayette a place where he could shine.

He secured quarters in a garage apartment on Convent Street, the street where author Katherine Anne Porter had once lived. The apart-ment was in a wood-frame, two-story building behind a large, tree-shaded home named Shadowlawn by its owner, who was a legendary character in Lafayette Parish. Mrs. Elizabeth Montgomery was a doyenne of Acadian society, a great defender of tradition, and one of the town's first Republicans. Ken was intrigued by the woman and her amaz-ing costumes. She favored wearing startling ensembles of red and pink and decorated her hair with camellias or cartwheel hats. For a Mardi Gras ball Mrs. Montgomery dressed in a kimono and put painted chop-sticks in her hair. The Carnival season in Lafayette was a scaled down but gaudy version of New Orleans festivities, and Mrs. Montgomery was one of its guiding lights.

Ken liked his landlady more than his lodgings. The small furnished downstairs apartment was dark and gloomy. There was one large bedroom/living-room combination, as well as a kitchenette and a very small bathroom. The trees surrounding the unairconditioned apartment kept air circulation to a minimum and the pesky insect population at a maximum. Mrs. Montgomery had advised Ken to keep the outside light off so as not to attract the bugs, but also because the rent included electricity. Always one to value his privacy, Ken did not encourage visitors and spent many hours alone reading, marking papers, and perfecting his party patter.

The second-floor apartment was rented to Elemore Morgan Jr., a young artist with degrees from LSU and the Ruskin School of Drawing and Fine Arts at Oxford University. Ken and Morgan didn't see much of each other, except for occasional chats over Coke or coffee. Because he was poor and had no television, Morgan read a lot of books from the library. His taste was eclectic, running from Russian literature to Thomas Hardy and the Brontës. Ken had not read many of these works. Once Morgan asked Ken what he thought about Dickens's *Nicholas Nickleby*. Ken was taken aback by the fact that there were whole areas of literature of which he was ignorant. It had never occurred to him that intellectually he might have become narrow and specialized. Morgan broadened Ken's view of literature, and in turn Ken introduced his neighbor to Evelyn Waugh, Kingsley Amis, and other twentieth-century British writers.

At the time Ken never let on to anyone that he was doing any writing of his own, but Morgan remembered him as a true observer of human nature. Ken had a detached but comprehensive view of things around him. Morgan's strongest memories of Ken concerned his New Orleans stories. Morgan would repeat these stories long before he knew that Ken had written a book about the city. Ken had a true fix on New Orleans that really crystallized it for Morgan. Ken's take on everyone who lived there was witty and entertaining, but the stories always had an edge to them. Often they would be about little men who sat around the house in their underwear drinking beer and getting yelled at by their wives.

Some of the stories Ken told were quite cynical and critical, concerning the disparity between the public façade and the private lives of the people he viewed as social climbers. A typical anecdote describes an uptown family who just had to keep up with their neighbors. They had to belong to the best Mardi Gras krewes, take the right vacation, and wear the right clothes. Yet they were so broke that if company came unexpectedly, the mother would run to the Toole house and borrow food to serve for dinner.

Ken related these tales complete with appropriate voices. He had a mimic's ability to briefly become a person he had observed. He could take someone apart in a few witty phrases. Although he would leave the listener helpless with laughter, Ken's wit was often shocking because he would dissect his friends as well as strangers. Everyone was fair game to him, and no one knew who would be skewered next and added to his repertoire. Ken pillaged the people around him to feed his sense of the absurd. He saw life as a passing parade and gave everyone equal time, never singling anyone out for particular attention unless he was truly original. Especially favored by Ken were people who were unusual and strong enough to not give a damn what others thought of them.

Such a person was Bob Byrne, English professor and certified eccentric. Byrne's Aunt May had taught Ken in elementary school, and both men were products of a New Orleans upbringing. In 1960 Byrne fascinated John Kennedy Toole, and according to many colleagues at SLI, he was the inspiration for the character of Ignatius J. Reilly in the novel Ken would write. Byrne's area of specialization was the medieval period. He and Ken had many discussions about Boethius and the wheel of Fortuna. Byrne later contended that Ken liked to talk about these things but had no deep understanding of them. It was Byrne's personal idiosyncrasies that caused Ken to take special note. Byrne, who was forever talking about theology, geometry, and his rich inner life, played the lute and worried about his weight, which had a tendency to balloon. Byrne had an aversion to driving a car and considered himself a devoted slob, wearing baggy clothes in an unruly mix of odd colors.

Then there was the hat. Just like Ignatius, Byrne had a deer-stalker hat, but in red not green. Byrne kept the ear flaps up and used the headwear as rain gear, and Ken gave him a bad time about it. Byrne admitted to others that there were some similarities between himself and Ignatius, but took care to point out the differences. The back garden of Byrne's house, although a fantasy landscape of stone lanterns and garden statuary, was neat and well tended, something Ignatius would never have been able to accomplish.

Still, Byrne was stuck with Ken's written exaggeration of some of his characteristics. George Deaux, who taught at SLI after Ken had left, recognized Byrne in Toole's manuscript. In a letter from his home in Fumisawa City, Japan, Deaux wrote: "When I first read *Dunces* in the early 1980s, it was immediately apparent to me that the protagonist was based on Bob Byrne. I was so persuaded of this coincidence that I suspected the improbable manuscript history that was recounted in the reviews was simply a publisher's fabrication to sell books. I thought Byrne was the author using a pseudonym. Not only does the Ignatius character seem to be based on Bob, but I am sure I have heard Bob express some of the opinions and tell some of the anecdotes that appear in the book."

Nicholas Polites, a fellow faculty member at SLI in the fall of '59, first met Ken in an English seminar class at Tulane in 1958. When Ken got up to read a paper, Polites had been quite impressed. He said it was the most impressive student paper he had ever heard. Their arrival at Lafayette gave them a chance to renew and deepen their friendship. Although they were both first-year teachers, Ken's salary was higher. Polites attributed this pay inequity to their differing credentials, thinking that a master's from Columbia University carried more weight than his own from Tulane. What did sting at the time was the unequal treatment the two new teachers received from the faculty, a situation that puzzled Polites for many years.

In 1960 SLI was a regional college that had not attained university status. The English faculty was small but very competent as well as very competitive. In the department newsletter that notes the arrival of Ken and Polites, there is mention of the fact that Polites had an aunt on the library staff. Although he never saw this article, when Polites heard about it years later he seemed to think it may have been written to alert the English department about possible nepotism. Whether this relationship figured into it or not, Polites said that he was snubbed socially during the time he was in Lafayette, while Ken, on the other hand, was lionized. The "icy social reception" Polites received was so blatant that he has long wondered over it. He was not invited to the faculty parties or asked to participate in activities that his friend was encouraged to attend. The faculty was extremely friendly and receptive to Ken, who, while he enjoyed the attention, downplayed it to Polites. Though to some extent Polites envied Ken's popularity, it did not affect their relationship. To amuse Polites, Ken would describe the parties in hilarious detail, skewering the guests and the goings-on with his usual harrowing wit. These conversations and Ken's recognition of the absurdity of it all went a long way to reassure Polites, who chose not to worry about his lack of social success.

Polites was drafted during the fall, but he was allowed to finish the semester before returning to New Orleans to await the army's call. During the time they taught in Lafayette, Ken and Polites enjoyed bachelor life, coming and going as they pleased. One Saturday Polites cooked dinner for Ken, and they stayed up drinking until four in the morning. Polites remembered it as "the most alcoholic evening I've ever had." They woke on a dreary, overcast day with raging hangovers. Even a Sunday drive in the country didn't clear their aching heads.

On another weekend Ken visited with Polites at his aunt's house to listen to music, including a Frances Faye album Polites had recently purchased. Ken loved the nightclub singer, whom he had seen perform in New York. He once jokingly asked another friend if Frances Faye was God.

Ken and Polites shared rides home several times, but after teaching together all week, they went their separate ways in New Orleans. They would spend the weekends with their families and then meet up for the ride back to college. At the end of the semester, Polites was living at home and celebrating his final days as a civilian.

On one of Ken's visits home, Polites invited him to a gay party in the French Quarter. It was being held at the apartment of an older man who was a prominent member of his family's law firm. Ken agreed to go, but the evening proved a disappointment. Polites recalled that he took Ken there "thinking he might find it entertaining on some level, or might have wanted to be introduced to gay life," but he remembers Ken "standing alone, bristling with discomfort and self-consciousness. It was

as if there was a moat around him and the drawbridge was drawn."
When Ken and Nick Polites arrived about nine o'clock, the party had
not really gotten started. They stayed for about a half hour, but Polites
was "well aware that Ken wasn't enjoying it." He was not sure if it was
he or Ken who suggested they leave.

Polites remembers being fascinated by Ken's reaction to the party.
When they got into the car, Ken was uncharacteristically silent. Instead
of heading down St. Charles toward home, he drove off in the direction
of Lake Pontchartrain. It seemed to Polites that since Ken wasn't heading anyplace in particular, he might want to talk. Polites suggested coffee, and they stopped at a nearby diner. At the table, Ken "unburdened
himself," strongly expressing his "distaste for the gay life," saying it was
not "worthy."

Polites, who was living the sort of life Ken had just disparaged, felt
confused and put down. He also felt sadness for his friend. He knew
that Ken could be "intolerant, censorious even," and Polites thought that
this lack of openness "cuts one off from a lot of things."

Not so long before this occasion, Ken had come by the Polites family
home with a handsome companion. Polites said that "it must have been
immediately after I met the young man that Ken told me they had been
in high school together, that the young man had taken a great fancy to
him and that they were or had been lovers. He was unmistakably proud
of his conquest." Polites was doubtful about the nature of the relationship. He took Ken to be "repressed sexually," and considering the young
man's good looks, he wondered if Ken's claim was more wishful thinking than anything else.

This was the only occasion that Polites heard Ken refer to a man in
a sexual way, and the only time he heard him talk about sex relating to
anyone, male or female. The high-school affair of which Ken had once
boasted to another friend, if true, seems to have been the first and possibly the only time he was ever in love. After the party in the Quarter,
however, it seemed that Ken was intent on denying any desire for a male
relationship, whether because of fear of disappointment or rejection, or
perhaps out of distaste for carnal contact. Ken certainly tried hard to
keep his emotional life in check. Because Polites valued Ken's friendship,
he did not bring up the subject again.

Pat Rickels, an English department colleague and dear friend of Ken's, later ventured the opinion that Ken had been "brainwashed by the priests and nuns" to believe that homosexuality was a mortal sin committed by choice and not a chance of birth. She believes that "this would have been a terrible burden for him, because he would never have felt that it was okay to be homosexual" and remain a Catholic welcomed by the Church. If Ken did consider homosexuality sinful, he may have determined to reject any attraction he felt toward men. His reaction to the party could have been a sign of that inner struggle. Though Ken often expressed interest in women, there is no indication that he engaged in a physical relationship with anyone of the opposite sex—not, at least, with his close female companions, who stated that they shared nothing more intimate than brief good-night kisses with him. Such chastity was expected at that time, however, especially of well-mannered, well-bred boys from New Orleans. It was hoped that men of good Catholic up-bringing would keep their libidos in check until marriage. Despite good intentions, there were many who failed to resist temptation. In this, as in other things, Ken seemed different from his fellows. He had abhorred outward shows of sexuality even as a teenager, when most boys basked in the heat their hormones were stirring up. It could be that the notion of a sexual relationship with anyone held little appeal for self-conscious Ken with his ingrained ideas of propriety.

With Polites's departure, Ken grew closer to the Rickels family—Milton, Pat, and their young son, Gordon. The couple was only a few years older than Ken and also just starting career jobs. None of them had any money to speak of, but that never stopped anyone in Lafayette from having a good time. There were parties with lots of spaghetti and cheap Chianti. Ken drank little around them, and Pat Rickels remembered him becoming intoxicated only once in the year he was teaching at SLI.

The Rickels had bought a tract of land near the Vermilion River on which they were planning to build a house. Once or twice a week Ken would come over for supper, and the four of them would go out to the property to cut grass and clear brush. Ken worked as hard as anyone, though he was unused to outdoor exertion. He had gained weight, so the exercise was good for him. Pat Rickels said that because Ken was so bright and entertaining it was easy to overlook how handsome he was. He was vain as well and forever worried about being fat. His clothes were preppy, and he always had a starched look about him. It was a real stretch for Ken to get sweaty and dirty cutting grass and raking the Spanish moss that had fallen from the live oak trees, but he loved it. The Rickels would sometimes pack a picnic, and they all would eat on the ground along the bayou, telling stories and enjoying each other's company.

Ken enjoyed those quiet moments with the Rickels, though he was much in demand on the faculty party circuit, where he displayed his ruthless wit. A friend said that constantly trying to be a live wire exhausted Ken, yet he felt compelled to play that part. Just as in childhood, when he was encouraged and sometimes forced to perform, Ken would enter a room armed with a quiver full of sharp stories and barbed one-liners. He would zing these out until his audience was weak with laughter, though he hadn't cracked a smile. Home life with the Rickels was therapeutic for Ken. He enjoyed baby-sitting Gordon, who was in the second grade, and often took him to the movies. Because the child loved to be read to, Ken gave Gordon a collection of books he had saved from his own childhood, including the Oz books, *Black Beauty,* and *Alice in Wonderland.* Gordon was killed years later in a motorcycle accident, and Pat Rickels has cherished the books that Ken gave him, as well as the good times they shared.

If Ken had one fault obvious to friends and colleagues, it was his concern over money. Finances had always been a great worry to the Tooles, and Ken was an old hand at squeezing a nickel. His close-fistedness finally affected his social life in Lafayette. Although no one there had much money, people did a great amount of entertaining on the little they had. Ken went to all the parties, but he didn't reciprocate. Pat Rickels said with great affection that he was just plain stingy and a constant freeloader. She suspected that he baby-sat Gordon because she threw in a free supper. Pat and others attributed the fact that Ken didn't date to his lack of funds.

Actually, such parsimony was part of the plan Ken had set for himself. He had decided to stay in Lafayette for only one year before returning to Columbia to work on his doctorate. By living on as little as possible, Ken was saving what he could to make life easier in the big city. In the meantime the SLI crowd was getting fed up with shouldering the social load and getting paid back only with jokes and stories. They ganged up on Ken and forced him to give a party.

With the help of Pat Rickels and at her insistence, Ken approached Mrs. Montgomery with a request to give a party in the Shadowlawn garden. Then he coaxed his landlady to help him fix the food. Everyone Ken knew in town and on campus turned out, partly to see if it were really true that Ken was going to spend money. The spring weather cooperated by cooling enough to keep the mosquitoes away, a factor of paramount importance in South Louisiana. The party was hailed as the best given that year, and not just because of its uniqueness. For a first-time host, Ken turned out to be a natural. He put everyone at ease and kept his grandstanding to a minimum.

Ken even sampled his own bar and got a little drunk. Pat Rickels remembered with great delight that Ken was having such a good time, he didn't want anyone to leave. The Rickels had to get home to Gordon and relieve the baby-sitter, but Ken held them up in the driveway. He kept sticking his head in the car and thanking Pat with kisses. Every time Milton would try to drive away, Ken would give Pat another little kiss until Milton got tired of it and rolled up the window to choke him off.

People in Lafayette knew only what Ken chose to tell them of his life in New Orleans. He told them little or nothing about his family. One Sunday, the Tooles motored in from New Orleans, and Morgan remembered their arrival. Immediately he could see that Mrs. Toole was the stronger personality. Mr. Toole cowered behind his wife in a furtive sort of way. She dominated the conversation all the way to the Rickels house while Ken drove the car in silence. Morgan thought that she was intelligent and interesting, but she didn't seem to know the rules of polite conversation. She addressed the group instead of allowing any give and take. At the Rickels' things took a turn for the worse when Thelma met Pat. Knowing how much Ken loved and admired his mother, Rickels had been looking forward to meeting her, but they butted heads from the beginning. Thelma considered Rickels a threat to the maternal bond and began to assert herself loudly. It was embarrassing for everyone, especially Ken, as Thelma held forth on his achievements and ambitions. Rickels said that Thelma "was absolutely convinced that he was without flaw and that all the hopes of the world lay in him. It was an extreme form of maternalism, where all your pride and all your hopes are in one person. He had had to grow up with that burden. She was a very ostentatious, shrill, loud-voiced, bossy, bragging woman."

John Toole sat and said very little. Rickels said that "he was absolutely cuckoo, but in a sweet, quiet, retiring way." Ken had been open with the Rickels about his father's oddities, but never voiced any criticism of his mother. That afternoon Mr. Toole related to Rickels his suspicions that people were trying to break into his house in New Orleans and get him. He had put two or three locks on every door, including the inside doors so that he could retreat one room at a time. On the last one, the bathroom, he had put four separate locks. One reason for the Tooles' visit was to install extra locks in Ken's apartment so that his dad could stop worrying about him. Although John Toole was only in his early sixties, to Rickels he seemed old and feeble next to Mrs. Toole's vigorous presence. Because he was so quiet, people might not have realized how "kooky" Ken's daddy was, but Ken affectionately thought that funny. On the other hand, according to Rickels, Ken was "ashamed of his mother being so conspicuous. He was aware that it came out of purest love, even though of a pretty destructive kind. Ken knew that we could see this. He knew we were not imbeciles. Everybody just never said anything. We could just pretend that it was okay, but he knew it wasn't."

Later, with the visit mercifully over, the Tooles and Morgan returned to Ken's apartment. Ken took his mother through the garden to meet Mrs. Montgomery. Mr. Toole went upstairs with Morgan to see his art studio. Out of his wife's presence, John Toole seemed to blossom. He and Morgan talked about baseball. Mr. Toole described a major-league game he had attended in the 1930s. He surprised Morgan with a display of wit and mimicry about the game and the players. Though he was a small man, Toole seemed to grow in stature as he told Morgan stories about himself and his family. Morgan said the same thing was true of Ken. He and other friends remarked that Ken was very quiet around his mother. In her presence he became the silent and submissive child. The natural fun and silliness that always burbled out of him froze when

Mrs. Toole came on the scene. Pat Rickels said that his mother expected great and special things of Ken, and he just couldn't be allowed to act like a comedian. She said that "Mrs. Toole adored culture with a capital C," and Ken hid things from her, like his love of practical jokes, his habit of writing silly graffiti, and other secrets.

At the beginning of May a notice in the English department newsletter stated that Ken had accepted a three-year fellowship to work on his Ph.D. at the University of Washington in Seattle. The field he had chosen was literature of the Renaissance. Soon thereafter he received an offer to return to New York in pursuit of his advanced degree at Columbia, an idea attractive to Ken, but the offer carried no fellowship. In late May, when he was tendered a teaching appointment at Hunter College, Ken could afford to accept the place at Columbia.

Six

The news that I have from Southwestern indicates new and hitherto unexplored fields for gossip and feuding. Ah, well. I have escaped from that to a college where the faculty doesn't even talk to one another. Which is better?

—*John Kennedy Toole, in a letter to Elemore Morgan Jr.*

I N THE SUMMER OF 1960 Ken made a new friend in Lafayette. Nicholas Polites introduced Ken to Joel Fletcher, whose father was at that time president of SLI. Before returning to graduate school at Stanford, Fletcher was wiling away the summer writing press releases for the college's news bureau, a summer job arranged by his father. Neither he nor Ken was thrilled at the prospect of three months of heat and tedium, and their common misery made them good companions. The two became fast friends and remained in touch long after that time.

In mid-July Fletcher took a break from the bayou and headed for the lights of the French Quarter three hours away. He offered Ken a ride to New Orleans so that he could spend a weekend on Audubon Street. After visiting with his friends, Fletcher joined Ken at the Napoleon

House on Chartres Street for a po' boy and beer. They had become such good friends that they wanted to enjoy the city together.

Fletcher was shopping for books about Louisiana to add to his father's collection. In one of the Quarter's bookstores, Ken and Joel spied a woman bending over a bookshelf. Her very large backside poked toward the ceiling. The clerk, in an awed voice, identified the big behind as belonging to Frances Parkinson Keyes. Fletcher and Ken both admired and delighted in the novels of Evelyn Waugh and Flannery O'Connor's southern Gothic writings, but popular romances like Mrs. Keyes's *Dinner at Antoine's* were not on their short list.

The young men's time in New Orleans was spent in the French Quarter and the old Faubourg Marigny. They never ventured uptown to drop in on the Tooles, and there is no indication that Ken wanted Joel to meet his parents. One afternoon while strolling the poorer sections of downtown, they happened upon a scene that fascinated Ken with its cruel absurdity. In this rundown area people sat outside their unairconditioned houses, hoping for a breeze and gabbing with neighbors. Grubby children ran everywhere, chased by equally grubby mothers as a summer thunderstorm blew up and began to pelt the street and its inhabitants. In the midst of this downpour, one obstinate urchin named Charlie refused to duck for cover. Spying an available weapon, his outraged mother cracked him with a board as she screamed for him to come in from the rain. In a further display of maternal affection, she whopped Charlie again, yelling that playing in the rain would make him ill.

Ken loved this incident, and throughout the afternoon he mimicked the mother's downtown dialect and bellowed commands to her offspring. The spectacle of a beating administered out of care for the child's health struck Ken as delightfully grotesque.

Back in Lafayette, Fletcher and Ken spent long hours driving down the bayous into the heart of the Cajun country. They also drank in local bars where English was a second language, with the chank-a-chank sound of Cajun music blaring from a jukebox. Through Ken, Fletcher met the faculty of the English department, among them the brilliant but sartorially challenged Robert Byrne. Ken, who shared office space with

Byrne, related amusing anecdotes focused on the older professor's aston-
ishing wardrobe. There was no doubt that Byrne was an oddball when
it came to choosing his ensembles. Once he arrived for work sporting
three mismatched plaids and a very silly hat that amazed his officemate.
Byrne's students also eagerly anticipated his every appearance in class,
and one young woman took notes on his haberdashery rather than his
lectures.

Because of Fletcher's important connections on campus and Ken's
reputation as a raconteur, the two were popular at parties. At a summer
dinner hosted by President and Mrs. Fletcher, Ken was seated between
his landlady and another woman. Mrs. Montgomery had recently traveled to Alaska and made much of her adventures on a dogsled. In a deep
drawl she preached on the culinary merits of raw blubber versus the
nasty boiled version. Mrs. Montgomery thought the Eskimo people were
nasty as well, but excused them by declaring that the white man was behind their problems. Ken was entranced by his landlady's monologues,
but there was more fun yet to come.

Seated on his other side was a married friend of Mrs. Fletcher. Ken
loved her lavish maquillage and strips of imprudently long false eye-
lashes. A possibly apocryphal story had been circulated that once, during
a social function, part of her eye makeup had fallen on the floor. Afraid
the black, curly object was a cockroach, the socialite shrieked and repeatedly crushed her eyelash underheel. This night at the Fletchers', the
woman wore a white frock with a plunging decolletage partially filled by
a necklace of large glass beads. She fancied herself a writer, and her generous husband had paid for a volume of her poetry to be published by a
vanity press. As usual in the presence of older people, Ken was quiet, but
in any case there was little room for group discussion. Throughout the
meal Ken's landlady and the poet engaged in a dialogue of one-
upmanship. Fletcher, sitting across from Ken, watched his friend's delighted reactions to the ongoing battle for conversational control.

Over coffee, Ken passed the sugar bowl to Mrs. Fletcher's friend, but
she was too busy pontificating to notice that his finger was still curled
around the handle. To tease her, Ken staged a small tug-of-war, but involved as she was with making her point, the woman did not notice that

she was wrestling him for the sugar. Ken, however, enjoyed the episode tremendously and grinned across the table at his friend.

A few days after this evening, Ken left Lafayette to spend the rest of the summer in New Orleans, and September of 1960 found the two friends on opposite coasts—Fletcher in California finishing his education, and Ken in his second-favorite city teaching English at Hunter College for Women. This return to New York fit in with his plan to begin doctoral studies at Columbia. Ken had long looked forward to realizing his ambitions, but it was wrenching to leave Lafayette and the friends he had made. Although at first he was homesick for SLI, Ken was soon too busy for any extended melancholy.

In a letter to his aunt and uncle, Ken wrote:

> The cool clear autumn weather here makes my schedule seem easier than it really is. I spend every morning here at Hunter on Park Avenue teaching; in the afternoons I make it across town to Columbia to take courses. From my office on the twelfth floor (this sounds as if I'm in an executive suite), I have a fine view of midtown Manhattan, which at the moment is hidden somewhat by the always present blue-gray haze that hangs over the city.
>
> The students here are, for the most part, very sharp, very eager and interested, very worthwhile. The all-girl student body is principally Jewish and Irish, balanced in about a 50-50 split, and all drawn from the New York metropolitan area. I'm even teaching a Dominican nun, Sister Martha. . . .
>
> I'm renting a room on Riverside Drive that is large, has a limited view of the Hudson and New Jersey across the river, and is inexpensive by New York standards. . . .
>
> New York is its usual busy, preoccupied, hustling self, and I find that I must readjust to this maelstrom after my leisurely stay on Bayou Teche.

Ken felt more confident about living in New York than he had two years earlier. Even with his hectic schedule, he found time to socialize with colleagues and a small network of expatriate Louisianians. Emilie Dietrich Griffin, with whom he had worked on the *Hullabaloo* staff, had accepted a job with a New York advertising agency following her graduation from Newcomb. Griffin renewed her friendship with Ken, and they began to date. The couple did some of the same things that Ken and Ruth Kathmann had done, like dancing at Roseland and strolling through Greenwich Village. As usual with Ken, spending money was a problem, but even in New York it is possible to have fun on a small budget. Ken and Emilie rode the subways or walked. They cooked and partied in their small apartments, visited museums, attended lectures and exhibits. They shopped at Gimbel's and Macy's, but bought very little.

Emilie and Ken were not in love and shared nothing more intimate than a good-night kiss. Griffin never felt that the relationship was going to become serious. They were satisfied with things as they were. But it was a very warm relationship. Griffin really did care for Ken and believed he returned that affection. Moreover, she felt that Ken idealized her in some way. She said that in general "he treated women very honorably," but the two were never serious enough about each other to press the question of intimacy. As with other women Ken knew and dated, Griffin found nothing strange in the fact that he never made sexual advances. She says that he would have known she wasn't "that sort of girl," and consequently, he would have behaved himself no matter how he might have acted with other women. It never entered her mind that he might not be heterosexual. "It wouldn't have," she admits. "We [women] didn't think in those terms at all. Things were more innocent back then."

Ken loved being back in New York City, but he missed New Orleans. At a distance he began to analyze his hometown from a literary standpoint. He mused to Griffin that no author had ever captured the real city with all the parts and people that make it unique. He asserted that there were more sides to the city than authors like Tennessee Williams portrayed, and he wanted to write about those unknown parts. He began to frame a novel that would explore the thread of "Latin madness" that runs through New Orleans, but he was not yet ready to write about it.

As autumn turned colder, Ken's excitement with his job at Hunter cooled as well. From the beginning Ken had felt out of place in the classroom there, but he had hoped in time to develop a rapport with his students. Ken appreciated their intelligence, but they lacked the polished quality he was used to in southern women. For their part, the Hunter students did not know what to make of Mr. Toole's peculiar sense of humor. He came off to them as provincial, ill at ease, and not a bit funny. One reason for this may have been that at twenty-two, Ken was younger than many of his students. In any event, he failed to charm them as he had done in Lafayette, and this bothered him, though he refused to take all the blame for this unhappy situation. He felt that there were other factors working against him, and he may have been correct.

This was the beginning of the "cause" decade, and it seemed that Ken's students were all looking for one. In Dalt Wonk's article on Toole, Ken is reported to have said that "Every time the elevator door opens at Hunter, you are confronted by 20 pairs of burning eyes, 20 sets of bangs and everyone waiting for someone to push a Negro." As a white male from the Deep South, Ken was the most likely suspect, which was something he resented. He was dismayed by the liberal brand of narrow-mindedness he discovered in New York. Although New Orleans had always been publicly and politically segregated, there was among its people a tradition of tolerance, both religious and racial. Ken was shocked to find that in an integrated city like New York there was a large degree of personal intolerance. In particular he had trouble with the anti-Catholic sentiment of some students and faculty.

Ken was a Christmas-and-Easter churchgoer, but he had a cultural commitment to Roman Catholicism. It was as much a part of him as his fair complexion, and he couldn't understand why he should suffer scorn because of it. Emilie Griffin once went to observe him teach and noticed that he had scrawled on the blackboard: "Anti-Catholicism is the anti-Semitism of the intellectual." This didn't make points with the students. Unfortunately his arguments with them further undermined his authority as their teacher.

Another friend recalls Ken's growing frustration with life in New York. Clayelle Dalferes was a displaced native of Lafayette. Joel Fletcher mentioned her to Ken, who called her out of the blue, complaining that he was just starved for talk with someone from home. They enjoyed each other's company but argued constantly about politics. She said that their differing attitudes toward the burgeoning civil rights movement came between them. Dalferes was liberal-minded and thought that the South had to be shocked into changing its segregated system. Ken was as liberal as she, but he called himself a "southernist."

Ken wanted integration to be attained peacefully, by letting the South handle its own problems. He was particularly upset at what he perceived as a second northern invasion of his homeland. Ken thought that the idea of a Freedom Bus was ridiculous and dangerous. He told Dalferes that taking a bus full of Yankees and Negroes into the small towns in Mississippi to register black voters was "just asking for trouble." Resentful of outside interference, Ken wanted the South to change by its own efforts. Dalferes suspected that Ken would have been more of an activist if the troubles had been happening in California or New Jersey, but because they were happening in the South, he felt obliged to defend his homeland. Still, he did often put himself into the middle of controversy.

Both Ken and Dalferes had been elated by the election of John F. Kennedy to the presidency. In a letter dated February 3, 1961, written to Joel Fletcher, Ken expresses optimism about the new administration, as well as relief that Nixon has left the scene. Recalling his former landlady's staunch Republicanism, Ken remarks on how disappointed she must be at the failure of the WASPs to capture the White House. Ken also felt a kinship with the new president for reasons other than politics. Part of it was their shared name, plus being committed Democrats, Catholics, and sharing an Irish heritage.

Because Ken was so fond of movies, he and Dalferes often made the cinema part of their dates. Once they went to see a revival of D. W. Griffith's silent film *Birth of a Nation* at the New Yorker theater on Broadway. The audience was very boisterous, whooping and hollering when the dialogue cards came up. Ken was very still, offended by the reaction of the audience to what they were seeing on the screen. A couple sitting behind Ken and Dalferes was discussing the movie. The woman called it racist and inflammatory. At one point in the film, when armed black thugs attacked a southern family and the Ku Klux Klan came to their rescue, the woman said that the author took one grain of truth and built an entire fantasy around it. The young man with her asked sarcastically, "What truth?" Ken turned around and in his thickest southern drawl told them that "after Reconstruction" things like that had certainly happened in the South. Dalferes, scared that this would start a fracas because they were in hostile territory, was relieved when the couple didn't pursue the discussion. She knew Ken to be "a ferocious defender of the South" who could have gotten them into trouble.

As put off as Ken was by his students, he was treated with kindness and respect by the administration at Hunter. John W. Wieler, chairman of the English department, regarded Ken as an excellent teacher and was anxious to keep him on the faculty. Wunderkind Ken was the youngest professor ever to teach at Hunter. He did not do quite as well with the hierarchy at Columbia and felt out of place with the professors, though Dalferes said he was popular with the support staff there. He would have long conversations with the waitresses and busboys in the cafeteria, and was at ease entertaining them with his stories and jokes. Ken felt that the teachers at Columbia were arrogant and took themselves too seriously.

Ken's studies were not progressing as well as he would have wished. Having completed his master's in a single year, he found his patience tried by the slow pace of the doctoral program. Earning a Ph.D. meant years of classwork and writing papers specifically designed to please his mentors. Add to this proposals and submissions that must be approved every step of the way. For the first time since entering Miss Mercadel's class, Ken seemed overwhelmed by schoolwork. Disenchanted with the academic process, he vented his frustration in a letter to Joel Fletcher, expressing doubt that the rewards of a Ph.D. would be worth enduring the boredom and penury ahead of him.

His daily schedule was fragmented by the necessity of earning his living. Besides teaching at Hunter, Ken would take substitute work teaching night classes at City College whenever it was offered. He spent tedious hours crossing and recrossing the city late at night, much as Thelma Toole had once bused across New Orleans teaching charm and elocution to young ladies and gentlemen. Ken wrote to his parents about the rewards of the work:

> Classes are all proceeding perfectly. The [Gertrude] Stein class, after a little slapping about the head and shoulders, has developed into one of the most interested, alert of the four classes. The professor whose classes I assumed in night school last week phoned me this af-

ternoon to ask, "what did you do to those classes? They said they were the most exciting classes they'd ever had, covering psychology, philosophy, history, and literature. All the classes want you back. They spent all the time telling me how thorough and fascinating you were." (One of those classes applauded when I finished one night.) So, there's some recompense aside from the financial for all this fatigue.

When Ken was home in New Orleans for the Christmas holidays, he made a day trip to Lafayette. Although it seemed a backwater to him after New York, he had a wonderful time seeing the SLI crowd. The holidays went by quickly, and Ken had to hurry back to the city, where he had a chance to start the new year in a new apartment.

Ken's new residence was at 128 East 70th Street between Lexington and Park, on one of the most beautiful streets in the city. The apartment was on the fourth floor, and there was no elevator in the building, but it was much nicer than his previous place. Another change for Ken was the fact that this apartment came with a roommate.

Kent Taliaferro (pronounced *Tolliver*) was six years older than Ken, a Tulane graduate and native of New Orleans working in the city. Taliaferro's memory was somewhat vague about the particulars of that time and at odds with the recollections of his sister, Susan. He had leased this expensive apartment with a man who became ill and returned home to recuperate. Because he could not make the rent on his own, Taliaferro said that he thought he advertised in, among other places, the Hunter College newspaper. He said that when Ken called and came over to meet him, they agreed to share the rent and expenses. Ken was thrilled because the apartment was so nice and right around the corner from Hunter, thus cutting down on travel time. Though it seems a great coincidence that two people with such similar backgrounds should come together by accident in a metropolis like New York, Taliaferro couldn't recall meeting Ken by other means.

If Ken had thought that his new roommate would become a friend and confidant, he was mistaken. Taliaferro was a very private person, and he found Ken that way too. There is no evidence that Ken was doing any writing in his new apartment. In fact, Taliaferro recalled never seeing so much as a book or notebook anywhere in the apartment. Popular with his own wide circle of friends in New York, Taliaferro was constantly invited to dinner and to cocktail parties, but never included Ken in these outings, nor did he introduce Ken to any of his acquaintances. Asked why not, he said that he "was not interested in having much to do with Ken on a social basis." He liked Ken well enough, finding him friendly and nice to be with, but that was as far as Taliaferro wanted to take the relationship.

Ken and Taliaferro spent little time together, partly because of their schedules. In the evenings when Taliaferro had the luxury of free time to spend with friends, Ken had papers to grade and schoolwork to do before he could think of going out. Neither man had a lot of money, but since many of Taliaferro's outings took place at someone else's invitation, he didn't have to budget much for entertainment. Because Ken didn't know many people, he just didn't have much to offer in the way of social connections.

Although they were never buddies, Ken tried to become better friends with Taliaferro. He introduced his roommate to Emilie Griffin, who cooked dinner for them several times at her apartment. Once Ken wanted to see Jackie "Moms" Mabley at the Apollo Theatre. Ken had the knack of seeming at ease wherever he might be, but Taliaferro and Griffin were not sure they should go. By nagging and cajoling Ken convinced them that they wouldn't be at all out of place. He said that as people from the South they would be welcomed in an all-black theater, and he was right. Although they were the only three white people at the show, they had a wonderful time. No one paid them any attention. The audience was too busy laughing at the hysterically funny Mabley to care about who was sitting in the seats.

Despite their common background, when it came to personality Ken and his roommate were worlds apart. Taliaferro was reserved and kept his own counsel. Although he felt Ken was "lonely and very shy" around strangers, Taliaferro said that he knocked himself out trying to engage Taliaferro's attention when they were alone. Then Ken "wanted to talk about everything." Taliaferro got the impression that Ken's mind was constantly working and he craved communication. Ken wanted to express his thoughts and ideas on every subject in long conversations that exhausted Taliaferro, who felt that Ken was looking for "someone to have contact with on his same wavelength," but Taliaferro just wasn't that person. Ken didn't seem depressed by this rejection, and in fact, he kept trying to get to know his roommate better.

One evening at the apartment, Ken broached the subject of sex. From the outset of their shared living arrangements, Taliaferro had said that he did not care to know what kinds of sexual encounters, if any, his roommate was having. Ken had never brought anyone home with him while Taliaferro was there, nor was there ever evidence that he had entertained someone in Taliaferro's absence. Ken did not spend his nights elsewhere, and if he sought to make connections on the streets, he kept these brief engagements to himself. On this one occasion Taliaferro said that Ken wanted to "share feelings" about his [Ken's] homosexuality and to question Taliaferro about his own sex life. Taliaferro was not interested in discussing private matters with Ken, who was very persistent. In a genial albeit tactless way, Ken kept asking questions, curious to know which of Taliaferro's friends were gay. Uncomfortable with the conversation, Taliaferro again cut him off. Apparently Ken got the message and never brought up the subject again.

Susan Taliaferro Grossman, Kent's sister, was not surprised that her brother refused to talk of his private life. He had always been extremely discreet. As for Ken, Grossman felt he was gay upon meeting him, though she admitted that it would not be easy for just anyone to see through his façade. Ken's "public face was absolutely straight."

It had always seemed to Grossman unlikely that Ken and her brother had become roommates by chance. Besides their similar backgrounds, both men had a deep interest in languages. Ken was fluent in Spanish, and Taliaferro loved German. Later he would move to Munich permanently. Grossman remembered many of her brother's friends from New Orleans, some of whom also knew Ken. Her brother professed no definite memory of any of his hometown acquaintances except for Clay Shaw, whom Taliaferro remembers with great clarity and affection.

Kent Taliaferro spoke of Shaw as an extremely courtly gentleman with exquisite manners. His recollections of the man are at odds with the sly libertine portrayed in the Oliver Stone film *JFK*. Taliaferro said that Shaw entertained on a lavish scale, but always with taste and dignity.

As with so many people in his life, Ken made a strong and lasting impression on Grossman even though she knew him for a short time. In 1960 she had left Newcomb College to become a New York–based flight attendant for Pan American Airways. Her brother and Ken were two of the few people she knew in the city. Ken would come over to visit her in her tiny apartment, but she was never invited to East 70th Street. Her brother would have felt that she was snooping, and she was not comfortable around his friends. Although they were educated, successful men, she was never happy around them and constantly had to pretend that she was having a good time.

It was different with Ken, because he seemed genuinely delighted to meet her. He loved people, especially people from the South. Naturally he wanted to talk about home, but he loved to talk about everything. She was sure that his mind never rested. Spending time with him was like being part of a comedy revue. Ken laughed all the time. When he would tell a story, he played every part. He had a bizarre, exotic sense of humor, but Grossman said that she got the impression that he did not make things up. There was no sense of fantasy in his life. He spoke about what was real to him. It was no surprise to her that Ken destroyed himself, because the seeds of his destruction were there in his humor. It was a crazy kind of comedy that fed on itself. She had been brought up with that kind of neurotic wit and said that it is difficult to live with from either side.

It was obvious to Grossman that Ken was quite intelligent, but she began to see that he was so brilliant that he "just didn't know what to do with himself." To her, it wasn't IQ so much as a "real eccentricity" in the way he perceived life. When she called him "a genius," there was the impression that she was not just flattering his memory but stating her longtime conviction about him.

Susan and Ken never discussed sexual matters. Though she believed he was gay, she considered it none of her business. She felt he fiercely protected his heterosexual image, and respecting her friend's privacy, she did not raise the issue. Grossman was the first person since Ken's college days to say that he drank too much. He never seemed intoxicated, but she noticed he would keep on drinking when other people had stopped.

In mid-January 1961, Ken's mother came to New York to spend a week with him. Ken had a three-week hiatus between semesters, and he was procrastinating about working on his dissertation. Kent Taliaferro said that for the first few days Thelma stayed in a hotel. When he would come home from work, mother and son would be there after having spent the day sightseeing. Thelma stayed late into the night, but would be gone when Taliaferro woke up in the morning. Later in the week, when Taliaferro went out of town on vacation, Thelma moved in to stay with Ken.

While he was still there, Taliaferro had an opportunity to observe them, but he stayed out of the way. They did not seek his company, since they were perfectly content by themselves. He said they "never stopped talking." He would go to sleep at night hearing the murmur of their conversation, and it would greet him when he returned home in the evening. They did nothing but talk, laugh, and drink beer. According to Taliaferro, "they drank lots and lots of beer until late into the night." Every evening the refrigerator was loaded with beer bottles, and every morning the trash can was full of empties. Mrs. Toole was civil to Taliaferro, but she had little to say to him. In fact, Mrs. Toole met none of Ken's New York friends. This may have been because her time in the city was limited, or, as Taliaferro suggested, because Ken wanted her to himself.

Following his mother's visit, Ken seemed to grow more discontented in New York. Nothing seemed to be going well for him, not studies nor his job. That winter was one of the coldest in years. Both Ken and Kent were housebound at times because of the snow, and Ken often reminisced about the mild, balmy winters in New Orleans. Added to this physical discomfort was his worry over his parents. His mother was still teaching her elocution class and planning for the spring revue. Mr. Toole, now retired from the car business, was not in very good health, either mental or physical. To be closer to his family, Ken decided to leave New York and move back home. He wasn't sorry to leave Hunter, and he felt that a Ph.D. could be pursued at Tulane as well as at Columbia.

As Pat Rickels said, "Ken had the curse of the only child." He had often spoken to her about the problems with his parents. She remembers that "he loved them, and he was grateful to them for all the affection that they had lavished on him. He wouldn't just abandon them. He said that his parents could not handle their affairs. They needed his physical presence. They couldn't handle their bank account, their bills, and things like that. He needed to be there to help around the house and maybe to drive them places. They really did need him, and one's obligation to one's parents is real."

Seven

The recruit . . . had a very special "Spanglish" which he formed from Spanish words. For example, "Juan Jose?" means, literally, "What you say?"
—*John Kennedy Toole, in a letter to his parents*

DURING THE 1961 spring semester Ken's decision to move home was rendered moot by the actions of the United States government. His student deferment had expired, and now it seemed that Uncle Sam wanted Ken to bear arms for his country. In April he received a draft notice commanding him to report for induction in the summer. Ken told Emilie Griffin that he was ready to go into the service "just to get it over with." When it was time for Ken to leave New York, he was alone in the apartment. Kent Taliaferro was in Europe, Susan Grossman away on flight duty. Only Clayelle Dalferes came to help Ken pack his belongings for the move south, and they made plans to meet back in Louisiana.

In June, at the close of the semester, Ken returned to New Orleans to bide his time until he had to report for basic training. Ken was twenty-four with two university degrees and partway to a doctorate that might never be completed. He had no money saved and no opportunity for regular employment, given that serving his country was the job that loomed in his immediate future. Back in the small bedroom of his parents' house, he was at their beck and call with no privacy. Faced with this situation, Ken might have been depressed and disappointed with his life, but instead he was looking forward to military duty. It would provide him a two-year breathing space before he must decide what to do about his future, his education, and the care of his parents. In the few months before he reported for duty, Ken decided to have a good time playing with his friends in the Big Easy.

That summer of 1961 Ken was back in his favorite city, but he maintained a correspondence with Emilie Griffin in New York. Her letter of July 10, 1961, is interesting because it indicates that Ken was doing some writing unconnected with his studies. She writes charmingly and with excitement about her newfound literary inspiration. Griffin, who had been reared in the Christian Science faith, had recently converted to Catholicism. She has since written several books on religious subjects, but at the time she was just beginning her literary career. Ken and Griffin had had many discussions about religion, but she knew Ken did not have her zeal for Catholicism. Her letter suggests that perhaps he was feeling even more distanced from the Church. It also forecasts a problem that would produce Ken's greatest disappointment.

Dear Ken,

It *was* nice, Sunday, wasn't it? New Orleans never looked dearer, nor more beautiful to me, than on that weekend home. I was so glad that you were there.

Ken, I am writing! I am writing! Pray for me that it will last. (Oh, some non-sectarian, non-religious prayer will do very nicely, thank you.) I hope your work is going well. I think it must be just that you have to be saying something that you really *mean* . . . not just dredging characters and situations up because they are charming. At least, that's the way it seems to be for me.

Didn't mean to be silent for so long. Letterwritingwise, I mean. Even my family has only had one note, very short, from me since my

return. Not a word from Kent Taliaferro. Will you write to me . . . I
do so like hearing from you.
Love,
Russ

Griffin signed this letter with her nickname, derived from her middle
name, "Russell." This missive, in the Tulane Archives, was listed as
being from an unknown "Russ" until summer of 2000, when Griffin informed the curator that she was the letter writer and friend of Ken
Toole.

While waiting to join the service, Ken got a short-term job in a factory on Poland Avenue assembling boxes. The work was easy enough,
and Ken had time to see his old friend Sidney Snow. One night Ken appeared at one of the clubs where Snow was playing and began hanging
around with the band again. Unlike some, who remembered Ken as
being close with a dollar, Snow recalled how generous Ken was to the
guys in the band. He often bought beer and food as well as offering them
transport to gigs. Snow said that this didn't sit well with Ken's mother.
Thelma didn't like the musicians or the hours they kept. She tracked
Ken around the city to see what he was up to when he was out with
them. Snow couldn't believe it when late one night he saw her driving
around Clay Square looking for Ken to make him come home. "She was
a real mean lady," Snow recalled. "Tooley wouldn't bring us around the
house" because she would give him a hard time. Still Ken persisted in
his association with the band members, who drank and partied as hard
as he did.

Snow said it wasn't that Ken *wanted* to be one of the guys, "He was
one of the guys. Tooley was an artist, and he wanted to be with fellow
artists. He talked a lot about what he was writing. He said he wanted to
write many New Orleans books." The band was among the very few
who knew about Ken's literary ambitions. He talked about writing all
the time to Snow and the others, but told them very little about himself.
Thinking Ken younger than he was, they thought he was just fooling
around. Later, when Ken's book came out, Snow was very surprised. "I
didn't think he was going to do anything. I thought he was going to be
a dropout like us. I was surprised to find that he went to college."

Around them Ken never wore his usual neat, preppy clothes. Often he would come straight from work and looking, to Snow, "as raggedy as us."

Hanging out with Snow and working didn't interfere with Ken's familial duties. He took his mother shopping, undertook the home repairs his father was unable to do, and helped pay the bills. The nights out with Sidney Snow were a deserved respite and outlet for Ken. He saw the army as a challenge. Ken was older than most inductees, and he was also better educated. Clayelle Dalferes remembered seeing Ken at a wedding in Lafayette in the fall, right after he had completed basic training at Fort Gordon, Georgia. Trim and handsome in his uniform, Ken bragged that he put forth the minimum effort and still received the assignment that he wanted. His excellent social skills had stood him in good stead. Ken claimed to have scammed his way out of difficult assignments by offering to do the sergeant's paperwork, but with the exercise he got, Ken was in better physical shape than he had ever been.

Because of his fluency in Spanish and his credentials as an English teacher, Ken was assigned to the U.S. Army Training Center at Fort Buchanan, Puerto Rico. As citizens of the United States Commonwealth, Puerto Rican men were encouraged to enlist in the American military. Until the end of the Korean Conflict, Puerto Ricans had been segregated from the regular army and not expected to know or to learn English. The teaching program at Fort Buchanan was designed to give the inductees an eight-week immersion course in elementary English before their assignment to basic training stateside. English-speaking military personnel at the fort were also required to take introductory Spanish classes.

Fidel Castro had been in control of Cuba for less than two years, but already the situation there was alarming the American government. Since President Kennedy was concerned about communist influence ninety miles from the shores of Florida, Puerto Rico, as part of Antilles Command, took on a greater importance. At about the time Ken arrived at Fort Buchanan in November 1961, the language program was at capacity with three companies of Puerto Rican recruits. He taught from Monday through Friday with no weekend duty. Following his promotion to group leader of the school, Ken was provided with a small private room where he spent much of his time on personal correspondence. The letters from this period of his life show a humor and originality of thought previously evident only in anecdotes related by others.

From May 22, 1962
Dear Parents,

The heat has been joined by rain now. May is the rainy season here, and the sun has hidden for a week. Nothing is dry. The red clay of the island has turned to paste; hanging from my mosquito net are some socks in their third day of drying. A heavy, cloying wet-heat hangs in the air.

We are in the middle (almost) of a cycle now. Fortunately, my current group of recruits is as pleasant as the others were. As I perhaps wrote before, these recruits are almost all volunteers, victims of unemployment in the mountains and, as such, are somewhat like characters from a Puerto Rican version of *The Grapes of Wrath.* One claimed he was a Cuban, an exile from Castro. However, it has developed that he is really from San Sebastian, Puerto Rico, and had read too avidly some stories of Cuba today. Now the class calls him *el cubano artificial.*

In Puerto Rican Pueblos, the usual number of stonings, incendiary suicides, and machete slayings are taking place. The police are shooting innocent bystanders, and the bleachers in the ball park collapsed Sunday. Caray! Que muchos accidentes hay!

I have been reading and reading and otherwise all is peaceful.

From July 5, 1962
Dear Parents,

Que calor esta tarde! What heat this afternoon! I am drinking from a large pitcher full of cubes and grape juice (through the courtesy of the mess hall), sitting in the office of Company A. With typical foresight, the Army sent about one half or more of the English instructors down to Salinas Training Area for the summer, and now we are understaffed and overworked.

Monday I was chosen "Soldier of the Month" of Fort Buchanan. Candidates were sent from every unit on post; a military board quizzed us on military subjects and knowledge and current events. We were also judged on appearance, bearing and uniform. For winning I am to receive . . . ten dollars.

My working hours have been long and one day seems to fade into the next. Yesterday, the Fourth of July, I went to the beach. Because it was a holiday, all the Puerto Ricans were out, creating the wild motley appearance that they do en masse. On the beach they scream, chatter, and giggle continually, pushing each other into the water, throwing sand at friends. And as always, there are several fully dressed people bobbing about in the surf. For a people who allegedly suffer from nutritional deficiencies, these are amazingly active . . . and the shouted, marathon conversations that they maintain are admirable. What do they have to talk about continually? Are they never afraid of being overheard? I imagine that all the Latin countries are this frenzied, volatile, and undisciplined.

From July 10, 1962
Dear Parents,

As I was looking out of the office a few minutes ago, I saw an ambulance drive up to one of the Co. B classrooms. The instructor of the class, whom I know, is a very passive, scholarly Yale graduate, and I suspected that he had finally passed out from asking, "What is this?"; "Who are you?"; "Do you like to eat fried chicken?" A moment or so later, the body of a trainee was brought out on a stretcher and slipped into the ambulance, while a group of excited trainees gathered around the scene screaming in Spanish . . . and Mish, the instructor, looked on with his slouch and his permanently doleful expression, probably wondering how fate had brought him to this erratic island. Later someone explained to me that the Puerto Ricans often pass out or suffer from closed stomachs whenever their diet is changed from rice and beans and dried salt codfish. And now I remember a trainee's telling me about his experiences during his first days in Chicago: "So I ahm eateen the deener wees my seester ahn' hair fahmelee and I ahm gate seek so they ahr take me to the Cook county Hose-peetahl foar a moanth and are many nice nurse in hose-peetahl."

Also in this letter Ken refers to his father's continuing paranoia about
home safety:

> That new refrigerator looks wonderful. All those solid ice cubes
> and hard ice cream! I hope this model had no ice "free-er" so that we
> can avoid the continual search and those doomsday warnings written
> on the kitchen wall in red crayola.

From August 14, 1962
Dear Parents,

There has been some delay in my writing you, due principally to
the series of inspections which we are having. I am now in charge of
the English instructors in Co. A, and this means that I am in charge
of their barracks, too. The benefit of this for me is a private room
which is a very pleasant, bright and airy one. It seems strange, but the
inspection preparation occupies so much of my time that I have very
little else to discuss. Our First Sergeant is unpredictable and more
temperamental than a prima donna. Now that my role in the company is principally disciplinary and supervisory, I have constant contact with him. Basically, he thinks a great deal of me ("you hahve
entelligence ahnd leadairsheep"), but there are his transitory whims
to contend with. And what strange ideas develop in his mind! Ideas
that must be changed tactfully and carefully. His paranoiac suspicion
of humanity is overwhelming. As someone remarked to me, "If I
were he, I would be suspicious, too." I am dealing with a veritable
Capt. Queeg of *The Caine Mutiny.*

The approaching Antilles Command Inspection has these Puerto
Rican officers and NCO's in a tailspin. They are basically terrified of
authority, and now their latent irrationality knows no bounds. In another company, a PR sergeant went into a hysterical fit while preparing for an inspection and began to throw tables around. This is all
very wild and strange and dreamlike. Ay Bendito!

With this background of information at your disposal, you can,
perhaps, understand current conditions here in the Training Center.
Therefore, yesterday when the First Sergeant came to inspect our
barracks for the first time, I was expecting to see a few tables begin to

fly in here. My room is furnished with two tables, a bookcase, an easy chair and several plants, left by the previous occupant. I was sure these would have to be discarded, for the appearance is not particularly barracks-like. Sgt. Ortiz looked at the chair, and said, "Ah, I see you hahve zees chair een here! (pause) Well, poot a leetle vahrneesh oan eet." Then he noticed the plants, which I really don't care about particularly but would like to keep on principle, and said, "Tole (my name is pronounced by P.R.'s so that it rhymes with sole). Ahr you wahtering zees plahnts?"

At any rate, our barracks in the inspection was far superior to the sergeants'—for the first time in Co. A history, Sgt. Ortiz was pleased in his curious way—and the English instructors (all of whom are terrified of him) were very excited in a remarkable juvenile way—for people who are all college products. Then Ortiz went off to harass the sergeants about their poor display, waving his swagger stick about like a demon. He even carries the swagger stick with him when he goes to the toilet.

From September 14, 1962
Dear Mother and Dad,

The heat and rain of the Puerto Rican summer seem to have ended—I hope permanently. The ranks of English instructors have been considerably thinned due to a series of departures for discharge during the summer. It is very disheartening to see people pack their duffel bags for the states and release from the Army. However, in less than a year, I will be out . . . if this Cuban confusion does not lead to a wave of extensions. We are now anticipating the arrival of several new instructors and everyone is eager to assess them in a way which our very small town way of life here makes particularly curious.

Actually, the English instructors are in many ways a hilarious group. All college graduates (some with advanced degrees), they exist here in an alien society. During the inspections several were used to cut grass and paint buildings and they inadvertently lost one lawn mower, a lawn mower wheel, and a shovel. Our immediate superiors, all of whom are Puerto Rican, are wild and excitable and unpredictable, and the combination of English instructors and Puerto Rican cadre is an uneasy alliance full of sound and fury and improbably funny happenings. The incident of the missing lawn mower wheel was magnified so greatly that it almost split Co. A asunder. As leader of the English instructors, I have a foot in both worlds with my psyche dangling between them. Sgt. Jose Ortiz, our ramrod-proud, swagger-stick erect First Sergeant, whom I've described previously, is intent upon beautifying our Co. A area. Huge urns filled with ferns and painted in the spectrum of colors line our road. Between the urns there is a heavy connecting chain painted yellow. Now there is a big blue sign in our parking lot that says "FIRST SERGEANT." Last week Ortiz sprayed all the leaves in front of the office silver . . . and they fell off and died the next day.

In a letter to Joel Fletcher dated September 23, 1962, Ken wrote of the malaise that had overtaken the company as a whole. A continued lack of students combined with high humidity had everyone dispirited. As a group they were looking forward to winter, when the tourists would arrive to perk up the scene and the weather would be delightfully dry. Ken comments that the English instructors were drinking heavily in a futile attempt to alleviate boredom. At the time their only bright spot was the anticipated production of *Macbeth* by some amateur thespians. A member of the English faculty, a corporal who was the brother of actor Stuart Whitman, had a part in the play. The entire company planned to turn out and heckle him. As usual, a great deal of drinking was planned, starting with early afternoon cocktails, which would continue until curtain time. The group was to travel en masse in a caravan of air-conditioned taxis to El Moro, an old Spanish Colonial fort with an outdoor stage beside the ocean. Ken laments that such foolishness as this constituted their only plans for the future.

From September 24, 1962
Dear Parents,

I returned Saturday from my two day tour of Ramey Air Force Base on the coast overlooking the Dominican Republic. In every way the Air Force has more style than the Army: it is neater, more civilian, seemingly efficient, newer. The morale of the men in the Air Force is quite implausible; their esprit de corps was a wonder to all the soldiers on the trip. But the sailors and marines with us had that same morale, that same devotion to their particular service.

I hope Fidel Castro does not have a complete paranoid breakdown at any time in the future and aim a weapon at Miami. Perhaps Russia realizes what a liability it has on its hands in Cuba. Again, I hope. Incidentally, a young Cuban "refugee" whom we had in our last cycle of English training was discovered by FBI agents at Fort Dix, N.J. (where he had gone from here for basic training), to be in reality a communist agent. Co. A was notified today that the Cuban is being deported. Nevertheless, it has caused a stir at Fort Buchanan . . . where we always expect an attack from Puerto Rican Nationalists who now have a vague alliance with Castro. Madness, madness. What will the world ever find to do with the Caribbean and Latin America?

From October 16, 1962
Dear Parents,

As for me almost nothing is happening. There are still no recruits in the Training Center, so I read. Sen. Kefauver of Tenn. is currently visiting here so the closed mess hall was opened and our very confused mess sergeant cooked hundreds of doughnuts and cookies for Kefauver. The doughnuts would be taken to the orderly room for Sgt. Ortiz to sample them ("Thees doughnuts ahr too brown!"); then, when the perfect result was achieved they were set out on beautifully set tables on great trays. At noon it became clear that Kefauver was not going to show; Capt. Gil de la Madrid and Sgt. Ortiz sat disconsolately viewing the piles of cookies and doughnuts as the mess sgt. munched on the fruits of his labor. Finally Ortiz said to me, "Take thees to your people!" So we all gorged on the doughnuts for the rest of another long, boring day.

From November 18, 1962
Dear Mother and Dad,

I always seem to begin my letters with a discussion of the weather; however, our long siege of heat created a preoccupation with this subject. The arrival of North Atlantic air has been accompanied by huge

20 foot waves which have washed away most of the beaches. In the slum, La Perla, which is on the ocean at the base of the cliffs on which San Juan is built, the gigantic and really awesome waves are tearing the little shacks to pieces; there the sea is filled with green tarpaper and old bits of lumber. Crowds of La Perla residents stand on the cliffs with battered suitcases watching their little dwellings below splinter and float away.

Friday night there was a dance for the guests at the pavilion of the Army-Navy beach and toward the end of the dance a great wave crashed into the pavilion drenching everyone. Several people climbed trees when they saw the wave coming, and as it washed back out to sea, it carried with it several shoes and caps. The girls for the dance were recruited from the San Juan YWCA and a motley crowd they were. Several of the "girls" were near forty, needless to say, the airmen and sailors were somewhat dismayed and many of them stayed in the men's room throughout the "dance." In addition to this, it seemed obvious that a few of the YWCA girls were rather identifiable prostitutes. After the wave struck, the outraged YWCA girls began to scream volubly, and somewhat dangerously, calling down the wrath of God upon the Army for bringing them to this dance. It took almost 15 minutes for our Puerto Rican bus driver to get them quiet, but not before one of the YWCA girls had tried to strike him. The San Juan YWCA must be a very special branch of that organization. At any rate, it was an evening that continually verged on the brink of hilarity.

From December 10, 1962
Dear Parents,

Last night I saw an amateur version of *"Bye Bye Birdie,"* the musical, done by a Puerto Rican group in San Juan. It was scheduled to begin at 8:30 P.M.—but because the audience was Puerto Rican, it did not get underway until well after nine. And there was great confusion and arguing about the reserved seats, etc. Nothing on this island can seemingly be subdued or rational or orderly. However, the elegance and style the Puerto Rican ladies present was pleasing, for when they attend a function, they turn out with a chic that makes Jackie Kennedy seem dated.

Kenny being held by nursemaid Beulah Mathews on the back porch of the Webster Street home in the Carrollton section of New Orleans. Thirty years later, Mathews would be one of three mourners at his funeral. *Courtesy Tulane University Manuscripts Department*

Like many New Orleans children, Kenny delighted in his yearly Carnival costume. This Mardi Gras (ca. 1940) he posed as a Cossack. *Courtesy Tulane University Manuscripts Department*

Both of Toole's parent were avid readers and encouraged his love of books. A snapshot preserved in the family album shows a grade-school Kenny relaxing in the sunshine while reading Frank L. Baum's *The Road to Oz*. *Courtesy Tulane University Manuscripts Department*

Like his father, Ken enjoyed baseball and described himself to one friend as "a pretty good ballplayer." Here he poses with his catcher's mitt in a neighborhood sand-lot. *Courtesy Tulane University Manuscripts Department*

The finale of the 1949 spring recital of the Lakeview School of Speech and Dramatic Art, directed by Thelma Toole. For his part in the program, twelve-year-old Kenny interpreted the dramatic monologue "Gaulberto's Victory." In a note accompanying this photograph, Thelma Toole wrote, "Ken's resonant, far-projecting voice, dramatic flair, and stage presence brought warm praise from the audience." *Courtesy Tulane University Manuscripts Department*

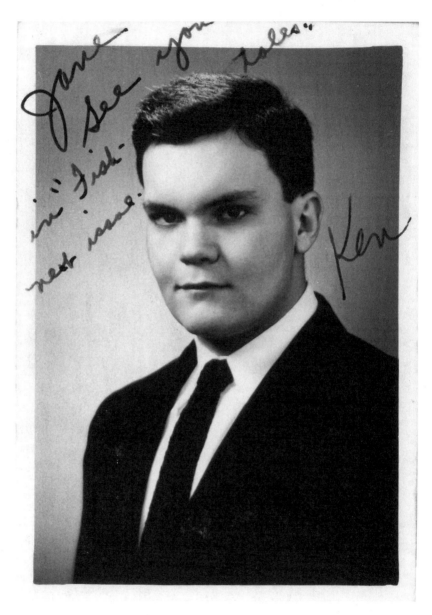

Ken's portrait in the 1954 Fortier High School yearbook *The Tarpon,* inscribed by Ken to good friend Jane McGee. *Courtesy Jane McGee Kingsmill*

After winning the Freedom Foundation Award, Fortier High School sent a select group of students, Ken among them, on a trip to Washington, D.C.; Philadelphia; and New York. Here Ken stands on the steps of the U.S. Capitol after meeting with Louisiana senator Russell Long. *Courtesy Tulane University Manuscripts Department*

Trim and fit, a collegiate Ken poses for a seaside snapshot. Ken loved swimming and often took Highway 90 east to the Biloxi beaches. *Courtesy Tulane University Manuscripts Department*

I don't know who she is, but she's been there for two days.

In this cartoon for *Hullabaloo,* Tulane's student magazine, Ken contrasts his idol in her "chanteuse" costume with the sweater-clad coeds. *Courtesy Tulane University Manuscripts Department*

1959–1960 *L'Acadien* yearbook portrait of the English department at Southwestern Louisiana Institute (SLI), since renamed University of Louisiana at Lafayette. Ken Toole stands on the fourth row, far right. Others pictured are (front row) Mary Dichmann, Louise Givens Williams, Esther K. Bodemuller, Joseph C. Broussard, Milton Rickels, Muriel M. Price, Patricia K. Rickels, Nicholas Polites, (second row) Eleanor Marionneaux, Sudie Carroll, Bolivar Lee Hait, Frank Meriwether, Anita Guillot, Marion Delaitsch, Thomas Sims, Ralph Lynch, (third row) Robert Osborne, Frank Flowers, Pearl LeBlanc, John Bennett, (fourth row) William Slattery, Paul Nolan, Robert Byrne, Joseph A. Ward. *Courtesy University of Louisiana at Lafayette*

Sergeant Toole surrounded by student recruits in the English language program at Fort Buchanan, Puerto Rico (ca. 1962). It was here, in his small private office, that Ken began work on what would become *A Confederacy of Dunces. Courtesy Tulane University Manuscripts Department*

While serving with the army in Puerto Rico, Ken traveled as much as possible through the Caribbean—alone and with other members of Company A. Here dressed in "civvies," Ken enjoys a quiet moment against the backdrop of a lush tropical jungle. *Courtesy Tulane University Manuscripts Department*

Eight

and there was another day, clear and in summer,
when right at noon, in the same mess hall,
Corporal Crabbe picked up his mashed potatoes
and gravy from his plate
with his hands, and rubbed them in his face.
                              —from a poem by David Kubach

ALTHOUGH KEN'S LETTERS exhibit great charm and spirit, they do not accurately reflect his daily activities or emotional state. They were written primarily for his mother's entertainment and peace of mind. The envelopes were always addressed to both parents, but the letters read as if Ken were certain that his mother would enjoy them while alone and then tell his father what was appropriate. Some of his messages seem unnecessarily cryptic, as if Ken were afraid his missives might fall into the wrong hands. In a letter from June 1962, Ken wrote:

I hope that "Operation Alert" at home is working. During the summer, I know, one must be more alert to search for ways and means. The new transportation aspect should pay off in positive results what it costs in time and inconvenience. The whole plan is admirable; the project must bear some fruit. Of course the "major issue" business must be attended to—and quickly. The procrastination in this matter seems to have taken the form of a phobia. I expect to hear from you that the matter has been handled.

There are many such mysterious references, and the one extant letter from his mother, in the archives at Tulane University, is equally oblique. No letters exist for the first eight-month period of Ken's service, though it was a rule of basic training that recruits write home once a week. Ken loved to write to his family and certainly did not need an order to do so. Given that over the years Thelma Toole saved much of the minutiae of her son's life, it is unfortunate that items as important as these early letters are lost. There may have been other letters from Ken, his father, or herself that Thelma felt too personal to share.

Ken loved and missed his parents as well as New Orleans, but enforced isolation gave him a different perspective on life back home. It also had the advantage of awakening his literary promise, in making him record observations on the world around him. When he began work on a novel about New Orleans, his letters may have served as Ken's lifeline to the city and anchored the story in his mind.

From all official accounts, Ken's short career in the military was brilliant. In less than a year he had risen to the rank of sergeant and had been honored with several awards and citations. On a personal level, however, his two years in the service were not all beneficial. The situation he encountered in Puerto Rico was a rather strange one. The people he worked with were liberal-arts graduates who were stuck teaching unskilled and uneducated inductees. Their job was frustrating, and a huge waste of time for men who never intended to make the army their life's work. The men were asked to do menial tasks like cutting grass and painting fence posts. Unused to discipline in daily life, they thought such labors foolish and beneath their dignity.

Added to this tension was the military hierarchy of Fort Buchanan itself. The commander was an officer of the regular United States Army, but middle management of the fort was entrusted to soldiers of the Commonwealth of Puerto Rico, who had difficulty understanding and dealing with the English language instructors under their command. Each group thought the other arrogant. There was much enmity and precious little cooperation on the post. Lack of communication and cohesion produced a disorganized group rife with suspicion and discontent.

Ken himself was intimidated by his Puerto Rican commanders. According to other instructors in Company A, Ken was terrified of his immediate superior, Sergeant Ortiz. Although Ken joked about the man in letters home, Ortiz was not the buffoon that Ken made him out to be. Ortiz was strict and did things the army way. Often this meant giving conflicting orders and expecting things to be done both ways at once.

To further complicate matters, Puerto Rico was in a crisis period, and that was reflected in the army stationed there. It was the height of the Cold War, and communists wanted to expand past Cuba into Puerto Rico to gain a foothold in the American Commonwealth and promote their cause among the population. There was a great deal of infiltration by Cuban agents, whose subversive activities were directed against the governments of both the United States and Puerto Rico. The island became strategically important to United States intelligence-gathering networks, which showcased their efforts to halt the spread of communism.

Barracks life is never easy for anyone, and it was especially difficult for someone as private as Ken. He made a few friends, but he made more enemies. Eighty men lived together in one barracks, and there was a constant transferring in and out as their service times elapsed. Each man had a bunk, a foot locker, and a wall locker for storage. The language program was under constant review by the Antilles Command, and inspections were scheduled and abandoned only to be scheduled once more. The teaching was frustrating because the recruits often came out of the eight-week training with little more understanding of the English language than they possessed at the beginning.

The climate of Puerto Rico was not appreciably different from New Orleans's, except that it was more extreme. The summers were hotter, the rainy season longer, and the threat of hurricanes greater. There were numerous tropical diseases that caused distress to victims and worry to everyone. A particularly nasty intestinal malaise called "spru" was one the Americans feared most because it was so painful and persistent. Sunburn and heatstroke were high on the list of everyday concerns, and pith

helmets were provided to all as preventive medicine. Ken took to wearing dark glasses and was seldom seen without them.

The most common complaint, aside from a general feeling of aggravation, was headache. A primary cause of this was the fact that the army
in Puerto Rico seemed to promote inebriation. The soldiers and especially the instructors drank excessively. Booze was cheap and readily
available on the post. There were free rum nights every week at the
NCO Club. Drinking in the barracks was continuous and caused no end
of arguments and trouble in the ranks. Some instructors stayed intoxicated for days on end, and no one cared enough to reprimand them.
Pharmaceutical drugs were readily available, and there was little control
over the gallon-sized containers of medication. The most popular drug
was ten grains of aspirin laced with caffeine. Known as APC or Empirin
Compound, these tablets were self-dispensed by the handfuls to alleviate
chronic hangovers. Medications of all sorts were available on a take-as-
needed basis.

This rough, constant partying became a problem for Ken, who
showed signs of becoming a heavy drinker even before coming to the
island. In a letter to Joel Fletcher, Ken describes the army faculty as dis-
similar draftees who shared an affection for liquor. He reports enjoying
a few rums mixed with lemon and water at the end of the day and also
praises the village of Ponce along the southern coast for having a hotel
with a great bar and an excellent staff to dispense his favorite tropical
libations.

When he first arrived in Puerto Rico in November 1961, Ken was
looking forward to his assignment in the Caribbean. This had not
seemed a bad place to put in two years. It was only a month later that
Emilie Griffin came to visit him. She was there as part of a pictorial
shoot for her ad agency. Excited about seeing Ken, Griffin added a day
to her schedule in order to spend time with him. They went to visit the
tourist spots like the old Spanish fort at El Morro and drove along the
beaches. As the day went on Griffin became increasingly concerned
about Ken. She found him to be horribly depressed. Some of it may have
been homesickness, but she felt it was more than that. He was deeply
dismayed about his lack of money. His preoccupation with money worried her. His dreadful embarrassment that he could not treat her to lunch

was inappropriate. They had often gone Dutch treat, and she was not at all offended to have to pay her share. Her sense that there was something deeper here than just embarrassment worried Griffin.

Although she was happy to see him and he seemed pleased enough to be with her, there was nothing she could do to bring him out of his silent black disposition. Griffin had always felt that Ken had a dark streak in him, and on this day it was obvious to her that he was suffering from more than just a mood swing. This was the last time she would see him, and Griffin's final memory of Ken is very strong. Because there is so much rain on the island, there are always rainbows in the sky. Ken and Emilie ate lunch in the Normandy Hotel dining room, which had a panoramic view of the ocean. Recalling that afternoon, she said, "the windows on all sides of our table were filled with perfect rainbows. Ken was sitting in a pocket of darkness surrounded by these brilliant colored arches, and he never looked at them."

Each company lived in separate barracks. Although the teachers worked together during the day, their off-duty time was spent in their own areas. In the evenings the men in Company A tended to stay to themselves, as was true with the other groups. Ken could be witty and entertaining, but he was also ambitious and soon set about becoming team leader. This position had two advantages. It required more administrative work and less teaching, which would give him more personal time, and the leader also got exclusive use of a small office with a door that could be closed. This sort of privacy was extraordinary and coveted in army life. Other men would rent rooms in small hotels near the camp just to have time alone.

Being in command had its disadvantages, as Ken would discover. He had to listen to every complaint and settle arguments. He had to make sure the school ran as efficiently as it could. He was responsible for the paperwork, but most of all he had to please his superiors while not losing the respect of the men. Ken chose his friends carefully. David Kubach was a particularly good companion who remembers their friendship as being an adolescent one with "a lot of silliness and exclusivity and making fun of other people." Kubach wanted to be a writer and owned a Swedish-made Halda in a bilious green color. He lent the typewriter to

Ken to put in his office. The two also shared a great devotion to alcohol. Kubach admitted that "in the service we all drank too much, and I think that I drank too much. . . . At that age you're so strong, you do not follow the rules . . . so you get sufficiently drunk to make some serious trouble from time to time."

In an interview, a former member of Company A said it was widely known that Kubach wanted to be a writer, and equally well known that his liquor consumption prevented him from making much progress. If that was the general impression of Dave Kubach forty years ago, he proved the skeptics wrong. He is a nationally published poet and poet-in-residence with the Arts in Education program of nine states. Much of his time is spent on the road, teaching the fundamentals of poetry to students of all ages and their teachers alike, but at the time he met Ken, Kubach was as miserable as everyone else in the outfit. He recalled the English instructors were a "bunch of aesthetic snobs" who thought of themselves as "little princes kidnapped by a foreign potentate." Ken wrote of him in a letter home:

> Last weekend I visited PFC Kubach, my intelligent and erstwhile friend, who is on temporary duty for the summer cutting grass with a machete at the Army's Training Area in Salinas down on the Caribbean coast. PFC Kubach has his little portable typewriter set up on a table in his large canvas tent, but finds that he is too depleted after a day over the hot grass to write anything and has turned to movies and beer instead. PFC Kubach, too, is determined to be a writer, but his prose (which is highly intricate and profound) is also unintentionally very atrocious and almost hilarious; in the past six months he has turned out about fifteen pages and last week threw them all out to start all over again. Sleeping in the tent with the side flaps up was really wonderful at night, but by day the tents are ovens. In addition, the mooing of the cows in the nearby cane fields and the meager facilities of the Salinas area make it a fairly horrible assignment. Someone from Fort Buchanan was supposed to drive me back Sunday afternoon for the long trip over the mountains, and I was so eager to escape Salinas that I sat in the Salinas NCO club for an hour before he was expected drinking beer and watching the road, poor Kubach ask-

ing me if I would come down for the next weekend, promising a possible boat trip.

Ken did get some chances to travel while he was in the service. He visited all parts of the beautiful island, either alone or with friends. Since soldiers were such an integral part of the economy, army rates were available everywhere. The thrifty Toole took advantage of these offerings whenever he had time off duty. The first summer Ken spent in Puerto Rico was the most exciting time he had while in the army. One promotion was followed by another. He won an award as soldier of the month at his post. In July he was chosen soldier of the month for the entire Antilles Command. For that he was given an all-expense-paid three-day vacation on the Dutch island of Aruba, near the coast of Venezuela. It was the first time this prize had been given, and Ken made the most of it. The letter he wrote about his trip is a perfunctory description for home consumption, with an air of detachment and loneliness.

From July 25, 1962
Dear Parents,

The three-day trip was a wonderful change of scene and quite an experience in itself. Aruba's bone-white sands, arid wastes barren except for cacti and boulders, and atmosphere of prosperity, cleanliness, and efficiency were a great contrast to Puerto Rico. A true desert island, Aruba was dry and burning hot. The sun, which hangs like an orange-yellow disk, and the sterile, blanched sands make the sky, in comparison, appear dark gray. The waters of the Caribbean there are crystal-clear, a lovely blue-green. It is difficult to convey the atmosphere of desolation and aloneness that the island creates.

The Dutch influence is obviously responsible for the order found on the island. Every home sparkles; the native population is quiet, well-behaved, courteous, and likable. They speak Papiamentu, a language combining Indian and Spanish.

An interesting aspect of the island is the great Dutch colonial population: Calvinistic women in plain print dresses wearing glasses and buns, fat burghers with German automobiles and broods of blonde children going to their private seaside Severn Klubs.

Today is constitution day in Puerto-Rico—and LBJ is here to offer the people a plebiscite on independence. If they accept it, all English instructors will have no jobs.

This summer was not as pleasant for his family. Ken's father was unwell and growing more paranoid as his senility increased. The house at 390 Audubon was involved in succession litigation, and as much as his parents wanted to stay there, it was unclear whether they would be able to. Ken hoped they could buy the house, calling it "a good deal." It is impossible to believe that Ken thought his parents could afford a house on their own. Obligating himself to help them would have meant he could never afford to leave home.

Ever on the lookout for a way to increase his finances, Ken applied for a hardship allotment from the army. His father's pension was very small, and without Ken there to handle his parents' affairs, things were getting desperate. In a letter home in July 1962, Ken details his plans for augmenting his army pay.

Dear Parents,

Whatever the long distance call last night cost you I hope to make up for if my current plans for getting an allotment go through. When I spoke to the Personnel Center last week, they explained to me that I pay monthly $40 out of my $99/mo. salary; the government puts up $70 to make a total of $110 which you receive. I also understand that the government will *pay more* if the conditions seem to make greater payment necessary. I believe that it is possible for you to receive much more than the $110 if the recipient (you) needs more money. At any rate, I intend to begin the paper work this week that will start the ball rolling. If I understand correctly, an Army investigator will call on you for an interview of some sort. I suggest that you make the case as financially clear as possible, for you should try to receive the maximum monthly payment. The payments depend (and this is important) on individual need, living conditions in the area. In your case make the amount of recent monthly income clear.

Remember: $110/mo. is *the minimum* monthly payment to which you are entitled under this Class Q allotment. You may be able to receive more and *should* be able to. Present a straightforward picture.

The summer of 1962 had been a good one for Ken, but an event occurred in August that again threw him into a bout of serious depression. He wrote a letter home detailing his feelings about the death of one of his great idols.

From August 6, 1962

Dear Mother and Dad,

Yesterday in the post library someone pointed out to me the headline in a local paper: *Muere Actriz Marilyn Monroe.* Surrounding one of those ridiculously leering photographs of her was the story of her suicide. It seems trite, I know, to say that I couldn't believe that she was dead, but I couldn't. Marilyn Monroe and death are such incongruous partners.

Marilyn Monroe made me happier (I can't think of another word) than any performer ever has. During my adolescence you know the overwhelming attachment I had to her. And although the enthusiasms of adolescence wane, the memories of those enthusiasms survive. There was a time, I think, when my interest in her had reached the stage of obsession. I don't imagine that anyone could understand my preoccupation with her.

On the screen she created the strangest and perhaps the most fascinating species of human being we will ever see. Her musical numbers had an entertainment value that few things in the world can equal. Will anyone ever be able to describe with justice—to a generation which will not know her—exactly what Marilyn Monroe was like in movies?

Her life itself was a gruesome Evelyn Waugh view of American life. The illegitimate child of the strange Southern California society. An orphan in the Depression. A defense plant worker during the war. A movie star whose effect upon the public was phenomenal even by Hollywood's standards. The wife of an Italian baseball hero and a Jewish intellectual. A suicide who could find no bearings in the soci-

ety which had formed her. Her life and death are both very sober-
ing—and even frightening.

   In my own way I loved Marilyn Monroe very much. Isn't that too
bad that she never knew this.

The letter reads more like an essay than a personal communication.
It is true that Ken had always been fascinated with movie actresses. Su-
zanne Pleshette and Dolores Hart were also two of his favorites. He
often spoke in a casual way about how much he enjoyed watching them
on screen. To army friend Tony Moore it seemed that Ken thought of
Hart and Pleshette as regular people who acted in the movies, but it was
not at all that way with Monroe. Moore knew that she was Ken's favorite
actress. Ken had always admired the grotesque, and Monroe's screen
presence was an exaggerated form of femininity that was so unreal as to
be nonthreatening to Ken's sexuality. Her history as an outsider who created her own identity made Ken feel that he shared a bond with Monroe.
In the weeks following her death, Ken wrote of wanting only to sleep
and rest, often a symptom of depression. Her suicide shocked and frightened him. It was the first real grief he had ever experienced, but aside
from writing home about it, Ken never mentioned how he felt. He
turned his emotions inward in what was to become a self-destructive
process.

   Even with his stultifying duties and depression, Ken rallied enough
to send a sweet letter to his father, marking it PERSONAL in bold print
on the envelope. The letter suggests that John Toole wrote his son often,
but none of these missives remain, and this one letter addressed singly to
his father is all that remains of their correspondence.

From September 4, 1962
Dear Dad,

   Mother wrote me that you are suffering from shingles, an infection which I know is extremely painful. Because you always enjoy
good health, I was especially surprised to hear of this. The illness is
obviously the result of too much work, anxiety, and too little food and
rest. Please take care of yourself for the sake of mother and me.

   Mother, I know, will nurse you excellently. She seems quite distressed over the illness, as well she should be. I am only sorry that I am separated from you at so great a distance.

Please rest. In your next letter I will hope to hear of some recovery.

I love you very much, Dad, and I hope and pray that this painful infection passes. You have always been so good, so kind to me that it hurts me to know that you are in pain.

All my love,

Ken

In the fall, with less than a year of service left, Ken began thinking of the future. He wrote Bill Wieler, his former department head at Hunter, asking about employment. Often army instructors who had teaching jobs were allowed to return to them at the beginning of the semester. Ken asked Wieler if he could return to Hunter in the spring of 1963. This would mean he could separate from the army six months earlier than his original date for discharge. Ken had also told Wieler that Cuban refugees were expected to be enrolled in the October classes in Puerto Rico, but by the time of Wieler's reply, September 17, 1962, another situation involving Cuba negated Ken's plans for enjoying an early return to New York.

In October 1962 the world teetered on the brink of nuclear disaster. The Cold War heated up as the Soviet Union and the United States locked horns over the placement of atomic missles in the People's Republic of Cuba, scarcely ninety miles from Florida. Even a thousand miles away Puerto Rico felt the pressure of such a dangerous predicament, and much of the rest of the world felt the same shock and disbelief. One of the English instructors was in charge of quarters the night the red alert came through. He was supposed to initiate a series of procedures designed to ready the base for the possibility of nuclear war. Problems developed immediately when the code book couldn't be found, and no one was sure what to do when it was located. When the Puerto Rican officers arrived, there was terrible confusion and lots of shouting in both English and Spanish. According to the officer in charge of quarters (CQ), the blame game lasted longer than the red alert and did much

more damage. But the panic was enough to stop Ken's plan for early release from the army.

According to Ken's letters, the Cuban Missile Crisis had little impact
on his work with the English school. It did greatly affect the economy of
Puerto Rico at the beginning of their tourist season, though Ken com-
mented that the tourists "are safer here than in Miami," which is only
ninety miles from Havana. In early November Ken voted absentee and
noted that "Brown is still leading Nixon in California—and I hope this
will effectively remove Nixon from the political scene for good."

The absence from his family and from New Orleans had been hard
on him, and Ken was looking forward to a Christmas furlough. He had
not enjoyed Puerto Rico nearly as much as he had anticipated. Promotion to a command position made the work easier, but the social aspects
of that job precluded close friendships with soldiers under his orders. In
November something happened that caused the first of many hard feelings between him and the men of Company A. His Tulane class ring
disappeared, and although Ken searched and questioned everyone, the
ring was not recovered. Fed up with barracks life, Ken wrote home that
"It's a wonder I haven't been stabbed yet or paralyzed by intestinal diseases on this insane little geological mountain top protruding from the
Caribbean. However, under any circumstances the loss of the ring affects
me deeply."

By the end of November Ken was desperate to get back to "just one
day of cool breezes" in New Orleans. The round-trip fare on Delta was
$190 if purchased in Puerto Rico before the Christmas rush, but Ken
didn't have that much cash in hand. When Mrs. Toole offered to send
him a ticket from New Orleans, Ken reminded her, "if you buy the
ticket in the U.S., you will *have to pay tax*—which I do not have to do
here." Pushing a little harder, Ken warned his mother that "the airlines
are almost completely booked." The $120 advance he requested came
quickly, since his mother wanted him to come home as eagerly as he did.

Nine

From my point of view, the Army gave me four invaluable things: time, detachment, security, and privacy.

—John Kennedy Toole, in a letter to Robert Gottlieb

F OR TWO WEEKS over Christmas and New Year's, Ken enjoyed a wonderful visit to New Orleans, never leaving the city. He spent the time catching up on sorely missed gossip over cups of the café au lait that the natives drink all day every day. In a ritual strictly observed in the Toole house, fresh ground coffee and chicory were measured into a small drip pot that simmered in a shallow pan of water on the back burner. While the coffee dripped in the pot, whole milk or cream was heated to boiling. Then and only then were the milk and the coffee poured simultaneously into a broad-brimmed cup, before being sweetened with pure cane sugar. There was nothing skim or artificial about Creole café au lait. Ken had missed the ceremony and the favorite pastime that accompanied it—conversation. After he declined repeated invitations from friends in Lafayette to come visit, Lafayette came to him. A group from SLI joined him for drinks at the Sazerac Bar in the old Roosevelt (now Fairmont) Hotel. Later Ken detailed the afternoon in a letter to Joel Fletcher, mentioning their mutual friend Nick Polites, who, like Toole, was on leave from the service. He was stationed at Fifth Army Headquarters in Chicago, but although this post along Lake Shore Drive overlooking Lake Michigan would seem to be a coveted one, Ken wrote that Polites spoke gloomily about the horrors of Chicago and life in general. Ken stayed at the party only briefly, joking in his letter that he feared an arrest of their suspicious looking group by the hotel detective.

Ken spent most of the time with his parents. Not unexpectedly, Thelma had been looking forward to doting on him, and he had missed being the center of attention. The visit home did little to allay his fears about his father. Although John Toole's physical condition had improved, he had deteriorated mentally, and his increasing deafness only added to his irrational feelings of fear and paranoia. Even with the GI hardship allotment, the financial situation on Audubon Street was precarious. Purchasing a home was out of the question, and the possibility that Ken could live apart from his parents was becoming even more remote. Even without his mother's constant reminders of how much she needed him, Ken could see that she did.

When he did get out on his own, Ken made the social rounds in New Orleans. He visited with his godfather and uncle Arthur Ducoing at the old home in the Faubourg Marigny. Arthur worked unloading fruit on the French Quarter docks at the end of Esplanade Avenue and had written often to Ken, sending the odd check when he could afford it. Ken traveled to the Garden District for a visit to the Byrne house and wrote Joel Fletcher about it, reporting that Robert Byrne and his younger brother were sitting around the table with their Aunt May and others. Ken noted that nothing much had changed except for the fresh pot of coffee, but that Bob Byrne (who would live another forty years) was looking old. Ken's own impeccable sense of style contrasted with that of the Byrne brothers, who entertained their guest while wearing nightshirts and slippers.

In the same letter Ken reflects upon his native city, praising its appeal and declaring it a mystery how its inhabitants manage to keep up one of the world's loveliest places. He had enjoyed relaxing in familiar and comfortable surroundings, but the holiday pleasures were forgotten when he landed back in the West Indies.

Returning to Fort Buchanan was a wrench to Ken, and not just because it wasn't home. Several things were obvious. There would be no separation from the army earlier than the end of summer, so he was stuck in Puerto Rico at least through hurricane season. And now Ken lagged behind his contemporaries who had gone on with their professional and academic careers. He still had no firm idea of what he wanted to do with his education besides the vague, generic notion of "teaching." Most obvious to Ken was the conclusion that without outside financial assistance, his parents could not keep their feet on the threshold of genteel poverty. Given the generally low salaries of educators, teaching alone would never be enough for the three of them to do more than just subsist. It was a paralyzing situation, and gave an already depressed Ken more to brood upon.

The cycles of teaching and graduation continued, as did army life in general. Although the routine had not changed, life in the Company A barracks was never easy. There was little feeling of camaraderie among the noncombatant personnel. Even the Cuban crisis had not inspired patriotism, and the duties were as boring as ever. Because he was in charge of the men and barracks, Ken was naturally set apart from the others, but he did little to bring cohesion to the group. In the early spring an incident occurred that ruined any chance Ken may have had to exert a positive influence.

To understand what happened it is necessary to understand the composition of Company A. Tony Moore, a former instructor in the company, retained clear memories of the uneasy coexistence between the army as an entity and some of the conscripted men in Toole's charge. Long before the "don't ask, don't tell" policy was in effect, gay soldiers kept their sexual orientation private and did nothing to call attention to that part of their lives. Company A was different in that its gay contingent was open and well organized. These men reserved one end of the barracks for themselves and set up a private platoon within the company.

David Kubach recalled that "the politics of that Company A were straight [or] gay; they had a gay component." By Moore's account the gay soldiers were a raucous group who indulged in outlandish campy behavior. By military standards it was scandalous, and in terms of common courtesy painfully annoying, given the close confines of communal life. Even so the situation was tolerated, if barely, by the other men. Moore remembered that the straight instructors did not feel threatened because the gays made no advances toward anyone outside their clique. All the men in the company were young, not long out of school, and inexperienced, and though few had been around gays, and certainly not in such proximity, most of the instructors were liberal minded and did not wish to nurture prejudice. They were also savvy enough to know that complaints sent up the chain of command could have ramifications more serious than the problems they already had. As sergeant, Ken was the logical person to weigh in and get control of the situation, but aside from criticizing the gay group behind their backs, he did nothing.

The group adopted what Moore called an "in your face" attitude toward the rest of the men. From reveille to taps they kept up a constant barrage of silly, flirtatious behavior. Every morning began with the "what should I wear" ritual. In the Antilles Command soldiers could wear regular army uniforms or tropical outfits consisting of Bermuda shorts and knee socks. One gay soldier pondered his choices aloud every morning. On the days he donned tropical khaki, he would ask his bunkmate, "Are my seams straight, darling?" This query never staled with repetition and always produced shrieks of laughter.

The gay group consumed much more alcohol than the rest of the men. The martinis they drank seemed to intensify their antics, which ended only when they passed out from too much gin. They were particularly fond of playing a recording of the Broadway show *Oliver*. Each time "Where Is Love?" came on, the volume was cranked up and the men would sing along with the boy soprano in loud falsetto voices. Tony Moore remembered the noise being as aggravating as fingernails scraping on a chalkboard. The group must have worn out the record by the time David Kubach returned from Salinas, because he never heard that score. He remembered thinking it was a real "comic opera" watching those guys in this "strange unit" dance on their bunks while Ethel Merman sang "Everything's Coming Up Roses" and other boisterous selections from the musical *Gypsy*.

Moore explained that it was "the lack of consideration toward others" that made barracks life insufferable to the straight soldiers. He said, "We wanted to ignore it, but sometimes the noise and silliness would get to us." Because all the men were teachers and not fighting soldiers, no one's life was at stake. The straight instructors were content to try to live and let live, but it was difficult with all the noise and cavorting at the opposite end of the room.

The other men in the company resented being so put out by an insensitive few. Sometimes the obnoxious antics got to Ken as well, but he was caught in the middle. During the early part of his tour of duty, Ken had become friendly with some of the gay men, even accompanying them on excursions around the island. David Kubach joined him on one of these outings. He later recalled that because Ken was their leader, some of the men in the company were annoyed that he and John were close. He said, "They probably thought I had an inside track on some things," and "some of the guys thought that John and I were having a 'thing.'" Kubach laughed about the idea, saying it didn't bother him as he "had enough trouble being me to worry about being gay too." Ken enjoyed the exclusivity of his friendship with Kubach, but did not encourage the sexual speculation. If the gay group suspected that Ken was in the closet, they may have held that over him. Though Ken sneered at the gay couples and spoke contemptuously about their behavior, his blustering was only for show. He never complained to his superiors about anything they did—until a circumstance arose that broke the unspoken agreement.

William Mason and Robby Rolfs were gay companions in Company A. On the inside door of his wall locker, Mason had taped a picture of the *Mona Lisa*. He had cut out the face and inserted a snapshot of Rolfs. According to another soldier, there was some sort of quarrel or disappointment between the two men, and Rolfs became very depressed. One night when Mason was away, Rolfs took an overdose of APC tablets. The next morning Ken discovered him unconscious and slumped over the desk in the administration office.

It was Ken's duty, after assessing the situation, to call an ambulance and notify the military police. He did not follow the proper procedure. In fact, Ken did nothing at all. For at least thirty minutes he just stood looking at Rolfs and waiting to see if he would wake up. It was apparent that Rolfs was unconscious and needed emergency medical attention, but Ken was terrified of calling the MP's. Because he stalled, fearing trouble with Sergeant Ortiz or Captain de la Madrid, the men in the company assumed authority. Only after they sent for another sergeant did Ken call for an ambulance.

David Kubach, who was there with Ken, admitted that on discovering Rolfs they did not know what to do and the "mistake was that we did not immediately call the ambulance." Kubach downplayed the drama of what he called a "pseudo-suicide." After all, he said, since Rolfs was "sitting in an office where the whole world could see him, his chances of managing to get dead under those circumstances" were slim. At first glance, waiting seemed like an option, because if Rolfs had been "hauled in for a suicide attempt, [he was] going to be in real trouble," perhaps ending up with a dishonorable discharge that would follow him after the service. It must be remembered, however, that Sergeant Toole, and not Kubach, was in command, and his responsibility for Rolfs's life took priority over concern for the man's reputation.

Rolfs survived, but the men in Company A were upset with Ken's lack of action. He did nothing to alleviate their consternation, adopting a cynical attitude about the incident. When someone asked why Rolfs did it, Ken replied, "Why did Robby ever do anything?" To make matters worse, Ken verbally attacked Rolfs to the men, saying that suicide was cowardly and that anyone who would contemplate it was wallowing in self-pity and should receive no sympathy or respect. This short, cold lecture, made even before it was known that Rolfs would live, did Ken a great deal of harm with the men. This nasty remark about one of their own was unusual coming from mild Sergeant Toole. The speech certainly displayed a lack of leadership and, indeed, hinted at a deeper, more personal, disquiet.

Ken had always hated confrontation. Any kind of emotional situation disconcerted him. Once there was an argument between Tony Moore and Dave Kubach over a science fiction movie. Moore hated it, and Kubach declared the film terrific. Ken put himself in the middle and caught grief from both sides. The angrier Moore and Kubach got with each other, the more anxious Ken became. He wanted to placate both men, no matter what his opinion of the movie was. Now, however, with something as serious as the life of a friend at issue, Ken was making no effort to placate anyone. In fact, he was making enemies on all sides. Unintentionally he managed to unify the squad for the first time, at his own expense.

Few had forgotten that Ken had made similar disparaging remarks about Hemingway's suicide. Dave Kubach and Ken had joked about a "macho man" like Hemingway taking the easy way out. He had made no such jokes about Marilyn Monroe's suicide, perhaps because she had always exuded an air of vulnerability. In any case the men were furious with his callous attitude on top of his inept handling of the situation. When William Mason got back to the barracks later that day, he got an earful of what had happened.

Mason was incensed about the whole episode, and especially Ken's part in it. He knew that Ken had been close to Rolfs, and it outraged Mason to think that because of Ken's delay in seeking help, Rolfs might have died. Mason wanted Ken called to account for his conduct. That night the company instructors held a closed meeting in one of the empty classrooms. One of the men from Company A recalled that Ken and Kubach refused to attend, but Kubach remembered it differently. He said that morale had been "really going downhill at that time." When Ken was first made team leader, everyone had looked up to him, but there were beginning to be some bad feelings, and some "people who were getting mad" at him. When interviewed, Kubach expressed doubt that the meeting was mandatory, saying "maybe we were not invited; I don't know. . . . I don't remember if we knew there was a meeting." Even if they had known, it may have been the kind of powwow they wanted to avoid. When the others had assembled, Mason demanded that the incident be brought to the attention of superior officers. He wanted Ken charged and removed as team leader. He was not alone in wanting Ken court-martialed. The entire company felt that he had mishandled the episode and that some punishment was required.

Ken was lucky that the meeting, which went on for several hours, was at times loud and emotional. The instructors spent their anger during the arguments, and the group's natural apathy reasserted itself. There was also cause for caution. An investigation by outsiders might bring to light embarrassing details about Rolfs's suicide attempt. The men decided not to pursue any action that might rebound and possibly prolong their stay in the army. Despite Mason's insistence, they concluded that it was best to hush up what had happened.

Ken had escaped trouble with the military authorities, but the incident was not forgotten or forgiven by his fellow teachers. There were few in the company who trusted Ken any longer or wanted to be friends with him. Some, like Tony Moore, shunned him altogether. Ken began to keep to himself, spending hours alone but not idle. Although he did not write home about the Rolfs incident or of earning his fellows' enmity, Ken did keep his mother informed about what he was up to in his little office:

From March 23, 1963

I am trying to leave this place with something to show for the time I have vegetated here. Lately, I have been doing a great deal of writing, and what I am working on—one of my perennial "novels"—is very good—and that criticism comes from a most reliable source whom I permitted to read one (the first chapter). It is rolling along smoothly and is giving me a maximum of detachment and release from a routine which had long ago become a somewhat stale second nature. I hope that nothing develops which will slow my pace of writing or turn me from this particular goal. The book is amusing and well paced; however, it is unwise to make comments upon a work which is so far from completion—and it is not my duty to judge it.

This letter to his parents provides the first mention that Ken had begun work on *A Confederacy of Dunces.* Depressed and homesick, Ken turned his thoughts toward the comfort of New Orleans. This missive also makes clear that it was not his first attempt at writing a long work since completing *The Neon Bible* nine years earlier. Thelma Toole asserted that she had not known about that book when it was being written, yet Ken's references to "perennial novels" shows that she was long aware that he had literary ambitions.

Ken was confident enough about the work in progress to show it to Dave Kubach, who encouraged him to continue and allowed him to keep the typewriter. The other men in the barracks could hear the clattering of keys late into the night. It was no secret that Ken was writing a book. Fred Mish from Company B knew that Ken was working on a novel, but he had not read any of it, and Ken was secretive about the details. Tony Moore was also working on a novel, but he did not have the luxury of a private office to use. Moore had to rent a room in an off-base hotel, where he could work undisturbed.

That Ken was anxious to be home is apparent in a letter that seems to disclose a drawing-inward feeling. Ken begged for pictures of his mother (and father, "if one exists"). Those along with the typewriter would content him until he got home. In a letter dated April 4, 1963, Ken complained about the tedious inspections and the menial labor required of the instructors. He lamented that the "command is changing; formerly conditions were very pleasant"—but it was Ken who was changing. He went on to say:

> In spite of these distractions, I am writing with great regularity. It seems to be the only thing that keeps my mind occupied; I have never found writing to be so relaxing or so tranquilizing, and I still like what I am working on. Quite a bit has been completed already. Some of it, I think, is very funny.
>
> The writing, incidentally, is making me save a great deal of money, something which I have heretofore not been able to do. But I do want to have a little money when I get out of here.

There was a decidedly different tone in a letter written only a week later. Deeply enmeshed in the construction of Ignatius Reilly, Ken began to sound like him. In his 1995 interview Bob Byrne contended that Ignatius was just a mask for Ken Toole, recalling that "Ken Toole was a strange person. He was extroverted and private. And that's very difficult. He had a strong . . . desire to be recognized . . . but also a strong sense

of alienation. That's what you have in Ignatius Reilly." Ken's letter of
April 10, 1963, had both of those characteristics.

Dear Parents,

This afternoon we were visited here by General Bogart (inspected,
rather, no one ever simply "visits" us), the Commander of the Caribbean, the gentleman most vocal in favor of sending us away from
Puerto Rico. I sincerely hope that he succeeds. So much of the money
which we spend could be used for welfare programs here on the island or back in the States.

Writing feverishly, I have completed three chapters and am deep
into the fourth. I only hope that my inspiration and dedication last
long enough to preclude abandonment of the project. I want to come
out of this experience with something to show for my time. What I
am doing will require a great amount of revision, editing, and rewrit-
ing, I imagine, but I should have a basis at least. In my private room
with the fan, easy chair, book case and plant, I settle down with a
borrowed typewriter (this one) and grind out my deathless prose.

I was surprised to see Charlie Ferguson's [a classmate from Fortier
High School] by-line on that article about New Orleans; he graduated
from the Tulane law school a few years ago. The article, incidentally,
was very badly written; some of it was almost painful to read. I
thought that he could do better than that. However, the quality of
the writing in the Picayune-States combine is uniformly childish and
clumsy. They are very poorly edited newspapers.

All is still going very well . . . and, surprisingly, for me, I am more
or less content.

Two weeks later Dave Kubach was sent to the Salinas Training Area
to do manual labor for the rest of the summer. Not only did this deprive
Ken of a trusted friend, but also the borrowed typewriter. Ken wrote his
mother on April 25, 1963, that the "writing, incidentally, is now over 100
pages and is still going strong." As much as Ken disliked spending
money, he was forced into putting out for a new machine. The novel was
moving along too well to stop because of mechanics and finances.

From May 8, 1963
Dear Parents,

This letter is written on the new Underwood-Olivetti typewriter I bought yesterday. It is a rather large portable that retails for something like $135.00. However, I bought it in the PX for only $69.00; the Olivetti name has become world famous, especially for portables, and this seems to be a fine machine.

I received today in the mail a letter of acceptance from Hunter for the 1963–64 academic year in my same position. I must admit, though, that I do not especially want to return to New York and therefore suspect that I will turn down the offer. I would be teaching at the Bronx campus, and that is certainly less than appealing. At the moment, I want to spend some time in New Orleans, at least until I can decide or return to some semblance of civilian behavior. In connection with this, I would appreciate your sending me the names and addresses of some private schools in New Orleans, including perhaps Loyola and Dominican . . . or even Xavier and Dillard. This also includes private high schools. It is rather late to apply for a position for the forthcoming year, but I can always try. The New Orleans Public School system did not want me once, and I doubt seriously whether it would want me now. Also, teaching in a public school seems a little overwhelming. I am preoccupied with this writing project at the moment and feel that with some time in New Orleans, I might be able to wrap it up and polish it. Therefore, the plans to return to the city.

Last night I had dinner with the parents of a fellow instructor who arrived here the same time as I in November 1961; he is from Flagler, Colorado . . . the parents, of course, from the same place. They are here on a two-week vacation, and, since they own the Dry Goods store in Flagler, have been able to rent a very pleasant apartment overlooking the ocean. I can not attempt to describe these people; it sounds unpleasant, I know, to say that they are appalling, but I can say nothing else. They look like two skinny haystacks, burr-like r's rolling from their thin lips. About them there is no hint of social grace, civilization, etc. Hillbillies are bad, but these people were worse. The mother, emaciated to almost skeletal proportions, wore a hair net, a house dress, and white keds with socks, smoking continually and assuming frontiersman poses on chairs and tables. The father is indescribable simply because I doubt whether he exists. When asked about Flagler, they both said laconically, "Dry and windy." For dinner I was served boiled chicken served in its own broth, a lettuce with Kraft French dressing, a slice of pineapple (fresh Puerto Rican variety, the tastiest thing on the menu), and pan bread and butter. That was it; however, as we were finishing our silent meal, a Tastee Freez truck jingled outside, and the mother ran down in her Keds to buy four sundaes for us. Both parents, incidentally, were particularly interested in fishing from the porch of their fine apartment and are hoping sincerely to catch some fresh ocean fish any day. So far, no luck. I have never seen such gray-white, sandy freckled powdery skins in my life. These people were almost inhuman and gave me at least a glimpse of what is lurking on the plains of the great central area of our nation.

The letter is interesting for the information it contains as well as for its tone, which is decidedly waspish toward the end.

Ken had waited until the last minute to make up his mind about future plans. Because he did not have a degree in education, the New Orleans Public School system would not employ him. His comment that they "did not want me once" before suggests that he had applied to teach there, likely at the same time he applied for the position in Lafayette in 1959. That Ken would desire positions at Dillard and Xavier, black universities, shows his liberal views as well as his willingness to take any place offered to him in the city, even those many whites at the time would have disdained.

The description of the couple from Colorado is pure Ignatius. With Dave Kubach away in Salinas, David Farr was the closest person to Ken, and in rendering his parents on the page, Ken proves again that everyone was fair game for his cutting humor. Letters like this one recall Bob Byrne's assessment of Reilly as a doppelgänger of his creator. The deeper that Ken got into the writing of his novel, the more his mask slipped, revealing the complex person beneath it.

In one of Ken's next letters home, Ignatius seems to have disappeared. Ken's communication of May 15 reads as thoughtful and introspective. The cryptic references to "intrigue and politics" concern the aftermath of Rolfs's suicide attempt. It's clear that Ken had not told his mother what had happened, and he probably never did. In later years Thelma gave only glowing reports of her son's army days.

Dear Mother and Dad,

One day, perhaps, when there is time and sufficient detachment, I will be able to fully explain the variety of my experiences here. I am sure that at one time I told you something of Army intrigue and politics; if not, I will have to use a thorough explication of this phenomenon as a foreword to my long duty here at the head of the English program. No one has occupied this position as long as I (since August of last year), and in maintaining this position I have had to survive so many microcosmic "crises" that my heart, head, and soul are thoroughly galvanized. However, this letter is not going to degenerate into self-analysis and evaluation.

The "creative writing" to which I turned about three months ago in an attempt to seek some perspective upon the situation has turned out to have been more than simple psychic therapy. I am now well over one hundred pages and feel that the story shows no signs of bogging or faltering; this is, of course, a first draft, but it is an unusual and entertaining first draft that is, at the very least, a solid foundation for whatever revisions, additions, and editing may be needed. My most immediate hope is that I will at least be able to complete the first draft before I am released from the Army; at the rate of my current progress, this may be possible. You both know that my greatest desire is to be a writer and I finally feel that I am doing something that is more than barely readable. As a matter of fact, I feel no particular anxiety about civilian life, and feel that I shouldn't anyway. If this thing can be worked upon, I am almost certain that a publisher would accept it and so do one or two others to whom I have shown excerpts. (I must not set my hopes too high.)

In my letters I realize that I tend to be rather self-centered and fail to discuss your activities; therefore, let me say that I hope that work is going well for both of you; that Mother's Day was pleasant; that the recital was a success; that Miss Avegno is behaving; that 390 Audubon is not being auctioned from under our feet; that the Corvair is still moving; that the cats are sassy and reasonably loyal; that my room will still be open for business in August.

I love you both very much and think of you more often than you imagine.

As summer set in Ken became more anxious to get home. Although he used his novel in progress as a reason to return, he worried about his role as referee in the often volatile relations between his parents. In an undated letter written probably earlier that spring, his mother referred to previous problems with her husband. She wrote, "Our surmising that his tyranny would reach new heights with your going was absolutely wrong. His mellow mood puts him in a cooperative, pleasant bracket. During a difficult time of rehearsing and picking up donations for an entertainment program, he was most helpful—and willingly so!" She closes the letter saying, "I love you very much, son and friend, and eagerly look forward to your return." All things considered, living in New Orleans seemed like the best possible decision for Ken to make.

The bureaucratic process of separation from the army had started. Ken had his final physical examination, given two months before a soldier's release. In this last sixty days he was promoted to the rank of specialist fifth class, the first such promotion given to an English instructor. He was also recommended for the Good Conduct medal, which is awarded shortly before discharge. Because there was a full complement of recruits and not enough instructors, Ken was teaching full time. This made the time go faster, but cut into his writing schedule. He wrote that his project "has been somewhat slowed at the current time."

Somehow he did find the time to begin boxing up his belongings for shipment back to New Orleans. He kept with him only "my radio and typewriter and my most valuable possessions" to pack carefully and ship at the last moment. By mid-June, Ken wrote that "the days seem to be passing very, very slowly; the month of June seems to have started years ago." There was a great deal of trouble with the group of trainees. Ken wrote that "so much military justice action has been taken against them on the Company level (courts martial, etc.) that the Company has run out of disciplinary action forms."

The teachers were exhausted by the sultry weather, as well as the unruly students. In a letter of June 4, Ken wrote that "the instructor who is supposed to succeed me as 'English Team Leader' suffered a nervous collapse as a result of it all, was sent to the hospital over the weekend, and sent home on leave yesterday. I know that it is unfortunate for him, but in a way it was amusing to see him lying motionless in bed for several days, his arm thrown over his face, especially because he has always been the coolest and most reserved and composed person. His departure made our 'faculty' even more minimal."

Ken celebrated his impending departure by taking some of his savings and spending a night in a luxury hotel in Condado Beach. Because it was the off-season, he got a military rate of $7.00 a day. He wrote home that "Between the couches and the beds in my lair, I didn't venture forth very much and chalked up fourteen hours of sleep at one stretch. I have never made a wiser investment. It is strange, but, in spite of the horrors of current life here, I feel very stable." Happy that his time was limited, Ken could "almost taste freedom."

Even in these last days Ken did not have a job waiting for him. This was of great concern to his mother, who had written him with suggestions of how to improve his (their) future finances. Ken's June 30 reply is uncharacteristically sanguine:

> On the writing. I have experienced a "renaissance," and have been regularly adding to the manuscript page by page. My one hope in civilian life (in the immediate months following discharge) is that I will have conditions favorable to trying to complete this thing and polish it. That is why I am planning to stay in New Orleans, for I feel that I should be able to do some work there while I am unburdened by having to shift for myself so far as housing and food are concerned. I must make one try at getting something published, and I feel that this is the time. New York, etc., would hinder my accomplishing this project. Upon my return to the city, I will have to find work; however, I am sure that something will turn up. At least, it appears to me that I can find a niche in the city. You will benefit from this, for I have never worked in the city. One point should be made clear: I do not intend to go to Law School or to any other school at the present time.

About the thing I am writing I have one conviction: it is entertaining and publishable, and I have more than a degree of faith in it.

In his last month on the island, Ken detached himself emotionally from the company, even though he was still in charge of the men. On July 30 he wrote home that the

casualty rate here is mounting: one instructor is seeing double out of one eye; another has an undefined headache; another got a bug in his ear and went to the hospital to have it removed; one claims that his cold has gone to his lungs and is becoming pneumonia. The pneumonia victim is coughing loudly outside my room at the moment. Everyone else is taking a nap and hoping that the rain will cease for a while. People who graduate from universities with degrees in the liberal arts certainly are often a species of prima donnas, ersatz movie stars, and eccentrics. Playing nurse to these instructors for over a year now has not been an easy job, principally because these instructors on this faculty were drafted into this particular academy and are forced to live together in the same barracks. The petty complaints which I get are very illuminating: "Make Corporal ——— turn his lamp off. It's shining in my eyes." The most ludicrous complaint which I've had to handle was this: An instructor claimed that the instructor in a classroom across the yard was shining a mirror which reflected sunlight into his classroom and, more specifically, into his eyes, thereby sabotaging his instruction. Handling a faculty anywhere is a problem because of the psychic structure of people attracted to teaching, but this is too much. However, teachers always nurse little grievances which they feel are quite justified and real.

Despite his concern about money and the uncertainty of his future, Ken decided to travel to St. Thomas in the Virgin Islands. It turned out to be one of the best times he'd had since arriving in the Caribbean. On July 15, he wrote his parents:

The brief flight from Puerto Rico really takes a person to another world, a very pleasant and "upbeat" one. After too long in the downbeat atmosphere of this unfortunate island, it is good to see a society

where there is some hope, at least. For one thing, St. Thomas is popu-
lated principally by affluent Americans who have made it their per-
manent home. And, let's admit it, there is nothing like a little money
to improve the atmosphere. St. Thomas is a lovely, clean, quiet, and
courteous island. The night life is sophisticated and entertaining (another change from Puerto Rico by night). The natives, West Indian
Negroes, are sensible and courteous, two adjectives which could never
be used to describe Puerto Ricans. The whole place is very charming,
and I seriously regretted the fact that I had neither the time nor the
money to remain there longer. It reminded me of the fact that there
are places in the world where people live in an atmosphere of relative
quiet and conduct themselves with at least some grace. And, in spite
of its sounding parochial, it was good to be surrounded by Americans
once more. I knew, however, that I must once again face reality when
I was sitting in the bar at the airport in St. Thomas awaiting the return flight late Sunday. The bar was quiet and pleasant and civilized
tourists were civilizedly drinking and maintaining civil conversations;
then three Puerto Ricans entered the bar (a man and two women) and
began their normal raucous screaming at one another in their inimita-
ble whine and wail and everyone in the bar ended up staring at them.
I don't want to appear a Mrs. Grunge, but I am afraid that Puerto
Ricans are really hopeless. They have neither looks, charm, manners,
sense, intelligence, nor decency. I await my impending rescue from
them.

Ken had always been quick to criticize, and his opinions of the Puerto
Ricans were based on little actual contact with the island's society. Most
of his dealings had been with raw recruits from the hills, army personnel, and people on the low end of the pay scale. He was afraid of the
officers, and his views were colored by daily contact with trainees, who
according to his letter of June 11, "are wearing stocking caps. It is a general practice for Puerto Rican men to use pancake make-up on their faces
and to use neutral polish on their fingernails, and it is not unusual to see
a trainee opening a compact during a break in the English classes or
working on his nails. What a frightening civilization exists on this island;
ignorant, cruel, malicious, infantile, self-centered, undependable, and
very proud withal."

Studio photograph of a beautiful Thelma at age twenty-one. Her blue velvet gown was designed for the occasion. *Courtesy Tulane University Manuscripts Department*

A star high-school debater, young John Dewey Toole Jr. was offered a scholarship to Louisiana State University and served in the U.S. Army during World War I. *Courtesy Tulane University Manuscripts Department*

The Hampson Street residence, where Ken Toole lived the last two years of his life. A plaque by the door reads "Toole-Hecker House, built about 1885 by John Paul Hecker, Jr., as his family residence and still owned by his descendants a century later. Last residence of John Kennedy Toole (1937–1969), author of *A Confederacy of Dunces,* winner of the Pulitzer Prize for fiction in 1981." The plaque was subsequently attached to a fence that now surrounds the property.

The site of Toole's suicide near Biloxi, Mississippi, is on the corner of Riverview Drive and Popps Ferry Road. In 1969, it was a rural and sparsely inhabited area.

Between sets, Sidney "Dr. Guitar" Snow relaxes in the Café du Monde as he reminisces about his friend Tooley and their shared passion for New Orleans music.

In the lower Quarter on Barracks Street is this local watering hole. Some New Orleanians say it provided the inspiration for Lana Lee's bar the Night of Joy. Toole set his creation on Bourbon Street, where nightclubs like the Gunga Den and the Sho-Bar featured such famous ecdysiasts as Blaze Starr, Linda Brigette, and Patty White.

Walker Percy, who championed *A Confederacy of Dunces,* began writing after completing medical school. He went on to win the National Book Award and to contribute a prestigious body of work to twentieth-century literature. Thelma Toole once sent him a check for his "services" to her late son. Percy returned the money. *©Jerry Bauer*

Actor John McConnell modeled for this bronze statue by sculptor Bill Lud-wing. It stands on Canal Street, welcoming visitors to the Château Sonesta Hotel, once the location of the D. H. Holmes department store. As he waits for his mother under the old D. H. Holmes clock, Ignatius holds the shopping bag presumably containing new strings for his lute.

In a photograph taken for *People* magazine, Thelma Toole sits before a giant poster of the character she called "that slob, known as Ignatius."
© *Christopher Harris*

In Thelma's old neighborhood along Elysian Fields Avenue, houses are crowded together on narrow lots. The imposing building on the right was once the old Schoen funeral home, where Ken's body was sent after his death. The small structure next door was Arthur Ducoing's home, built in the 1960s, where in later years Thelma would live with her brother. Nearby sits St. Peter and Paul Catholic Church, where Thelma and John D. Toole were married and where Ken's requiem mass was held.

In her last years Thelma braved illness and fatigue to attend every function honoring her son. Just a few months before her death, she attended the premiere of the musical production of *A Confederacy of Dunces* at Louisiana State University. She is pictured here flanked by (left) Scott Harlan, who played Ignatius Reilly, and (right) writer and director Frank Galati. *Photo by Jim Zietz*

In her role as "mother of the book," Thelma was invited to participate in many civic events. She described herself as "a worthy and cultured representative of my son." Here, in a 1981 Christmas parade in New Orleans, she waves to the crowd. © *Philip Gould*

Greenwood Cemetery along Canal Boulevard is the resting place of John Kennedy Toole and his mother. The Ducoing tomb pictured in this "city of the dead" has the tallest cross.

Ten

One wonders how your masterwork is doing. . . . I wonder if it has been sent to "your publisher" and when it may see the light of day and the book store's shelf.

—*Joe Hines, in a letter to John Kennedy Toole*

B Y THE END OF JULY Ken had shipped his typewriter and crated the rest of his belongings. He was scheduled to be discharged from the army on August 8. In a hand-written note he informed his parents that he had obtained a position in the English department of a small Catholic all-female college within walking distance of his home in New Orleans. With two years of patriotic duty (such as it was) behind him and a job ahead, Ken's future looked promising.

This optimism carried over into his dealings with the men of Company A. Reluctant to leave with bad feelings on either side, Ken went out of his way to mend some fences. Tony Moore remembered what happened in his final meeting with Ken. Moore was engaged to a woman who was teaching in Puerto Rico. He had never spoken of her to Ken because he did not want to subject the relationship to Ken's scrutiny.

The night before Ken left, he saw Moore in town. Ken crossed the street to meet him and said that he had heard Moore was serious about a girl. Ken congratulated him and wished him well. Grateful for the chance to part on good terms, Moore was surprised by Ken's sincerity. It touched Moore that Ken seemed rather envious of him as they shook hands.

With his manuscript tucked safely in his carry-on bag, Ken departed for Charleston, South Carolina, on Wednesday, August 7, to receive his formal discharge. In one of his last communications from Puerto Rico, Ken wrote his mother a long, introspective, and philosophical letter, which reads in part:

> While I have had unusual success in the Army, I have also had unusual problems (This is a statement, not a complaint. I believe that I have matured sufficiently to avoid complaining—previously one of my more apparent characteristics). Handling a contingent of English instructors trapped here together for almost two years and half-maddened by continual exposure to the trainees has not been easy. Some aspects of this have almost been tragic. I can sincerely say that nothing could faze me anymore, and that nothing is all-inclusive. I feel that I will return to civilian life strangely rejuvenated and energetic. If I am fortunate, I will be able to forget many things that have happened in the last few months; however, this place is so far removed from reality that the happenings here tend to fade from your mind when you get away for only a day . . . My own outlook is more positive than it has been in many years and I feel quite calm.

Ken made only one request of his mother: "I would like to sit in the living room and talk for hours and hours and hours . . . over black coffee, lemonade, bourbon, or whatever you are willing to serve me." No matter what problems were waiting for him there, home had never looked so good.

Don't do it was Bob Byrne's advice to Ken on hearing that he had taken a position at Dominican College. Byrne felt that teaching at another girls' school, especially a Catholic school, was not in Ken's best interests. Byrne referred to it as a "Byzantine" situation, rife with intrigue and unwholesome for Ken. Dominican was the sister school of Loyola University. Staffed by nuns of the Dominican Order, the school was small, with a student body of about four hundred white upper-middle-class young women from the New Orleans area. There was a great emphasis on a strict adherence to the tenets of conservative Roman Catholicism at Dominican, and suspicious objections to the changes enacted by the Vatican's Twenty-First Ecumenical Council. Not a school that encouraged independent thought, Dominican did not seem to be a place where Ken would flourish.

Ken dismissed Byrne's objections. For one thing, the administration was thrilled to have a teacher with Ken's credentials, and he was flattered by all the attention he received from the nuns, as well as by the proffered salary. In a letter written July 31, a week before he left Puerto Rico, Ken boasted to his mother of his impending employment.

> The administration hired me with breathtaking dispatch. Later they asked for a photo, and, after I had sent one, asked whether I would be willing to teach a course on WYES-TV also. I will not commit myself on that particular subject. However, Good Dominican is paying me $600.00/mo for 10 mos. or $6000/yr . . . and for N. O. that is quite a sum. They strained their budget. . . .
>
> I receive two-page letters from Dominican almost daily; the nuns, apparently, are growing more and more excited as my date of arrival nears. Who knows? It might be a relatively pleasant experience . . . and will certainly provide me with the financial security for writing.

Ken did enjoy that first year at Dominican. He taught only ten hours a week, which gave him the time he needed to write. The staff of the English department was small, but close-knit and congenial. Everyone there encouraged him to work on his novel. As for the students at the St. Charles Avenue school, they were convent-trained young ladies, southern born and bred. Unlike the black-stockinged Hunter students, who were careless of their appearance, the women at Dominican were impeccably groomed for every class. The New York students had no compunctions about venting their views and challenging the teacher. The gently reared belles in New Orleans were content to listen, learn, and keep dissenting opinions to themselves. After two fractious years teaching rough-and-tumble army recruits, Dominican was a welcome change.

The nuns loved Ken from the beginning. His exquisite manners and charm were a hit with the faculty. One of the lay teachers whom he often walked home complained that he would keep her talking on the corner until her feet hurt. Ken loved women, especially safe women. Pat Rickels had noticed this long ago, but thought it was not unusual among young men who did not want to be trapped into marriage. Nuns, married women, and students were all hands-off, which suited Ken just fine. He had traded in the old Corvair and paid cash for a good new Chevrolet, but walked to school to save money on fuel.

Ken had abundant leisure time, and his mother was delighted to wait on him hand and foot. Thrilled that he was back, his parents encouraged him to work on his writing, since that was an important reason for his living at home, but it was not easy. For the past five years Ken had been in New Orleans for brief periods in between moves. In that time his father's mental condition had deteriorated, and he would often wander around the house lost in a world of his own. Although money was scarce, Thelma was too proud to ask either the Toole family or a service organization like the Veterans Administration for help. She constantly reminded Ken that she depended on him to take care of them and their problems.

Ken complained about his situation to a few people, one of them J. C. Broussard of Lafayette, who related his concerns to a friend, describing how Ken, after several drinks, had confessed that he felt imprisoned by his parents' demands and frailties. Broussard urged Ken to save himself and not waste his youth.

Thelma loved her son and wanted him with her, not just because she missed him, but because she felt incomplete without him. She wanted to orchestrate Ken's adult life as she had his childhood. Each time he went away (to graduate school, to Lafayette, to Puerto Rico), it had been with a certain anticipation. Now that he was home of his own free will, she intended to see that he never left again. The question is why Ken, after years of independence, allowed himself to be manipulated.

Clinical psychologist Mary Lou Kelly has speculated that guilt was only part of the reason he returned. Of course his parents needed help and he was their only child, but many children abandon aging parents for the sake of a job or a chosen lifestyle. Ken was raised in a very controlling situation and made few decisions on his own. Kelly said that people with such backgrounds often don't feel confident about making choices for themselves. Even though home was not a happy place, it was secure. For someone reluctant to make a decision, even an unhappy home can be a refuge.

Kelly commented that the jobs Ken had were also in controlled environments. For a teacher, rules, class hours, instructional materials, and grade scales provide a structure that can be comforting. His military experience had its own set routine, and as a soldier Ken had to follow a rigid code. He was told when to get up and when to put the lights out. It was easy for him to obey orders, but when Ken was given command of the barracks, his confidence faltered. As with any large organization, the army would often issue conflicting orders. When this happened, Ken would get upset, and he feared facing the master sergeant, often the one who had caused the confusion. When Ken had to make an important decision on his own (as in Rolfs's suicide attempt), he ducked the responsibility. Afraid to fail, he froze and did nothing, perhaps unaware that this act of denial was a decision in itself. Equally unable to bear the consequences of his inaction, Ken lashed out at Rolfs, who he felt was responsible for his dilemma. Avoiding accountability is neither a healthy nor effective style of coping, and Kelly did not find it surprising that Ken opted for a sheltered life, no matter how miserable it made him.

Sidney Snow remembered that Toole was very unhappy at home. Ken had taken to following the musicians around after his release from the army, and he would hang around the Snow house in the Irish Channel. Ken helped Snow paint his 1950 Oldsmobile and told him that once he wanted to go into the car business as his father had done, but now he had other plans. He talked about the book he was writing, saying it was the first of many he planned to do about the city of New Orleans. Sid's mother liked Ken, and he often stayed for dinner at her request. Ken enjoyed hanging around the Snow house, where there was a constant flow of people and conversation. He did not talk much about his family, except to say that they never had such impromptu gatherings.

Ken spent many evenings in the clubs where Snow and his friends played. There were a lot of girls who hung around the band. Ken was acquainted with them all, but never spoke to one in particular. Snow did not know whether or not Ken was gay, but it would not have mattered. Ken was so much fun, and he just loved the music. Snow taught him how to chord some simple tunes on the guitar, but the only tune he mastered was "Malaguena." Mostly Ken just relaxed and drank beer with them. New Orleans has always been noted for embracing alcohol, and this was a hard-drinking crowd.

The GTO was a black nightclub where Snow and the band sometimes played. "We were all white kids," said Snow. "In the early sixties we played the Beatles' songs, and the audience loved it. Tooley was with us then." On one tragic occasion, Snow didn't show up for the rehearsal of a group that had asked him to play with them at the GTO. The group shot up some tainted heroin, and all of them died. "Tooley was with me when we found out," Snow recalled. The incident scared both of them.

The November 1963 assassination of President Kennedy devastated Ken. He became depressed, so depressed that he quit work on the book and began to drink quite heavily. Friends like J. C. Broussard saw Ken during this time and noticed this deep melancholy, but did not realize the cause. Some years later Ken recalled this extreme reaction to Kennedy's death in a letter to editor Robert Gottlieb.

It was not until February that Ken recovered enough to go back to the manuscript. He made no revisions, merely picked up where he had left off several months before. He typed what he had, tacked an ending onto it, and mailed the manuscript to Simon and Schuster in New York City. It was the first time he had subjected his work to public scrutiny since *The Neon Bible.* He chose that company for a specific reason, which he later detailed in a letter to his editor. The novel came unrecommended, "over the transom," and fell into the firm's slush pile. In those days Simon and Schuster was a small family-owned publishing house. The relationship between editors and the staff was warm and casual. Secretaries and assistants did the first reading of a manuscript. If the initial reader liked a book, he or she would then recommend it to an editor.

In 1964 Jean Ann Jollett Marks was assistant to Robert Gottlieb, a senior editor at Simon and Schuster. It was she who picked Ken's manuscript from the slush pile. She remembers reading the book and loving its energy. She knew that the novel was not ready to be published, but she felt it had great potential. She passed the manuscript on to Gottlieb.

When interviewed, Marks was effusive in her praise of Gottlieb's care and compassion toward his writers. It was Gottlieb who coaxed Joseph Heller into finishing *Catch 22*. Gottlieb also pioneered the practice of auctioning paperback rights, which meant greater royalties for authors. At Simon and Schuster a successful editor like Gottlieb was given leeway in encouraging new writers. If Gottlieb liked Ken's novel, he would fight for it. Marks's main job was to put emerging talent in contact with Gottlieb.

Although he did not like the book as much as Marks did, Gottlieb felt that Ken had talent. It would take a lot of work to mine the book, but Gottlieb was willing to do his part. At this time the blockbuster complex had yet to take hold of New York publishing. The atmosphere of Simon and Schuster was a nurturing one for writers, and there was a strong commitment to literature.

For two years Gottlieb worked with Ken to develop *A Confederacy of Dunces*. It was a trying and painful experience for editor and author, ending unhappily for both of them. Ten letters exist that chronicle their professional relationship. All are photocopies, and the whereabouts of the original letters are unknown. Within the collection there is reference to three missing letters from Simon and Schuster, as well as some missing notes from Ken to Gottlieb. The surviving letters tell a story of disappointment and frustration, and hint of a descent into madness.

Confusion has long surrounded Ken's dealings with Simon and Schuster and his relationship with Robert Gottlieb. Marks had great respect and admiration for Gottlieb and thought that he had taken undue criticism over Toole's book.

Later, in her bitterness over Ken's suicide, Thelma Toole made racist remarks about Gottlieb. Showing great restraint and charity, Gottlieb chose not to comment, but his refusal to clarify his dealings with Ken created a cloud of mystery. Other industry insiders tell conflicting stories about who knew what. These varying accounts may be the result of faulty memories, or a wish to stay out of the story. Whatever the reason, denial and double-talk make an accurate, detailed reconstruction of those two years next to impossible.

The correspondence starts out with a joyful, optimistic letter from Jean Marks. Some previous communication, perhaps an exchange of letters, now lost, must have passed between Gottlieb and Ken. By summer, scarcely four months after Ken submitted it, Gottlieb had read the manuscript, and Ken wanted to meet him in New York to discuss how best to proceed with the revision.

From June 9, 1964
Dear Mr. Toole,

Thank you for your good letter to Robert Gottlieb. He's at the American Booksellers Convention in Washington, but will return here on Thursday. He asked me to write you that he'd call you or write you immediately upon his return.

There's going to be a slight problem—this: Bob is leaving New York for Europe on June 27. However, he will be in the office the day before he leaves, on the 26th. Can you jiggle dates and be here a few days early (I'd like it to be even before the 26th—good intentions and all, I know that day will be chaos itself). Can you? At any rate, that's the story—I'm sure you all will work something out. This is just to explain the delay in his getting back to you.

Is now the time for me to tell you that I laughed, chortled, collapsed my way through Confederacy? I did.
Sincerely,
Jean Ann Jollett

A week later Gottlieb wrote Ken reiterating his one great objection to the novel. He felt there was a fundamental flaw, which Ken would never correct to Gottlieb's satisfaction. It was the same point that Russ Griffin had made to Ken years before, when she wrote, "You have to be saying something that you really *mean* . . . not just dredging characters and situations up because they are charming." In all the time they worked together, Gottlieb never changed his opinion about what was wrong with the book. It was on this point that negotiations eventually foundered, sinking Ken's hope for publication with Simon and Schuster.*

From June 15, 1964
Dear Mr. Toole,

Apparently we're to miss each other in New York. I'm sorry, but not so sorry as I would be if I weren't off to Europe. Anyway, in case I don't speak to you before I go, I wanted to say one thing more about your book having read your letter. And this is it:

It seems to me that you understand the problem—the major problem—involved, but think that the conclusion can solve it. More is required, though. Not only do the various threads need resolving; they can always be tied together conveniently. What must happen is that they must be strong and meaningful *all the way through*—not merely episodic and then wittily pulled together to make everything look as if it's come out right. In other words, there must be a point to everything you have in the book, a real point, not just amusingness that's forced to figure itself out.

Does this make sense? I hope so because it's vital.

Please, no matter what, let me see the book again when you've worked on it again. I understand completely why you had to stop and put it aside, get it finished at all costs. That happens even to editors—books are sent to press that demand at least another go-through because one simply can't look at them for another moment. A period away from the job usually does help, though.

I hope to see you at some later date if we can't make it in June.
Sincerely,
Robert Gottlieb

This letter and all subsequent letters from Gottlieb to Ken were composed on the former's typewriter and sent out with handwritten correc-

*PUBLISHER'S NOTE: The publisher acknowledges that it incorporated Mr. Gottlieb's letters in this book without his permission. Mr. Gottlieb viewed the inclusion of his letters in this book as failing to comply with the requirements of Fair Use, that such an inclusion would be in error, and that he would be justified in preventing their use. We are grateful that instead of interfering with publication, he has graciously allowed us to proceed.

tions. Gottlieb rarely dictated the letters he sent to his writers. Although they corresponded and spoke on the phone for two years, Gottlieb and Ken were never on a first-name basis. It is possible Gottlieb did not know that Toole went by the name of Ken in New Orleans, since all the letters are addressed to "Mr. John Toole."

Two days after this letter from Gottlieb, Jean Marks wrote to Ken.

From June 17, 1964
Dear Mr. Toole,

By all means call when you get here, and come in. I can see what the writer of The Book looks like, and you can see, at least, how we live here.

Did someone forward the enclosed from New Orleans? I'll probably have no more editorial thoughts from Bob for you, but perhaps your vacation from the manuscript plus the enclosed will be sufficient, and you can take it away knowing exactly what you want to do. We shall see. Come.
Sincerely,
Jean Ann Jollett

When this letter was written, Ken had been back from Puerto Rico for almost a year. His time in New Orleans had been productive and successful. The two semesters at Dominican were easy and delightful, with such a mutual satisfaction between teacher and school that Ken had no intention of seeking another position. Despite his complaints, living at home was not as disastrous as he had feared. Although he didn't have much privacy for writing, his novel had been completed and submitted, unsolicited, to a first-class publisher. In a Cinderella twist, the novel had caught the eye of a senior editor who agreed to take it on. This was heady stuff for a beginning artist, and Ken was thrilled about the response from Simon and Schuster.

Even though Gottlieb and Marks warned him that there was a great deal of work to do on the book, Ken was irrepressible in his excitement. He wrote to all his friends, telling them his good luck. Ken was confident that he could revise the novel to the editor's satisfaction and toyed with the idea of visiting in New York, finally deciding that the expense of the trip was better left to another time. Also, Gottlieb had a hectic schedule, and there was no assurance that Ken would get to meet with him. Gottlieb had sent all the editorial comments he thought necessary for the time being, but Ken was not ready to begin a rewrite. He was disappointed that Gottlieb thought the book couldn't be published as it was.

Having worked on his novel constantly for over a year, Ken felt that he needed a break from it, thinking some distance would stir the creative juices. He decided to spend the summer relaxing and soaking up the atmosphere of his home city in preparation for the revision process. There were visits to see the Rickels in Lafayette, and Robert Byrne made his annual August trip to New Orleans. Also in August, one of Ken's army friends, Joe Hines, made a trip from New York to visit Ken and meet his family. He thought it was funny that he went to see "John" and left knowing "Kenny."

In August of 1964, Joel Fletcher saw Ken for the last time. On this occasion he also met Ken's parents, lunching with them at their home on Audubon Street. The family seemed in good spirits, and Ken praised his mother's stuffed tomatoes. Amid the conviviality, Mr. Toole popped in for a moment, inexplicably dressed in the uniform of a Boy Scout leader, short pants and all.

The fall semester was well underway before Ken sent the revised manuscript off to New York. When that was done, only the waiting was left, which is hard for any writer. Ken's creation was now out of his control and in the hands of strangers. The stakes were high, and his pride was on the line. Everyone in Ken's small world knew that his book was in New York, and they questioned him constantly about its progress toward publication. His parents found the waiting extremely difficult, which made Ken feel even more helpless.

Eleven

"Micawber!" exclaimed Mrs. Micawber, in tears. "Have I deserved this! I who never have deserted you; who never WILL desert you, Micawber!"

—*Charles Dickens,* David Copperfield

WITH NOTHING TO BE DONE on the writing front, Ken threw himself into teaching. His first year at Dominican had been very successful, and now, with his classes filled with eager students, Ken was clearly the most popular new teacher on campus. Delighted that he had chosen to continue at Dominican, the staff praised his professionalism and ability. The department head knew that he was a writer and made no demands on his time outside the classroom. Ken did not attend school events or monitor any of the many organizations there. When his classes were over, Ken headed away from campus.

The students knew nothing about his private life. Because he wore no wedding ring, they assumed he was unmarried, though he never spoke of anything personal. The women in his classes did not know where he lived. Male teachers were required to wear coat and tie while on campus, but none of them dressed as well as Professor Toole, whose shirts were the whitest and most starched. His wardrobe was the best turned-out, and he never had a hair out of place. Former student Charlene Sperling Stovall said that "his photographs do not do him justice. He was really very good-looking." Some of the girls had crushes on him, but his demeanor was purely professional and discouraged them from approaching him. One day a student came to class wearing a micro miniskirt and parked herself in the front row. Professor Toole told her she had to leave because he was serious about the study of literature and refused to teach her while she was dressed like that. She left embarrassed, but Stovall reported that the other students thought she had deserved the reprimand.

From the beginning of his career at Dominican, Ken had many repeat students. Some, like Stovall, signed up for his classes no matter what he was teaching, even if it meant having to spend all day on campus and riding the last bus home. In her three semesters of English literature under Professor Toole, Stovall never missed a lecture. Her explanation was that she "just loved to watch him teach." She said that he was hysterically funny and could make the class weep with laughter while he barely cracked a smile. He never repeated a joke or a story.

Although his students did not know Ken was a writer, they knew that he was very creative. One of his favorite class pastimes was the study of names. He was fascinated with what characteristics names bring to mind. The students would think of a name or choose one from the story they were reading, and he would make up a complete persona to go with it. For example, Professor Toole's "Betty" was a poor white woman wearing run-down work shoes and carrying a bucket. By the end of each semester the students had been privy to a gallery of Professor Toole's creations.

Right before the Christmas break, Ken received a reply from Robert Gottlieb.

From December 14, 1964
Dear Mr. Toole,

   I've taken a long time to get back to you, but not for want of thinking. And I still don't know what to tell you, after thinking and after consultation with one person in town whose opinion I needed.

In many ways I think you've done an excellent job—of pulling the plot together, and of making sense out of certain non-sense things, of strengthening certain characters, of eliminating certain others. The book is much better. It is still not right.

Let me interrupt to say that the other opinion I wanted was that of Candida Donadio, a young woman who is probably the best literary agent in town (one of my closest friends). She handles Joe Heller, Bruce Friedman, John Cheever, Nelson Algren, Thomas Pynchon, Harvey Swados, Philip Roth, ad infinitum. I wanted to know what she thought for various reasons: because she is the agent for you; because what you're good at would delight her; because her judgment is accurate; because, frankly, if she and I can't figure out [what] to do with you, it's not likely that anyone else will be able to. Anyway, having introduced her: we talked for an hour on the phone Sunday night, and as often happens had exactly the same reactions—liked the same parts, didn't like the same parts, had the same doubts and the same excitements.

What we think is this. That you are wildly funny often, funnier than almost anyone around, and our kind of funny. That many of the characters are wonderful—Burma, Santa, Irene, Mancuso, Lana Lee, and others (Miss Trixie too). That certain things don't work: Myrna, in particular. That Ignatius is in trouble—that he's not as good as you think he is, and there is too much of him. That the Levys are not so hot. That the book is considerably too long. That certain scenes, particularly my favorite—the civil rights demonstration in the factory—are glories. That others are washouts (What Joe Heller called "Black eyes" and "Feathers in my cap"). But that, all this aside, there is another problem: that with all its wonderfulnesses, the book—even better plotted (and still better plotable)—does not have a reason; it's a brilliant exercise in invention, but unlike CATCH [22] and MOTHER'S KISSES and V and the others, it isn't *really* about anything. And that's something no one can do anything about. Certainly an editor can't say: "Put meaning in."

Which is all very well, but what to do? The book could be improved and published. But it wouldn't succeed; we could never say that it *was* anything. On the other hand, we can't abandon it or you (I shall never abandon Mr. Micawber). We won't. But we know from experience that when Candida and I know something is basically for us, but not right, it is very difficult to have it right for other people in town on our wave length, and the others are out of the question.

So I don't know what to tell you.

What I really would like would be to talk. But you are there, not here, and I'm not likely to be there soon. Is there a chance of your coming North?

If not, and if you are not disgusted with me, perhaps C. and I will figure out a next step. Or perhaps you will.

In any case, write to me without nervousness, because I am here for you whatever way things work out. Let me know what you think. My own guess is that you will feel you can't do more on this book without specific editorial suggestion. I wouldn't blame you. If so, I'll try harder to think of something.

Or if you give us up, tell me and I'll send back the manuscript. But I don't want to, and it wouldn't be a good idea.

Or just brood for a while.

Don't despair.

Best,

Bob Gottlieb

Excuse the typing; I can't dictate letters like this.

Gottlieb's letter is both interesting and confusing. The reference to Charles Dickens's "Mr. Micawber" suggests that there must have been other correspondence between Gottlieb and Toole, or a note included with the revised manuscript. All that is known of Candida Donadio's assessment of the novel is found in this one letter. No other mention is made of her.

What Gottlieb calls "letters like this" makes one wonder what sort of letter it is. Amid the generous praise for the book and Ken's talent, there is a definite note of firmness that the work, as far as Gottlieb is concerned, has reached an impasse in its present form. Equally definite, however, its the editor's commitment to helping the author through "specific editorial suggestion." Although he states that the book as it stands is "not right" for him or "other people in town on our wavelength," Gottlieb strongly affirms his desire to maintain a connection to Ken.

Though he sees no ready fix for the problems he details, Gottlieb discourages Ken from asking for the manuscript's return, perhaps hoping that Ken himself will find a solution to their common problem. Having taken him on as a potential author, Gottlieb does not want to abandon the young writer but finds himself at a loss as to how to proceed. Unfortunately, Gottlieb could not know how desperate Ken was to have the book published.

It wasn't just that Ken believed in the book and Gottlieb didn't. No editor (even at LSU Press, the book's eventual publisher) ever thought the book would be much of a success. Ken had an unrealistic idea about what the publication would do for him. He thought it would provide additional income for his parents, that he could get away. Ken wanted to return to New York as a famous writer with all the right doors open to him. Gottlieb thought he was helping a talented albeit stranded writer, but his letter of December 14 stunned Ken. Methodical as he was, Ken must have taken the letter apart to weigh, sentence by sentence, all aspects of the editor's comments. Although he saw his chance at glory slipping away, he refused to let it go without a fight. The day he received Gottlieb's letter, Ken penned a hasty, importunate reply.

From December 16, 1964
Dear Mr. Gottlieb,

Ironically, I found your letter encouraging. Perhaps this sounds masochistic; however, I'm grateful for attention you've given the book.

Now I should "think the book over." But while I'm doing this, I would like to communicate with you about the book in more specific terms; in some detail, what is wrong, etc., where things go wrong . . . I don't know whether you find telephone conversations successful, but if you do, please call me collect here in New Orleans person-to-person at University 1-0162. I'm at that number most nights.

I must appear to be a very "ambitious" writer. But I'm not despairing.
Sincerely,
John Toole

Ken had suffered a shock. His Cinderella tale had quickly turned into a horror story. Afraid to confront his mother with the downturn in his fortunes, he fobbed her off with talk about the editor demanding more revisions. Repeatedly affirming his faith in Ken's talent, Gottlieb had placed the decision of what to do with the manuscript in Ken's hands, but Ken was not equal to the task. As with the Rolfs episode some years before, Ken just sat confused and impotent before the seriousness of the situation. This sad state of affairs continued for a month, until Ken, unable to rebound from this setback and unwilling to advance in a new direction, determined retreat was his only option. He communicated this decision to Gottlieb.

From January 15, 1965
Dear Mr. Gottlieb,
    The only sensible thing to do, it seems to me, is to ask for the manuscript. Aside from making some deletions, I don't think I could really do much to the book now—and, of course, even with revisions you might not be satisfied. I can't even *think* of much that I could do to the book. So there's little point in your being burdened with the manuscript. Will you send it to me?
    I must say very honestly that I've been fortunate in having the manuscript receive your notice; I hope that you'll be willing to look at anything I might send in the future.
Sincerely,
John Toole

The next six weeks stressed Ken to the breaking point. He seems to have suffered a serious emotional collapse during this time. Reconstruction of these weeks is sketchy at best. What is known is that along with the returned manuscript, Gottlieb sent Ken a letter (now missing) that greatly confused him. It was apparently not a blunt dismissal of either the book or the author. There was something in it that gave Ken hope that his novel could be salvaged, and indeed, Gottlieb had said from the beginning that there were parts of Ken's book he greatly admired. Ken's sophistication wasn't much deeper than his Ivy League wardrobe, and his lack of publishing experience left him unequipped to interpret the seemingly mixed message. Unable to be dispassionate about rejection, he determined unwisely that some action was required of him.

Gottlieb is known for his dedication to his writers, and according to Jean Marks, he is also renowned for his elaborate rejection letters. She said writers turned down by him have saved the letters with pride. Gottlieb must have penned just such a charming and glowing missive to Ken. Unfortunately, the editor did not realize that in Ken's unsteady state of mind, he would not know what to make of the correspondence. On the strength of this note, Ken planned an impromptu visit to the offices of Simon and Schuster.

Sometime in February, Ken arrived unannounced at Gottlieb's office, only to discover that the editor was not in town. In a subsequent letter to Gottlieb, Ken recounted a distressing and disastrous meeting with Jean Marks. He confessed that he caused a scene by cringing and babbling in her presence. He was beside himself with humiliation and remorse at the way he acted. The truth is that he never saw Marks. She left at the end of January, taking a month's leave from the firm to get married. She said that she never met John Kennedy Toole, then or at any other time.

Marks said she did not know who it was that Ken saw the day he came, but she doubted that the scene was anything like he imagined it. Whoever Ken saw, whether it was a receptionist or a secretary, did not mention having a horrible encounter with a writer, and Marks certainly never did. No one at the office remembered meeting Ken.

There is no doubt that Ken went to New York, and to the publishing house. The most likely scenario is that on being told the editor was unavailable, Ken spoke to someone from Gottlieb's staff. If Ken assumed that the woman he met was Marks, it is odd that he didn't speak up, since he was acquainted with her by correspondence. He may have been too upset to do more than leave a message for Gottlieb. However boorish or crazy Ken may have thought he was that day, he made no impression on anyone in the office. When Gottlieb returned to work, there was a note saying only that Ken had called in person and asking Gottlieb please to phone him in New Orleans.

Although Ken had withdrawn his manuscript from Simon and Schuster, Gottlieb felt enough connection and good will toward Ken to do as he asked. He called the writer and they spoke for an hour on the telephone. Gottlieb did make it clear in the conversation that he would not accept the manuscript as it was. He suggested that Ken write another book and put some distance between himself and the old project. Many writers have been forced to abandon a beloved work, and Gottlieb could not have realized that Ken was unable to do this. Talking to Gottlieb just made it worse for Ken and prolonged the agony of a final break. Unable to let go, Ken wrote another lengthy letter in which he bared his soul to the editor.

From March 5, 1965
Dear Mr. Gottlieb,

I've been trying to think straight since speaking with you on the telephone, but confusion and depression have immobilized my mind. I have to come out of this, though, or I'll never do anything. Writing a letter might be a good beginning; I hope you'll bear with this letter and follow through to the end. It may be long. If I had been less inarticulate when speaking with you, all of this might not have been necessary. Perhaps this is the letter I should have written you in December rather than that brief stiff-upper-lip of a note that only served to prolong things.

After the telephone conversation, I was certain that I was simply hanging on by overeager fingernails. Perhaps I still am. When it was suggested that I write another book if I could, I felt that you were offering me an opening to withdraw with at least a little grace. My feeling might have been accurate.

Whenever I attempt to talk in connection with *Confederacy of Dunces,* I become anxious and inarticulate. I feel very paternal about the book; the feeling is actually androgynous because I feel as if I gave birth to it too. I know that it has flaws, yet I am afraid that some stranger will bring them to my attention. The worst example of this was my apprehensive, incoherent meeting with Miss Jollett, during which I, bent with obsequiousness, almost sank through the floor in between my silences, cryptic comments, and occasional mindless (for it had left me) absurdities. I didn't fare much better on the telephone. But one or two of the few things that I did say seem to have been misinterpreted (which, in view of their source, is understandable). A question follows, I guess: why did I want to drop in to Simon and Schuster, why did I ask you to call me? At any rate, this reticence on my part has succeeded in my being confused, which is ironic. I'm not given to discussing myself, but I have to say some things.

This book began actually in 1961. At the time I was teaching full time at Hunter and doing part-time doctoral work at Columbia by day and regularly substituting at Hunter night school in order to pay tuition, [and] survive. I was in the frustrating cycle of someone who wants to write, had decided to teach, and must get a PhD to do anything decent academically. The mind goes off in three directions, and the writing suffers most. When I got my Master's from Columbia in 1959, I was in the womb of a Woodrow Wilson Fellowship and succeeded in rewarding the Ford Foundation with a series of pseudo-poems and short stories which were never submitted to anyone, like most of my earlier attempts. The 1959–60 year was spent teaching at a Louisiana state university and suffering through a neurotic apathy induced by the stark horror of rural Louisiana.

In the summer of 1961 I had the time to work on that earlier version of the book, in which Ignatius was called "Humphrey Wild-blood." The Army ruled out both writing and the Hunter-Columbia game by drafting me in August and sending me to Puerto Rico, where I became supervisor (something called "English Team Leader") of a surrealistic English-training program for Puerto Rican recruits. My duties consisted principally of blowing a whistle to change classes and exuding great waves of Hispano-American understanding to assuage the understandably hostile and smoldering students and the vilified and broken North American instructors. I coveted my job because with it went a comfortable private room with a desk: the chance to write. And I blew my whistle so well and exuded such understanding because of my private room that I won all sorts of military honors—even a free vacation in the Dutch West Indies. A room has never prompted such ambition; I really shaped up. There the book began all over again, and for the first time in my life I was able to write without having to worry about survival and problems that had any contact with reality. From my point of view, the Army gave me four invaluable things: time, detachment, security, and privacy. Also, the irony and absurdity of life in Puerto Rico was more subtly valuable. The whole span there was very valuable. When the time came for my release from the Army in August of 1963, I had a decision to make. I had completed more than half of the book, and, as opposed to my earlier writing, I could reread what I had done without feeling painfully embarrassed. More than that, I was totally involved and preoccupied with this book; it had overtaken me completely. Before me lay a return to graduate work and, for the 1963–64 year, the Bronx campus of Hunter, which would have meant hours consumed in traveling between Morningside Heights and Bedford Park Blvd. W. In addition, there was Hunter's requirement of a PhD in three years or out which would mean that I had two years left in which to jam courses, dissertation, and orals. I would be able to write nothing. So I wrote to Hunter, then got a job at a carefully selected small, quiet local college, where as I had hoped, there's little demand on time and almost none on mind.

The book went along until President Kennedy's assassination. Then I couldn't write anymore. Nothing seemed funny to me. I went into a funk. At last, in February of '64, with no changes and revisions, I typed up what I had, briefly concluded it, and began sending it around in the hope that someone might take an interest in it. Thus, the first version of the book never developed into anything.

That brings me up to your first reading the book (though perhaps you've stopped reading this letter); now I'd like to talk about the book itself. These comments have nothing to do with the "quality" of the book. The book is not autobiography; neither is it altogether an invention. While the plot is manipulation and juxtaposition of characters, with one or two exceptions the people and places in the book are drawn from observation and experience. I am not in the book; I've never pretended to be. But I am writing about things that I know, and in recounting these, it's difficult not to *feel* them.

In the revision plot threads were tied together, but sometimes this turned out to be only sound and fury. Myrna turned into a cartoon, in a book where almost everyone else was basically real, but she was supposed to be very, very likable; if, to an objective reader, she is a "pain in the ass," then she's a debacle. But when I sent you the revision I was certain that the Levys were the book's worst flaw. In trying to make them "plot" characters, they got out of hand, becoming worse and worse, and turned into cardboard whose conversations I was embarrassed to reread. (I think that they began to turn into a hazy remembrance of the old *Easy Aces* TV show in which the husband [Goodman Ace, if I remember correctly] and his wife argued and the wife's mother made sporadic appearances.) I don't know whether I can describe just how that couple kept slipping from my grasp as I tried to manipulate them through the book. Irene, Reilly, Mancuso—these people say something about New Orleans. They're real as individuals and also as representative of a group. One night recently I watched again as Santa bumped around while Irene sat on a couch guffawing into a drink. And how many times have I seen Santa kissing her mother's picture. Burma Jones is a not a fantasy, and neither is Miss Trixie and her job, the Night of Joy club and so on. There's no need to burden you with an itemized list.

In short, little of the book is invented; the plot certainly is. It's true that in the unreality of my Puerto Rican experience, this book became more real to me than what was happening around me: I was beginning to talk and act like Ignatius. No doubt this is why there's so much of him and why his verbosity becomes tiring. It's really not his verbosity but mine. And the book, begun one Sunday afternoon, became a way of life. With Ignatius as an agent, my New Orleans experiences began to fit in, one after the other, and then I was simply observing and not inventing. The old "Humphrey Wildblood" version of the book had been a painful and protracted, unfelt and stilted, thing; this one came to life, at least to me.

I was unsure of the revision that I sent you: too often it was more (and mere) plotting than anything else. Therefore, when I received your letter in December, I was both encouraged and discouraged. I was encouraged by the kind comments, the indications of continued interest, and very discouraged by "The book could be improved and published, but it wouldn't succeed." Did you mean the book as it stands or ever? The telephone call turned my doubts into despair. The book seemed to have become nothing—and there I stood frozen at the other end of the line, abjectly eager, dulled by apprehension, weakened, inarticulate, frustrated by an inability to make sensible comment. (If I don't overcome this, writing will turn me into a mute, an incoherent Mr. Hyde.) Your letter following my request for the manuscript is what confused me very much; after the telephone conversation, I was convinced that the book's chance and opportunity had come and gone.

You mentioned Bruce Jay Friedman on the phone in an oblique connection with this book. *Stern* is my favorite modern novel; I had an intense personal reaction to the book. It was after reading *Stern* that I mailed this book to Simon and Schuster. Since I liked *Stern* so greatly, since something about the book caused me to respond to it so sincerely, I thought I'd try sending this book to its publishers. When I received your first letter, I knew that I had been correct. While blacking out in Miss Jollett's presence, I managed to convey this news beautifully with one or two non sequiturs that climaxed that eventful visit. But Ignatius is only a farce. *Stern* appealed to me for various inexplicable reasons that had to do with attitude or impulse. I don't know. I can't explain this. If I could put myself into fiction with the humanity and perspective that Bruce Jay Friedman manages, I'd try. I can't write that sort of thing well, at least not now. I know because I've tried in the past. There's enough boring spreading of self across pages today, and I don't think that I should try adding to it. I'm not interested in trying; I don't think that I'm that interesting. I can only do what this book represents, and this is to write about things that I know, what I've seen and experienced. What was very accurate in your commentary about the revision was your separating the real characters from the unreal.

I don't want to throw these characters away. In other words, I'm going to work on the book again. I haven't even been able to look at the manuscript since I got it back, but since something of my soul is in the thing, I can't let it rot without my trying. I don't think that I could write anything else until this is given at least another chance. Will you bear with me?

Sincerely,

John Toole

Gottlieb took his time replying, composing a long letter that was aimed to soothe Ken and make him feel less isolated.

From March 23, 1965
Dear Mr. Toole,

I've let several weeks go by before answering your letter—partly because I'm not sure what to say, partly because I've been looking for a time when I could write something unfrantic and relatively thought out. That time will never come. Between my work, civil rights activities, and the accumulated psychic garbage and practical frenzy of one's private life, that Time never turns up, I hope—and I hope you will get from this letter the absolute knowledge that there is someone here sympathetic to your book, your problems, and you. For that is the case.

I can't say much sensible to you about your mortification over your performance on the telephone with me, or here in the office with Jean Jollett. Six years of analysis haven't robbed me of my own brand of insecurities or neurosis, and why should I try to rob you of yours? But remember that if to you, we are threatening Figures in a complicated and confusing world, to us you are an attractive and important mystery. *You* don't have to put yourself on the line in person, since you've done your job on paper; *we* are the ones who have to appear and behave strongly and well. Besides, silence never seems frantic—it didn't occur to me that you were anything but cautious and relatively easy and pleasant about accepting criticism from a total stranger.

I'm glad you wrote all you did about your history. First of all, curiosity is satisfied, then it means that we have a connection, since you wouldn't have talked that way to an un-connection. Just as I liked your book, I like your letter—which means I like you. Which means a possibility of friendship—which is good. Of course you don't know me, since you haven't had the advantage of reading a novel of mine. (I haven't written one.) You must take me on faith, while I have living proof of your you-ness.

About the book. Everything you write about makes sense to me, including your doubts, and your ultimate determinations. Since we agree on what is real and what isn't, there's not much point to recounting the areas I approve and disapprove of. You know, and you knew them before I mentioned them. As you explain yourself, I see that it is essential that you work on into the book, and I'm glad you are. My words—"it wouldn't succeed"—I can't tell you now what I meant by them. Probably that the book as it stood wouldn't sell. But the trouble is—and always is—that when someone like yourself is living off from the center of cultural-business activities, with only a thin lifeline to that center, through vague and solitary contacts, everything gets disproportionate, difficult to analyze, to give the proper weight to. It is like those odd people who turn up in New Zealand or Tanganyika or Finland, writing or painting masterpieces—they have their own power, but they read or look as if the artist has had to discover the form for himself. They don't have the assurance of worldliness and mutual interest and energy with others. So I can see that to you I (or Jean) is not merely a person, but a voice with more authority than it could possibly deserve. Not that I'm not good at my job, because I am and no one is better; but that I'm just someone, and a good deal less talented than you.

I don't know just what I've said here, and I don't know that I want to turn back to see (a Lot's wife complex). What I want basically to have said is this: you have nothing to apologize about; you are a good writer and a serious person and are doing your job seriously and modestly and of course it isn't easy. And as for the actual rewrite, I tell you as I may already have told you, "I will never abandon Mr. Micawber." A writer's decisions are his own, not his editor's. If you know you have to continue with Ignatius, that is of course what you should do. I will read, reread, edit, perhaps publish, generally cope, until you are fed up with me. What more can I say?

Please write me short or long at any time, if only to say that you're working (or not). Or if you like, show me bits of what you've done. Or don't; whichever would be more useful. Cheer up. Work. We are overcoming.

Best,

Bob Gottlieb

Although she was somewhat out of the loop when it came to Gottlieb's dealings with Ken, Marks had definite opinions of the situation.

She knew that the novel was not ready to be published when it first came in. There was "great energy there, but the book was going to be very difficult to mine." In her view, if the work was to progress, "a writer and an editor must be simpatico." If a writer has a problem or irritates his editor, it is "almost impossible to do the creative work necessary" to finish a book. Gottlieb was not averse to hard work, but it had become apparent to Marks that he felt Ken was too difficult to deal with on a professional and commercial basis.

In his letter, Gottlieb mentions Ken's supposed meeting with Jean Marks. The editor had accepted Ken's version of events and didn't discuss it with Marks when she returned from her honeymoon. She learned only later that Ken thought he had seen her in New York. Ken's reply, some days later, strikes a professional tone.

From March 28, 1965
Dear Mr. Gottlieb,

That was a calming letter, and I appreciated it.

In that it was an unburdening, my letter to you was itself a relief—as unburdenings are. I had to talk; thanks for having listened. I had lost perspective on the book and on myself, too. But basically I have a sense of the ridiculous and of the absurd (including my own absurdities) which keeps me afloat.

What happened, I think, was this: ten years of suppressed feeling surfaced when I first heard from you about this book. In 1954, when I was sixteen, I wrote a book called *The Neon Bible,* a grim, adolescent sociological attack upon the hatreds spawned by the various Calvinist religions in the South—and the fundamentalist mentality is one of the roots of what has been happening in Alabama, etc. The book, of course, was bad, but I sent it off a couple of times anyway. After that I wrote pieces and beginnings that were never inflicted upon any editor. For one thing, my mind was diverted during those years by other things. Then, as I wrote, with Puerto Rico there came a physical and mental detachment, and the relatively unused energies of almost ten years came flooding into this book and created too great a concentration of emotion. Had I been submitting things regularly during those years, I might have received some editorial comments and suggestions that might have provided me with some degree of perspective or at least a little "cool."

I've been rereading the book. What is most apparent is the need for a red pencil through a lot of it. There are hints in the book of developing themes and ideas, but they seem to be abandoned before they become consistent statements. I see a possibility of having the book say something that will be real, that will develop out of the characters themselves and what I know of them, that will not simply be a superficial imposition of "purpose." The book as is evades certain logical consequences of the nature of the characters themselves, and in this way wastes a character or two. Am I making myself clear? This does not, I hope, sound too confusing, but I do have ideas for the book, and I am beginning to work on it. I hope that I'll be able to send you a reworking of the thing in the not too distant future; since I am able to "see" and "hear" these characters, I can always work with them.

We'll see what happens.

Incidentally, if you are interested in a commentary from my particular vantage point, I might say that the events in Alabama have had profound effects, the results of the civil rights activities there have been the most successful so far. And the Klan, ironically, has been one of the Negro's best friends.

And I have rallied, have begun to work. And Spring is here.

Sincerely,

John Toole

Two months later Ken wrote to Nick Polites and Joel Fletcher, who were living in Italy. In the letter he quotes some of Robert Gottlieb's praise as well as his criticism of *Confederacy,* though the letter ends on a decidedly upbeat note. Ken had pulled the manuscript from consideration by Simon and Schuster, but he tells his friends that he is continuing to revise the novel. He also credits the publisher with helping him gain confidence in his writing by lavishing so much time and effort on his book. Though he jokes about publication coming when he is an old, toothless man, the overall tone is light. For his friends, Ken seems determined to put a bright face on his setback.

In the fall of 1965, Jean Marks left Simon and Schuster because she was expecting a child. Robert Gottlieb heard from Ken again at the beginning of 1966, in a card or letter that was either lost or discarded. The editor's letter of reply was the last in their two-year correspondence.

From January 17, 1966
Dear Mr. Toole,

I was glad to hear from you, particularly since a week or two ago—when the year changed—I had wondered how you were coming along.

My interest in the book remains what it was. I liked a lot of it a lot; thought it needed much work; and have a small doubt that something so long agonized over is ever going to live up to (at least) your own expectations. I certainly want to read it again, when you're through doing what you're doing.

I didn't think your purpose in writing me was vague. Everyone wants to feel outside, professional interest in what he's doing. "Writing," we live on it. But you are not working in a void, not as far as New York publishing is concerned: at least this editor is interested. And hoping that you've made the right choice in continuing with this book rather than starting something new. But that decision has been made; now to see what you do with it.

Best,
Bob Gottlieb

In this last letter, Gottlieb expresses his concern about the future of the novel, even as he extends best wishes to the author. It isn't known how much revising Ken had done at this point, but it is clear that he did not continue long with the project. Capturing the interest of a New York publisher on the very first try, although thrilling, had not led to a happy ending. The experience had been extremely stressful, and at least for the moment, he did not have the courage to try again. It was more than just a blow to his dreams and the embarrassment of having to tell friends that his novel was not up to snuff. By his own admission, something of his soul was in the work, and the book's failure was deeply personal.

Ken's world was small by choice. Each time he pushed himself out into the wider world, he returned to the security of his family. Rarely risking a bruise to his ego, Ken shied away from situations he could not control. He used his charm and wit successfully in small settings like his own classroom, a friend's party, or the teachers' lounge. Living a narrow life kept pressure to a minimum and larger responsibilities at a distance. The book's failure was the greatest stress he had endured, but his reaction to it was predictable. Ken did with this novel what he had done with *The Neon Bible* twelve years earlier. He consigned it to the graveyard— the top of the armoire in his bedroom—and did not look at it again. With this act began a gradual process whereby Ken disavowed accountability for the failure of the book. The next few years would find him concocting a distorted view of events, featuring fantastic rationalizations and projections of evil intent that were troubling to others and fatal to himself.

Twelve

"I'm not touching him, lady," the policeman said. "Is this here your son?"
"Of course I'm her child," Ignatius said. "Can't you see her affection for me?"
—*A Confederacy of Dunces*

T O SUPPORT HIS FAMILY, Ken continued teaching at Dominican. He referred to his position there as "a substantial cushion." His classes remained popular and filled to capacity well in advance of the official registration. The world of politics, especially the zany politics practiced in Louisiana, provided Ken with wonderful raw material for his lectures. His stand-up comedy routines were the high point of the students' days, and probably the best part of Ken's days as well. The rest of his time was spent close to home in a dull routine that became a downward and destructive spiral. Outside of class he interacted less and less with other people.

Although Ken had put *Confederacy* aside in an effort to distance himself from disappointment and failure, he did not quit writing. He told Pat Rickels that he was working on a new novel tentatively titled *The*

Conqueror Worm, a reference to death in Poe's "The Fall of the House of Usher." Ken kept a journal of sorts in composition books, but as always the privacy he needed to work with any dedication was difficult to find. Mrs. Toole hated being alone and would constantly interrupt Ken when his door was closed. If he protested and a fight ensued, that was all right with her. Any sort of attention from Ken was preferable to being ignored.

Ken was also her drinking companion. Booze had become an integral part of their relationship. The constant drinking and partying of Ken's army days carried over quite easily into his civilian life. In a letter from Puerto Rico, Ken had written of how much he looked forward to sitting and talking over "black coffee, lemonade, bourbon or whatever." More and more the choice was bourbon, and the "whatever" became beer.

The Tooles' home life had always been a secretive one. Most of the information about what went on within the walls of 390 Audubon comes from the family's few visitors and fewer comments that Ken made to friends. Interviews of Thelma and information she imparted to friends do not gibe with the others' accounts. Some things can be agreed upon, such as Thelma's reaction to what she saw as Simon and Schuster's refusal to publish Ken's book.

She took it as a Jewish conspiracy against her son, whose Myrna Minkoff, the Jewish liberal firebrand, was an unattractive and unsympathetic character. Thelma was furious with Robert Gottlieb and remained so until the day she died. She could see her precious Kenny suffered from the rebuff and determined to help him. Like most native New Orleanians, Thelma read every word printed in the *Times-Picayune,* believing that local newspapers were the only ones that could be trusted. She came upon a small notice about Hodding Carter Jr. coming to Tulane as a writer in residence for a semester. Carter was famous as a crusading journalist and publisher of the *Delta Democrat Times* in Mississippi.

Thelma found out the particulars of his stint at Tulane and persuaded Ken to speak with him about the novel. As skittish as Ken was about rejection, he had been able to interest a prominent New York house, which was no small accomplishment. Surely he must have reasoned that with its strong regional flavor, the book might have as good or better a chance of catching the eye of a fellow southerner. Ken met with Carter and left the manuscript with him. When Ken returned to collect the book, Carter was less than effusive in his praise of Ken's work.

In a later interview with the *Times-Picayune*, Thelma reported that Carter told Ken "It's worthy of publication. If you can't have it published, I'll put it in the right hands." There is no way to know what Carter meant by this, or if he said it at all. Known as a courteous man, Carter would have been exquisitely polite even if he'd disliked the novel. Obviously he was not impressed enough to pull out all the stops and help Ken. It is hard to believe that Carter would have promised to forward the manuscript to a publisher at some later date if he thought it was ready to be sent as it was. It is more likely that, having heard the history of the book, Carter told Ken that he was the best judge of where to send his own work.

The long-distance, if cordial, relationship with Gottlieb had resulted in great personal disappointment for Ken as well as the return of his manuscript. Devastating as that may have been, it did not have the crushing effect of a face-to-face meeting with Hodding Carter. As with the visit to New York, Ken blew the Carter situation out of proportion. He felt humiliated and took out his shame and frustration on the person nearest him. Blaming his mother for sending him on a fool's errand, Ken railed about her meddling in his life and in his work. He told her most emphatically to stay out of his business. From her account of the scene, Thelma acquiesced readily to his wishes. Such sweet surrender seems unlikely for the feisty Thelma, unless Ken had threatened to leave home and not come back. Whatever happened, their relationship from this point changed. Although he stayed home, Ken was no longer his mother's best friend. He refused to confide in her and spent little time in her company. He wouldn't join her for cocktails, and instead began to drink alone. Nursing his anger and wounded pride, Ken became estranged from his mother, even though they were living under a single roof. Thelma, watching her husband and her son deteriorate in front of her, was powerless to help because John couldn't hear and Ken wouldn't listen. The last three years of Ken's life were spent in a self-imposed hell.

Thelma would later say that Ken never left the house except to go to school, but this may not have been so. There is some indication that Ken had found another source of comfortable misery downtown in the old Faubourg Marigny. His Uncle Arthur still lived there, and this would have given Ken a good excuse to visit the area. Filled with despair, he may have dropped in to drown his sorrows in the bars in the Vieux Carré, and some evidence suggests that he began indulging in a lifestyle he had claimed to despise. Though Ken may have found some comfort in his cups at places like the Napoleon House, Laffite's, or at the bottom end of the French Quarter at the House of Joy, as his drinking increased and his self-control faltered, he found it harder to compartmentalize his life. Some parts began to bleed into others.

In the summer of 1967 there could have been just such a spillover. Chuck Layton remembers encountering a man at that time who bore a striking resemblance to the author later pictured on the dust jacket of *A Confederacy of Dunces*. Then, Layton was a Tulane undergraduate, and because his summer-school schedule was not as hectic as the regular semester, he spent much of his energy honing his social life. At the time he had a severe drinking problem. His days and nights were planned around the acquisition and consumption of Scotch. The ambience of the Big Easy promoted the sort of partying Layton enjoyed. The freedom of the French Quarter also encouraged Layton to indulge in another pastime. Like many others in this part of town, he was a closeted gay man who engaged in anonymous sex. Hit-and-run promiscuity fueled by alcohol brought him pleasure, but even more pain.

Layton said it took him years to break this cycle of self-inflicted degradation, and many memories of the sixties and the seventies are a blur to him. The time he spent with the man he believes to have been Ken Toole stands out in his mind for a particular reason. One very warm summer night in the Quarter, he was drinking at one of the gay bars and struck up a conversation with a stranger who introduced himself as John. They sat at a table together for some time, drinking heavily. Layton got the impression that John was not comfortable in this public setting. He said it was obvious that "John was equally closeted, but did not cruise the bars very often."

John suggested that the two men carry the party back to where he was staying on Elysian Fields, a walk of about about ten blocks. Asked why he went with a stranger alone to a part of town he was unfamiliar with, Layton answered, "John was obese, unkempt, and *very attractive.*" Layton also recognized that John was "monumentally depressed," a condition Layton shared at the time. There was a great deal of conversation during the walk, but very little humor. John spoke about his position as a college professor, but said that he was also a writer. He said that he was not teaching at that time and was trying to work on his writing.

John told Layton that he lived in a rooming house in the Faubourg Marigny, and that his family lived there as well. On arriving at Elysian Fields, the two sneaked into the rear of a very old house and into John's room. John cautioned Layton to be quiet so that he would not disturb anyone. It was very late. The men had sex and drank until Layton passed out. Sometime in the early morning, despite a terrific hangover, Layton left to go to class. He was thoroughly disgusted with himself and thought John did not look nearly as attractive in the morning light as he had the night before. At this time in his life, Layton was very concerned that his partners look handsome. Still, he was interested enough in John to make another date for the next afternoon.

Layton came alone to the old house, and he and John picked up where they had left off. The two men spent some hours together, again drinking and having sex. Layton had arrived sober and did not get as drunk as he had on the previous visit, so he was much more aware of what was going on around him. John admitted having lied when he said that he was living there with his parents. Layton thought the lie was a precaution in case he was dangerous. This time John said that his parents were living off St. Charles Avenue and claimed he was staying at the boarding house and running the place in order to get some writing done in privacy.

The men didn't stay cooped up in the room as they had done the night before. As they moved about the house, they ran across some of the boarders. Seeing that they were all young, good-looking gay men and "obviously street hustlers," Layton immediately realized what was going on in this old Creole cottage. John was picking up young male prostitutes and giving them a place to stay in return for sex, a common enough practice in the gay community. In Layton's words, "Nothing else explains the presence of such guys as I saw coming in and out of there as well as the weird way of it all." Although it was supposed to be an ordinary rooming house, John spoke casually of his concern that his mother would "pick up on what was going on." Layton was amazed that John seemed so offhand about what was a suspicious position for a closeted gay man. For someone who declared himself scared of his mother finding him out, John was being extremely careless.

Layton recalled this peculiar affair well, because late in the afternoon John's mother made an appearance while they were lounging around drinking. When John stepped out into the hall, his mother began a tirade aimed at her son, who fired back at her. The pair had a terrible fight as Layton sat out of sight listening in absolute amazement. As Layton remembered, the battle between John and his mother had "nothing to do with my presence or the reason for it, which was obviously sex." She totally ignored the wispy young men lurking around the place, blatantly advertising how they earned a living. Instead she railed at John over the general untidiness of the house. Layton couldn't believe she was scream- ing at him to wash the dishes and clean up the place.

Either John's mother was totally accepting of the sordid situation or she was in complete denial. Whichever it happened to be, Layton de- cided to leave, and determined not to meet John again. He said it was not so much John himself that turned Layton off, but "the pathology of the situation." Layton had had his own problems with an abusive mother who refused to either accept or acknowledge his homosexuality, and the love/hate relationship John had with his mother was all too familiar.

"John's mother was a harridan," Layton said. "John was a mess. I was not surprised when years later I heard that he had committed suicide." It was only because Layton was able to give up booze and put a thousand miles between himself and his mother that he survived. Although he empathized with John, Layton could not deal with the sort of turmoil John was going through. He never saw John again, not even in the bars Layton continued to visit. Over the years Layton asked others in the New Orleans gay community if they recalled the now-famous author and his suicide. Though Ken was believed to be gay by many in those circles, no one had a story to tell. Perhaps, as Layton said, this is because "there have been so many deaths in the gay community" and "the kind of street people Ken was dealing with were most at risk." It is either that or no one "ever made the connection with the book [*Confederacy*] that I did. As soon as I saw his picture on the dust jacket, I knew that the author was the 'John' I had spent some time with a dozen years before."

After the book came out, a friend took Layton riding down Elysian Fields and pointed out the house where Mrs. Toole now lived with her brother. Layton recognized it, but said that the rooming house where he visited Ken was one of the older cottages to the side of it. Without getting out and poking around the back entrances, Layton could not be sure which house it was, but felt that his curiosity had been satisfied.

During that same summer of 1967, Ken made a motor trip through the northern United States, stopping in Madison, Wisconsin, the home of David Kubach, his old army buddy. It was the second time Kubach had seen Ken since their service at Fort Buchanan. Months earlier, in the winter of 1967, Kubach had come south by train to visit Ken (whom he called "John") in New Orleans. Ken must have been between semesters, because they spent every day together driving around and talking. When visiting with Ken in the Tooles' home, Kubach remembered feeling that his friend was "living an awful life for a thirty-year-old man." After meeting Ken's parents, Kubach sensed they did not have equal impor-tance in Ken's life. Kubach recalled that "his mother was very big in his life. She was sort of a detached gray eminence. She was definitely a presence. His father, in John's mind, [was] a kind of comic character, and I don't think he was of any great significance to John."

Kubach also remembered "one thing that he told me years ago; his mom and dad had planned to not have kids, but she fell down the stairs and kicked her ovaries back and consequently he was conceived quite by accident. I don't think he had a lot of physical love at home. I think it was a very detached family, and I think it was a mess, as I say; he grew up too cerebral, too solipsistic, a hard person to rescue, a hard person to heal."

Even then Kubach noticed that his friend "took no pleasure in the small things of life." During his stay in New Orleans, Kubach com-mented to Ken about "how nice his cat was and how cute and all of that, and John said, 'Kittens are so obvious. Everyone is so obvious.' "

Although it seemed to Kubach that Ken was not particularly happy with anything, he was surprisingly upbeat about his returned manuscript. He told Kubach that there was still a chance to get the book published, although he never elaborated on how this was to be accomplished.

In their travels around the city, Ken bragged about the fortune he was going to inherit from his uncles Paul and Arthur Ducoing. He said they were going to leave him so much money and property that he wouldn't ever have to work again. Another time he told Kubach that one of his ancestors had been a pirate with Jean Lafitte. Although this seems a fancy designed to impress, both Lafitte and the first Ducoing immigrant did fight with General Andrew Jackson against the Redcoats.

Two incidents from his visit to New Orleans stand out in Kubach's memory. One afternoon while driving around the city, Ken checked his rearview mirror and said he was sure they were being followed by a car. He said the woman driving and her passenger must be students from Dominican. Kubach recalled that "quickly, we took evasive action. John drove down a couple of alleys and made a couple of swift turns and proudly mentioned that he had eluded them." Kubach thought Ken's reaction to this supposed pursuit was odd. He said that had he been single, Kubach "would have been flattered" to have young women chasing him, but Ken's view was that "they were to be gotten rid of."

While in the army Ken had boasted that he had left many women in New York "in a tizzy" over him, but he never mentioned being intimate with any woman. While they were in Puerto Rico, Kubach never saw Ken "sample the night life . . . as far as the women that were available." Kubach said that the Ken he knew was "unfocused" where sex was concerned. He thought that the physical act would have been difficult for his friend because "Ken had such a sense of the absurd that he would not have been able to do the strange animal antics that it takes to make love."

The second memorable incident of Kubach's trip south happened when Ken took his friend to the Mississippi Gulf Coast. They turned off the beach highway and drove away from the water on a country road edged with slash pines. Describing the scene, Kubach said, "It was a place you pulled off the road, and I was trying to say 'Why are we here?' It was not a really beautiful spot. John's love of nature was certainly under control. I just looked at him and said, 'Why are we here?' It had significance to him. He said, 'I kind of like this spot, you know.' I looked around and could not see anything especially to like or dislike. . . . I'm a guy who spends a lot of time in the country. I thought, 'This is okay, but I certainly wouldn't drive a long way to show it to somebody.'"

A few months later, Ken traveled north to visit Kubach in Wisconsin, and again they enjoyed each other's company. On Ken's return, the family began looking for a new place to live. At one time the Tooles had wanted to buy the duplex where they had lived so long, but abandoned that plan for financial and personal reasons. Besides the fact that their combined incomes would not have allowed it, the trio had outgrown the small residence. Ken took the lead in finding a larger place that would suit them better and possibly afford him more privacy.

Anything near the universities and the exclusive Garden District was too pricey for the Tooles, but Thelma refused to consider moving out of the area. With his salary and a V.A. loan, Ken could have afforded a small place in the suburbs, but he would have considered that another failure.

Instead of buying, he found another, larger rental house on Hampson Street in the favored part of the city. The corner house sprawled across a shady lot. The Tooles, as ever, shared the duplex with another family, but Thelma loved the place, especially the garden. For the rest of her life she would say that the Hampson Street house was the best one she had lived in. With its wide front porch, the house looked like a single-family dwelling. Today it is marked with a plaque noting it as the final home of John Kennedy Toole.

The family took everything with them from Audubon Street. The old baby-grand piano traveled to its new home, as did the pieces of furniture from Thelma's family. Ken had few personal belongings other than his typewriter and his clothes. One thing he was careful to bring was the box containing the manuscript of *A Confederacy of Dunces*. He was not ready to give up on it, but he could not face a rewrite. He hid the box on top of the chifforobe in his bedroom. It is doubtful that he ever looked at it again.

Ken's work at Dominican went on much as before. Charlene Stovall was enrolled in his classes for the spring and fall semesters. The only change she noticed in him was that his humor had become more pointed and political. The radical sixties had only served to strengthen Ken's intolerance for institutional hypocrisy, but though the times were liberal, the climate of the Deep South was not. Stovall said Ken's mockery of religion and the foibles of Louisiana politicians upset some of the young women in the class who did not see the humor in making fun of how fast nuns could say the rosary. Although his classes remained full of devoted followers, Ken's acid wit was playing to the wrong crowd.

By the end of the school year, Ken was in sad physical shape. Unable to curb his drinking, he had put on more weight. As he packed on the pounds, his clothes no longer fit him and he had to spend precious money on a larger wardrobe. Fastidious as he was, his bloated appearance distressed him. His friends and coworkers were aware of his weight problem, but not the reason for it. They all knew that his home situation was not an easy one, but it had always been that way. Ken had never been forthcoming about life *en famille*. He had coped so long that people close to him did not see that he was breaking.

In the last year of his life, Ken did reach out for help. He had begun to have severe headaches that could not be controlled by over-the-counter medicines. At that time aspirin in various forms was all that was available. The favorite remedy of southerners was a BC headache powder chased with a cold six-ounce Coca-Cola. If this one-two punch of aspirin and caffeine failed the sufferer, it was time to seek professional advice.

Dr. Cornelius Gorman Jr. was a general practitioner in the Carrollton section of the city. He and his family lived above his office in a beautiful Elizabethan-style home with sixteen-foot ceilings and marble mantels in every room. Dr. Gorman's wife and her sister, both wearing starched white uniforms, shared nursing duties in the office. As a family physician Dr. Gorman had a varied practice doing everything from deliveries to dermatology.

A scholarly and kind man, Gorman was extremely discreet and nonjudgmental. He had transvestites and a few hermaphrodites as patients, and a significant part of his time was devoted to treating a number of gay men who were having difficulties. They needed to bring their particular problems to a doctor they could consider a friend. Many of his gay patients were frightened of discovery, and Dr. Gorman never made small talk about them, even to his family.

Some patient notes were kept on small index cards, but most of the information about a person and his problems was kept in Dr. Gorman's head. When he retired, Mrs. Toole was contacted to see if she wished to have the family's cards sent to her, but she was not interested, and the cards were destroyed. Dr. Gorman's son, a physician himself, remembered most of what was on Ken's card and the conversations he'd had with his father after Toole's death.

Dr. Gorman knew Ken as John Toole, and he was very concerned about John's headaches. John had suffered from headaches as a Tulane undergraduate, but they had not been this severe. John was otherwise in good health, having never had surgery or any chronic illness, other than the transient respiratory difficulties associated with living in humid New Orleans. John's pain and a diagnosis of its cause were the predominant reason for seeking medical treatment.

In addition, there was a note on the card referring to John's anxiety. In hopes of alleviating this and perhaps stopping the headaches, Dr. Gorman may have prescribed Butisol Sodium, a brand name for buta-barbital. In pre-Prozac years this green liquid calmant was the only medicine readily available for "nerves." When after a few visits the headaches had not lessened, Gorman suggested that John see a neurologist. There was no mention of mental illness or the need for a psychiatrist. This drastic step would have been a last resort because it might have included hydro- and electrotherapy (shock treatment), which was destructive to the patient's memory.

John remained under Dr. Gorman's care, but there was no visit to a nerve specialist. Before a referral was made, Dr. Gorman heard of John's death. He was very troubled that he had not seen it coming. Because Ken was such a good performer, Dr. Gorman did not notice the symptoms of mental illness that Ken's friends were to witness in the last few months of his life.

That there were few entries on the office card indicates that Ken had not made many visits to Dr. Gorman. Although he trusted the doctor, Ken never fully confided in him. Certainly he minimized his drinking and any sexual problems he may have had.

Contributing to Ken's depression were the assassinations of Robert Kennedy and Martin Luther King Jr. earlier in the year. President Kennedy's murder five years previously had thrown Ken into a well of sadness. Now the violent deaths of the senator and Dr. King added a new twist to Ken's grief. Paranoia had always been an accepted part of the Toole family life. Ken's father had his multilocked doors that kept unnamed intruders at bay. Thelma was convinced that there was a Jewish conspiracy behind the rejection of Ken's book. When Ken was healthier he had shrugged off such suspicions. At this time, however, in a state of emotional confusion, he began to give credence to wild fancies of his own.

From the pretend kings of Carnival to voodoo queens, New Orleans has always been a place that encourages mystery. Following the death of President Kennedy, even the district attorney's office began an investigation of the assassination. D.A. Jim Garrison was convinced that a plot to kill Kennedy had been hatched right in the Crescent City, with Clay Shaw as the mastermind behind it. Reports of these intrigues had swirled around New Orleans for years, and by 1968 Garrison was ready to try Shaw in open court. It was during this time that Ken's personal paranoia shifted into high gear.

Thirteen

I stand at the crossroads, baby,
Now there's no turning back;
I'm here to make a deal,
Let the Devil deal the pack.
                    —*Blue Bob Crawford, blues song*

D ESPITE HIS FRAGILE MENTAL STATE, Ken tried to go on with his life. Since teaching put food on the table, he wanted to upgrade his academic position. He enrolled in the doctoral program at Tulane, encouraged by colleagues who thought him a brilliant scholar. A Ph.D. carried with it both prestige and a salary increase, but though Ken tried to view the pursuit of a higher degree as a positive move, his heart wasn't in it. He was older and more experienced than the majority of students, and having failed to become a published writer, Ken saw a return to school as another step backward.

One of the classes Ken took that fall semester was a seminar on Theodore Dreiser taught by Dr. Donald Pizer. Ken had taught Dreiser's *Sister Carrie* to his Hunter students. In Professor Pizer's class, students were allowed to choose their own research focus. Ken was interested in the intense and affectionate bond between Dreiser and his mother as well as the author's anti-Catholic views. Years later, upon reading *A Confederacy of Dunces,* Pizer noted the connection between those topics and the character Ignatius Reilly.

Anyone looking for hippies in New Orleans in 1968 would have found them taking English courses at Tulane. Sitting in class with his short haircut, starched shirt, and dark tie, Ken looked stuck in the fifties and found little common ground with his fellow students. Ken's notes in graduate classes are written in a strong, clear hand that shows no evidence of the turmoil in the rest of his life. Since putting his novel away, Ken had divided his time between home and Dominican. Now the forced proximity to so many strangers lowered his threshold of paranoia, and he began to confide in friends and colleagues about the fears he had kept to himself. Most bizarre and frightening to his friends was the seriousness with which Ken regarded these fancies.

When Nick Polites had visited Ken in the summer, he had noticed Ken's deep depression. Polites did not know the cause, but he suspected Ken's low spirits stemmed in part from alcoholism and the problems connected with having to hide his sexuality. Though he saw no signs of mental illness, Polites was distressed by Ken's behavior and home setting. He remembered that the sole topic of conversation during the visit was "The Book." Thelma was present and raged at the New York editor who refused *Confederacy* after multiple rewrites. In recalling the scene, Polites said, "Ken was depressed, and she was angry and bitter. I didn't stay long. Upon leaving I told Ken I would call him and that maybe we could get together again before I left New Orleans. But that visit depressed me, and I couldn't bring myself to call him until safely at the airport." Polites then apologized for having been too busy to see Ken a second time. Ken's reply was curt. He said, "We saw each other just the right amount of time." It was a sad, abrupt end to a decade-long friendship. Polites felt hurt and cut off. He never saw or spoke to Ken again.

This was the same summer that Ken drove north to meet up with David Kubach, who was dismayed at the change that had taken place in his friend in only a year's time. He noticed a great decline in Ken's personality and saw definite episodes of "paranoia and strange behavior." Once, when they were walking in downtown Madison, a friend of

Kubach's greeted him. Ken ducked into a storefront to avoid having to meet someone new. Ken seemed in a trance much of the time and was not at all forthcoming as he had been before. When he spoke it was in monologues about persecutions he was enduring. He told Kubach a dark tale of being victimized by Simon and Schuster and losing control of the manuscript. He no longer believed he would get his work published and said that was just as well because he now worried that the book was such a savage satire of New Orleans, if it were published people would hate him so much he would never be able to live there.

Kubach would interrupt these ramblings to dispute Ken's version of events, but these objections were dismissed. Kubach said, "I suppose with weaker personalities than John, you could say, 'Hey, get off this; this is just bizarre.' But John, he was absolutely convinced that last summer." It was difficult for Kubach to help because "John had such faith in his own take on things." Even though Kubach could see that this situation was serious, their time together was short, and Kubach had no expertise to offer. He said, "Obviously no one was close enough to him, that he respected anyway, who could really drag him out of it," and if he continued in that direction, "I don't think there was much salvation possible."

Bob Byrne knew that Ken was suffering from more than just depression. During his summer stay in New Orleans, he'd also had a visit from Ken. Byrne contended that Ken had no true confidants, but this time Ken shared his problems as he had with no one else. Byrne had always been very blunt with Ken, and this occasion was no exception. He had once told Ken not to return to New Orleans, not to live with his parents, and not to teach at Dominican—and now Byrne was concerned that the atmosphere in the Tulane English department was wrong for Ken. He knew that given all the other stresses in his life, Ken would not have an easy time working on his advanced degree at his old alma mater.

In an extended interview with Carmine Palumbo in Lafayette, Byrne spoke about that August day in 1968:

> Well, he was going into paranoia. . . . He was living in that house with his father and that overbearing mother. This was on Hampson Street, between Tulane campus and Broadway. Ken's problem was that he was extremely parsimonious. Money hagged him, and he wor-

ried. What he really wanted to do was to make enough money to go to New York again. I think he thought New York was the *centre de tout bon.* He was going to go there and take care of his parents, so he could get rid of that obligation. . . . He came here and we talked. . . . My little brother was with us in the house on Bordeaux Street. He'd gone into therapy, but evidently it didn't work. . . . I remember the windows were open. It was hot. He walked over. He said that people were passing his house and honking, that people were plotting against him. It was pure paranoia. . . . I talked to him, and by the end he seemed pretty stable. He said, yeah, maybe it was all his imagination. That was in August. And then I didn't see him at Christmas. I wasn't in that long, but my brother said, Ken's going mad. I said, Yeah, he's in a bad way. That was my little brother's comment. He was well into paranoia, and part of it was the book. It was a tremendous frustration. He was defeated. He was frustrated. He was completely disoriented. He was just—because the book was his—I think he pinned a lot of his hopes on it. Of course, they had encouraged him to begin with. Then he got an editor, and the editor objected to the picture of the New York Jewish girl; they said it was anti-Semitic or something, but she's a typical Hunter girl . . . other things like that, you know, and Burma Jones, and the guy at Schuster was giving it a bad time. It was the sixties, you know. And the book isn't politically correct. He was thoroughly frustrated and utterly defeated. As I say, he needed to escape. It was a very bad situation. It always reminded me of *The Glass Menagerie.* . . . Well, he [the brother in the play] finally just opts out, because he just can't take it anymore. It's exactly the same type of situation. . . . That book was his; it was private. He had extended himself, and it was rebuffed. He was humiliated. The last time I talked to him he was just devastated. . . . I mean, he told me things, when he wanted to, because I knew certain things, and I could tell him some things. I told him about my aunt when she had that run-in with Thelma Toole [when she referred to him as a genius]. And he was surprised at that because he said, My mother spends all her time telling me how stupid I am, and he would tell me things like that, about the family. . . . That was the last I saw him, that dreadful session, which disturbed me a great deal, because he was obviously paranoid. I know enough about psychology to know paranoia when I see it; I've had enough paranoid friends to know when someone is paranoid, and he was. The girls [at Dominican] were whispering about him, people were writing nasty notes behind his back, people were driving by the house at all hours of the night honking their horns, and all sorts of things like that. He said, Do you think I'm imagining these things? I said, Yes, Ken, I do. I said, You need to get some professional help. They say he did, but evidently it didn't take.

Byrne's 1995 interview is enlightening because it shows that Ken was aware of his mental condition and wanted to improve it. There is no indication, however, that Ken underwent any form of therapy other than to visit Dr. Gorman. There is also no evidence to support Byrne's statements about Robert Gottlieb's opinion of the book. Nowhere in the extant letters between Ken and the editor is there mention of a problem with anti-Semitic or racist portrayals of the characters. It is true Ken worried that the Jewish firebrand Myrna had become more of "a cartoon" than the other characters. This concern may have been discussed with Gottlieb in a phone conversation or in some lost correspondence, but there is nothing to show who, if anyone, initiated this subject.

The returned manuscript was no doubt a hot topic in the Toole household, giving rise to furious discussions behind closed doors. In trying to distance himself from the failure of the book, and suffering from paranoia, Ken may have seized upon the Judaism shared by the Myrna character and Gottlieb as a the root of the editor's problems with the book. Ridiculous as this interpretation was, it gained credence in the Toole family, as witnessed by Thelma's remarks before and after the publication of *Confederacy*.

In mid-November and mid-December, Ken called on the Rickels in Lafayette. On the first visit they were alarmed by his depressed condition. He was not at all the sweet, funny person they had known for so long. His personality had changed so much that it was clear this was no ephemeral case of the blues.

On Ken's second visit, the Rickels knew Ken was suffering a major crack-up. When Pat Rickels saw him pull up in the driveway, she fully expected him to come up to the door, but he remained in the car. When she went out to greet him, he would not believe that he was welcome. He asked repeatedly, "Are you sure you want me?" Despite her assurance, he wouldn't bring his bag in the house. He said the Rickels had asked him to come only because they felt sorry for him. Pat Rickels grew even more concerned after she coaxed him into the house. Although he was bloated and looked ill, it was his mental state that astonished the family.

Ken's conversation at dinner was bizarre. He recounted some of the same improbable tales of persecution previously told to Bob Byrne. The wildest concerned a plot to steal Ken's book. The supposed conspirators were another author, his wife, and the publishing firm of Simon and Schuster. In Ken's story the second wife of George Deaux (a former English instructor at SLI) worked at Simon and Schuster. Aided by Robert Gottlieb, Mrs. Deaux was supposed to have stolen Ken's manuscript to prevent its publication while George Deaux rewrote it as his own.

Pat Rickels listened wide-eyed to the story while her husband just shook his head. There was no doubt that Ken believed what he said, and the story shows how paranoia can twist facts to suit the fantasy. George Deaux got a job at SLI in August 1961. This was a year after Ken had left Lafayette, and he had been drafted into the service. Ken never met Deaux or his family. While Deaux was at SLI, he was one of a group of bright, aspiring authors on the faculty. One of his colleagues, James Lee Burke, would later find fame as the author of the Dave Robicheaux detective novels. During his time in Lafayette, Deaux was plagued by misfortunes. His first wife suffered a nervous breakdown and took her own life. Deaux and his baby daughter moved to Philadelphia in the summer of 1963.

In 1964 Deaux met his second wife while teaching at Temple University. Both of them state that she "never met Bob Gottlieb and did not work as a literary agent or in any other capacity in which she could have influenced publishing decisions at Simon and Schuster." Ken's tortured mind made a connection based on two unrelated facts.

Simon and Schuster published Deaux's first novel, *Exit,* in 1966— shortly after *Confederacy* was returned to its author. Deaux's editor was Robert Gottlieb. Deaux said that although "I had extensive professional association with Robert Gottlieb throughout his tenure at Simon and

Schuster, we were not close personal friends. He never asked my opinion of other people's manuscripts under consideration at Simon and Schuster. However, since Toole would have known that I was published at Simon and Schuster, that Gottlieb was my editor, and that I had recently lived in southwest Louisiana, it would have been reasonable for him to assume that Gottlieb might ask my opinion of the manuscript of *Dunces*. In fact, no such thing happened, but Toole would have had circumstantial evidence to suppose it might have."

In another coincidence, the second Mrs. Deaux's given name was Myrna, the same as Ignatius Reilly's girlfriend. Ken may have picked up on this as the reason for her interest in his manuscript. In truth, Myrna Deaux had never read the novel. She and George Deaux, who are divorced, had not heard these stories linking them to Ken Toole and were surprised to learn of them.

The Rickels too were surprised to hear Ken's story that strange evening years earlier. Late in the night, with Ken sleeping only a room away, Pat and Milton held a whispered pillow conference. Pat had not been a fan of Deaux's during his stay in Lafayette, and she was incensed at the thought that Ken was being cheated by folks up east. She fumed to her husband, saying, "Don't you think it's terrible what they're doing to Ken?" Milton Rickels short-circuited her by murmuring, "Darling, Ken Toole is going mad."

Ken's Lafayette friends were appalled at the state he was in, but they were among the last to know. Although Professor Pizer noticed no signs of emotional disturbance in Ken's "quite quiet" behavior, another Tulane professor had gone to his superiors with concerns about Ken's state of mind. That teacher was told to ignore the problem and do nothing. It is probable that had Ken been in Lafayette, caring friends would have forced him to get help before he reached so low an ebb.

His position at Dominican had been in jeopardy for some time. Charlene Stovall was not a student of Ken's during the fall of 1968, but if she had been, she would have noticed a great change in him. His comic monologues in the classroom had become harangues against church and state. His wry humor turned so vicious and bitter that it became cause for complaint. Many of his students, especially freshmen, had never gotten the point of his jokes. Now even the ones who understood didn't think he was funny. Some of them complained to the nuns that Mr. Toole was a "communist." When he was called to account for these complaints, it was clear that Ken was not in command of himself.

The former head of the Dominican English department would not speak of Ken except to say how much she liked and respected him. She stated that she had made a promise never to reveal confidences he had entrusted to her at the time. This could mean that she knew what Ken was going through and perhaps tried to help him. She did say that toward the end of his time at Dominican, some of his students were afraid of Ken. His wild ranting upset them, and this situation could not continue. Considering the respect and regard in which he was held by his fellow faculty, it is possible that Ken was asked to take a leave of absence from the school instead of being fired. Professor Pizer recalled knowing that Ken was teaching part time at Dominican, but late in the semester Ken stopped coming to class at Tulane. He did not turn in any written work and received an I (incomplete) on his transcript. At the same time Ken stopped teaching his classes at Dominican.

Christmas of 1968 was little cause for celebration at the Toole home. Lost in dementia, father John wandered around the house like the ghost of Christmas past. Ken searched everywhere for the electronic devices that he thought were reading his mind. Thelma was stuck in the middle, screaming at both of them. Set in the southern quadrant of *The Twilight Zone,* this holiday season was the Toole version of a yuletide in hell. And hell is what broke loose in the first month of 1969.

Most of what has been written about the final months of Ken's life was based on interviews with his mother. The inaccuracies and gaps in her recollection could be credited to the lapses of old age, though it is just as likely that she lied to protect herself and her son's memory. This is understandable if not commendable behavior, but adding the facts available provides a more accurate history of what happened to Ken Toole.

In early January, when Ken did not resume his teaching duties, the administration at Dominican was forced to hire a replacement, and Thelma hit the roof. It was aggravating enough that Ken should have a nervous breakdown, but unacceptable to do so without a paycheck coming in every month. After all, he was the breadwinner of the family.

There was no one else to provide for his elderly parents. As always, Thelma saw problems only in relation to their effect on her. She was sure that Ken could get a grip on himself if he would stop drinking. The skirmishes between mother and son became open warfare.

On Sunday, January 19, they had a horrible final quarrel, and Ken left the house. It isn't known where he went, but possibly to his uncle's, or perhaps the boarding house, on Elysian Fields. Thelma said that Ken came back unexpectedly the next morning at 9:30. She had gone to the market to (as New Orleanians say) "make groceries." When Ken asked his father where she was, the old man didn't know, and without another word, Ken left again.

It was a mild winter in New Orleans, with the temperature getting up to sixty degrees plus on most days. Ken was dressed in dark pants and a black zipper jacket that would have been plenty warm enough, yet he also brought his gray-and-white woven wool overcoat, as well as his eyeglasses, his watch, and possibly a .32 blue-steel automatic pistol. After leaving his father, Ken withdrew fifteen hundred dollars from his savings account at Whitney Bank. He drove west out of the city in his 1967 Chevrolet Chevelle, possibly headed for what he had considered his second home.

There are differing versions about what happened the first week following Ken's departure from the city. Thelma Toole told police that her son had called from Lafayette and was visiting friends there. Later she would tell reporters that a few days after he left she received a note from him saying he had gone to see the Rickels. Regardless of whether either account is true, it seems clear that Thelma thought Ken had returned to his old stomping ground.

Within days of her son's disappearance, Thelma began calling the Rickels home and asking for Ken. She wouldn't believe that he wasn't there or that he hadn't been there. She accused Pat Rickels of hiding Ken. When asked why he'd left home, Thelma said they had quarrelled and parted on very bad terms, but she would not say over what. Time after time she called and begged Pat Rickels to tell her if Ken was all right. She said she didn't want to speak to him if he didn't want to, she just wanted to know he was safe. No one in Lafayette was able to give the Tooles any information.

Like many busy and organized people, the Rickels kept a detailed engagement calendar, and theirs from 1969 showed that on the evening of
January 20, they held a book-discussion meeting at their home. If Ken
had come by that night, he would have seen the driveway full of cars.
Given his despondency, it is unlikely that he would have braved a group
of strangers even to reach the friends he loved. Without knowing if he
drove to Lafayette or not, Pat Rickels has lived with regret for years—
wondering if Ken did attempt to seek her out that night, and whether
she might have been able to prevent the tragedy that followed.

The following Monday, January 27, Thelma reported her son's disappearance to the New Orleans Police Department. Detective John G.
April called at the Toole home on noon of the same day. The report he
filed noted that Ken had never been missing before and his probable des-
tination was unknown. Thelma told Detective April about a single
phone call from her son from Lafayette, but admitted that no one there
had seen him. She had not heard from him since that time. She also told
police that Ken was suffering from a nervous breakdown and listed Dr.
Gorman as the treating physician. Unfortunately, she did not mention, if
indeed she knew, that Ken had a gun with him. This might have made
the police a bit more interested in tracing Ken's whereabouts.

With so little to go on, the police were unable to do more than type
an incident card and file it in the pending pile. Thelma was much too
frantic to sit and wait. She called the Rickels constantly during the next
few weeks. She told them that she had reported Ken missing, and from
the number and tone of her phone calls, the Rickels expected a visit from
the authorities, but they heard only from Thelma. As weeks grew into
months, she still refused to believe they did not know where her son was.
She kept in touch with the police, but they had no information. It was a
frustrating and helpless time for everyone who cared for Ken. Adding to
Thelma's misery was the death on March 18 of her beloved elder sister.

Less than a week after Dollie's funeral, Thelma received news of her
missing son. On Wednesday, March 26, an anonymous caller reported a
suspicious car to the city police in Biloxi, Mississippi. The year 1969 was
long before 911 service, electronic recordings, and computerized docu-
ment-keeping. Later that same year Hurricane Camille would drop in
on the Gulf Coast, flooding the basement of the Harrison County court-

house and destroying the records stored there, including those about Ken Toole. The bits and pieces that remain merely sketch what occurred before and on that day.

The Biloxi police referred the call to the Harrison County, Mississippi, sheriff's department. At 4:20 in the afternoon, the message was radioed to Deputy Ralph Diaz, a native of D'Iberville, Mississippi. He was twenty-five, new to the force, but with a calm and observant manner. Diaz drove for ten minutes down country roads through the back bay section of the county, a marshy area dotted with tidal pools and hummocks of pine trees. He turned onto the Popps Ferry Road that leads to the beaches along the Gulf Coast.

It was a warm, clear spring afternoon, and the temperature had climbed into the mid-eighties. The white Chevelle was backed onto the side of a gravel road surrounded by pine woods. What caught Diaz's eye was the bright green garden hose running from the exhaust pipe to the rear driver's-side window. As soon as he spotted that, Diaz knew he was dealing with a serious situation. He parked in front of the Chevelle and walked toward it with the glare of the sun in his eyes. Even before he could see into the car, Diaz smelled death behind its doors.

Diaz ignored the sick feeling in his stomach and examined the vehicle. All four doors were locked, and the key was still in the ignition. The motor had died when the car ran out of gas. One end of the hose was shoved a foot or more into the exhaust pipe. The other end was stuck in the window and trailed down to the floor. Diaz knew from the sight and smell that the man in the front seat was beyond his help. The deputy returned to his squad car and summoned the coroner.

Gladys Gorenflo was a registered nurse who had been elected coroner of Harrison County. She arrived at the scene within a very few minutes and convened an inquest, authorizing Diaz to break into the car by smashing open the small window vent on the front passenger door. At her direction, Diaz reached in, unlocked the door, and began his examination of the car and its contents. Ken's body was sitting behind the wheel. His head was tilted back, resting on the seat. He was neatly attired in a white shirt, dress pants, and a tie.

Diaz had never seen a suicide and was struck at how peaceful and orderly it looked. Ken might have been asleep except for the small trickle of yellow fluid at the left corner of his mouth. His body and clothes were clean. His hair was washed and combed. He had a day's growth of beard, as if he had been in too much of a hurry to shave that morning.

The inside of the car was so clean and neat that it looked as if Ken had been gone a day instead of two months. The seats and floor were spotless. A sport coat was carefully folded on the back seat, but Diaz found nothing in its pockets. The trunk held only a jack and a spare tire. There was no sign of luggage or other clothing. The woven wool overcoat that Ken had taken had been discarded somewhere on his journey. All else that Ken had kept with him to the end lay next to him.

A ten-inch stack of papers, folders, and notebooks had been placed on the front seat. In the center of this stack was a black attaché case. Diaz moved the folders and opened the unlocked briefcase. He found the .32 pistol inside, lying on top of more manila folders. Diaz did not read the papers or notebooks, but he noticed that some were handwritten and some were typed. He did not see any maps or souvenirs. As far as Diaz could tell, there was nothing on the surface to indicate who Ken was or where he had been. His wallet was in the briefcase among the papers. Diaz saw no suicide note.

By the time an ambulance arrived from Bradford-O'Keefe Funeral Home in Biloxi, Coroner Gorenflo had completed her report. She determined that Ken had committed suicide by carbon-monoxide poisoning sometime that morning. She found no evidence of foul play or suspicious circumstances. Deputy Diaz watched as Ken's body was taken away and saw that rigor mortis had already set in. Diaz put Ken's coat and papers into Gorenflo's car. He stayed behind to wait for the tow truck, and the coroner went back to her office to inform the next of kin. An investigation into Ken Toole's death had been opened and closed in a single day.

Later that same day, the Tooles' worst fears were realized. Prompted by a call from Gorenflo, two New Orleans policemen visited the house on Hampson Street to break the sorrowful news that Ken had died by his own hand. At that time, suicide was rare along the Mississippi coast, attributable, perhaps, to the strong influence of both Catholic and Protestant faiths in that region. Ken's was the only self-inflicted death that Diaz knew of in his five years with the sheriff's department. Gorenflo could not have seen but a handful of suicides herself.

Before Ken's body could be released for burial, it would have to be formally identified. Without calling anyone for help or sympathy, his parents got in their car immediately and drove to Biloxi. Perhaps they still held out hope that it would not be Ken they would find there. They drove east out of the city on Highway 90, across the marsh and along the beach. It took them over two hours to get to Biloxi and find the funeral home.

Mr. Murray, the funeral director, and Gorenflo met the Tooles, who identified Ken's body. Despite the shock of the situation, decisions had to be made and papers signed. Together the director and Thelma began to hash out the details. Ken would be sent back to New Orleans to be buried near his Ducoing relatives in Greenwood Cemetery. The Schoen funeral home, next door to Arthur Ducoing's house on Elysian Fields, would prepare the body. The old Church of Saints Peter and Paul, where John and Thelma were married some forty years before, was across the street from the Ducoing house. Thelma wanted the funeral mass held there, but first she had to get permission from the priest. Although this was post–Vatican II, burial rites for suicides were still in a state of flux. Some priests made it difficult for suicides to receive funerary services in the church, even refusing to be in attendance at the grave. Thelma called Father Patrick Cunningham at Saints Peter and Paul and explained the situation. She wanted Ken to have a private requiem and a service at the cemetery. Thelma told the priest that she did not want anyone to know what had happened until Ken was in the ground.

Father Cunningham knew the family very well. Arthur Ducoing attended daily mass and was most devoted to the church. Thelma had taught charm classes to the older girls in the parish. The priest also knew that Ken was her only son. Because of the awkwardness involved with the suicide, Father Cunningham agreed to hold the ceremony as soon as Ken's body could be prepared. Hours later Thelma and John, in separate cars, followed the hearse back to New Orleans. In Ken's car were the briefcase, notebooks, and papers that had been with him when he died.

The service was set for 3:30 that same afternoon, less than twenty-four hours after Deputy Diaz had been called to inspect a suspicious vehicle. Thelma asked only one person to be with them at the funeral.

Beulah Mathews had been Ken's nursemaid on Webster Street. She came to pray with Thelma and John at the church. She stood with them at the cemetery to watch the flag-draped coffin slip into the tomb. The first three people in Ken's life were also the three to see him out. When the ceremony was over, the priest returned to his rectory and Mathews went home. The Tooles drove to Hampson Street. They were as they started so long before—a childless couple. This time, however, they were old and sick with little to look forward to. There was only grief and darkness ahead. In choosing death, Ken had put out the lights for them as well as for himself.

Fourteen

It is not possible that in the end the miracle will not occur.
                                                              —*Artaud*

THE DAY AFTER THE FUNERAL was in many ways worse
than the funeral itself. Ken's obituary, written by his mother, had
come out in the *New Orleans States-Item* newspaper, and word
quickly spread of the sad circumstances surrounding his death. For
months Thelma stayed home talking on the phone to friends, neighbors,
and her son's coworkers, grieving and analyzing what had gone wrong,
trying to make sense of his self-destruction.

In Wisconsin David Kubach received a card in the mail from Mrs.
Toole. At first, because it was decorated with drawings of small pastel
flowers, he thought it was an Easter card, and the language of the note
confused him further. Mrs. Toole wrote that Ken had "been taken from
us" and "Mr. Toole and I are just devastated." Initially Kubach thought
she may have meant that Ken had gotten married, but then he realized

the terrible truth. Later, when he learned the particulars of Ken's suicide, Kubach remembered the odd stop they made in the back-bay section of Biloxi, Mississippi. Kubach believed that lonely spot they visited must have been the same place where Ken chose to die.

Any suicide has a share of mystery, and perhaps the unknowns are what make these deaths so difficult to accept. Certainly even in such a private act there are enormous public consequences for the survivors, who must live with questions and doubts, not to mention the judgment of others. Thelma struggled to understand what had happened to Ken in the months before he died. She knew from his visits to Dr. Gorman that Ken had suffered from anxiety, and she had told the police about his nervous breakdown. Years later she would tell the new parish priest at St. Peter and Paul that she knew Ken had been an alcoholic. These conditions, sad as they are, do not always lead to suicide. Desperate for an answer, Thelma explored the few clues remaining to try to discover why Ken had broken so completely.

The only physical evidence of Ken's two-month mystery tour was inside the Chevy Chevelle, but none of these personal effects is found in the Tulane library. Years after Ken's death, Thelma would reveal what she had found in the car and how she reconstructed her son's cross-country trip. She said that she had discovered a ticket to the Randolph Hearst estate of San Simeon on the coast of California. Because Ken had idolized Marilyn Monroe, Thelma theorized he had gone to visit the movie star's Los Angeles grave. Thelma said there was a tour ticket to the late Flannery O'Connor's home in Milledgeville, Georgia, though the writer's residence has never been open to the public. If Ken did travel to Georgia, it was perhaps from there that he took the coast road back toward New Orleans.

A trail of credit-card receipts would have been easy to follow, but Ken had paid for everything in cash. How much money remained in his wallet is not known, but he did leave a two-thousand-dollar life insurance policy, a few thousand in savings, and the Chevrolet for his parents to sell. There is no reason to discount Thelma's reconstruction of events. Two months would have given Ken plenty of time to travel to both the West and the East Coasts. He may have hoped to use the trip as a time of recovery and then found it was a farewell journey.

In listing the rest of the car's contents, Thelma may not have been quite so accurate. She claimed that among Ken's papers she found an envelope addressed to her and John containing a suicide note. It must have been well hidden, since Deputy Diaz found no such note in the car—although he did not go through all the papers. If Coroner Gorenflo discovered a note, she never mentioned it to him.

Thelma said that Ken's note "concerned his feeling for me." She also told *Times-Picayune* interviewer Dalt Wonk that the letter was "so bizarre and preposterous. Violent. Ill-fated. Ill-fated. Nothing. Insane ravings." Only a small percentage of suicides leave written messages, and most of those are found at the scene in plain sight. Of that percentage, a still smaller group leaves negative or hostile messages. If there was a note among Ken's papers, Thelma took it as a cruel attack on her, and maybe it was. No other opinion is possible, however, because Thelma said that she destroyed the note after she read it.

What she did with the rest of the writings in Ken's car is not known. The manuscript of *A Confederacy of Dunces* given to Walker Percy seven years later was a smudged carbon copy, because the original no longer existed in a complete form. The writings at the Tulane archives are only bits and pieces of Ken's student work, as well as letters saved by his mother. Of the notebooks, folders, and loose paper lying next to Ken's body, nothing is known for certain of their nature or their fate. It is possible that Thelma destroyed the papers because they evinced Ken's disturbed state of mind. It is just as likely, given Thelma's raging grief and unsettled life, that the papers were lost, or discarded by someone who could not have foreseen their importance.

Another part of the mystery of Ken's death is what happened to his luggage. There was no suitcase in the trunk and, according to Deputy Diaz, no clothes save the sport coat in the car. The clothes Ken wore were clean, but there was no ticket to show where they had been laundered. In a two-month journey Ken must have stayed many places, but there was no evidence of those stops, and, from the neat condition of his car, no reason to suppose that he had been sleeping there. Ken had covered his trail very thoroughly.

It is most likely that Ken spent his last few days near Biloxi, revisiting his past and possibly deciding if he could bring himself to cross the Pearl

River into Louisiana. When he decided not to return to New Orleans, his final actions were carefully planned. Suicides often give away their possessions to friends and family as a farewell gesture, but Ken dispensed with his belongings somewhere along the way. Coroner Gorenflo told Deputy Diaz that Ken had eaten breakfast on the morning of his death, but nothing among his effects told where. Although there was an article in the *Biloxi-Gulfport Daily Herald* on the day of his funeral, no picture of Ken was included, and no one from the coastal area ever contacted the police or the Tooles to say that they had seen Ken or had found any of his things.

Besides the papers in the seat next to him, two other interesting items were found in the car: the gun and the green garden hose. The hose was new, but there was no receipt to show where and when it was purchased. The gun was not new, but it was clean and loaded. Ken may have brought the pistol with him as protection on his travels, but Thelma never mentioned a blue-steel .32 to the police or to any interviewer in later years. If Ken had purchased the gun in the time he was away, it was probably with the idea of using it to kill himself.

Louisiana State University psychologist Owen Scott reviewed the circumstances of Ken's death and the events that led up to it. Scott advanced the supposition that John Kennedy Toole was becoming psychotic. According to Scott, the onset of schizophrenia and the various forms that disease takes usually occur before a person turns forty. At thirty-one, Ken was well within this range. The causes of schizophrenia are not well understood, and there are many theories. The mental illness is thought to be a biological problem that causes some kind of breakdown lasting months or years. The paranoid subtype of schizophrenia may be characterized by delusions and sometimes by auditory hallucinations.

Before he left home Ken had mentioned to friends and coworkers that strangers were spying on him and reporting his movements to some unknown authority. He also told Robert Byrne that the students in graduate school were whispering about him, and that odd cars going by his house were honking horns to disturb his sleep. The paranoia always present in the Toole household intensified in Ken, and alcohol was not always a factor. When Ken told the Rickels his delusions about George

Deaux, he was not intoxicated. There were other instances at work when Ken, completely sober, recounted his bizarre imaginings. It is impossible to know if there was one reason for Ken's emotional turmoil or if it was a combination of depression, alcoholism, and psychosis that interfered with his ability to deal with the ordinary demands of life. Psychologist Scott said it is not uncommon for people to commit suicide as they deteriorate into mental illness as well as depression or prolonged substance abuse.

Ken was not so raving mad that he couldn't make and carry out the decision to leave New Orleans early in 1969 on a trek across America. There is no record of him having been detained or arrested by law enforcement during those two months, and certainly no one anywhere called New Orleans to say Ken's conduct had caused a problem. Whatever disarray his mind was in, the plans for his suicide were exact and effective, giving the appearance of a methodical rather than a spontaneous act. Just as Ken plotted his novel, he may have plotted his death.

Ken's method of suicide, for instance, seems carefully chosen. Although he had a gun (one of the most certain means of death), he did not use it. There are those who have ventured to link a suicide's method with his personality, and it is tempting to speculate as to why Ken opted for another way out. Ken loved cars, for example, and the fact that he ended his life in one may not have been coincidence. Death by gunfire is such a violent and messy exit that, given Ken's passive and fastidious nature, it is unlikely this choice would have appealed to him. Not to mention that a bloody death would have ruined Ken's car and lowered its resale value. As careful as he was with money, it is doubtful that he would have wasted it so wantonly. Vanity may also have played a part in his choice of asphyxiation, which leaves the body intact. Deputy Diaz said that there was no evidence to show that Ken had suffered. His face was quite peaceful.

In this terrible situation Ken, consciously or otherwise, showed two signs of kindness to his parents. He did not disfigure his body, which must have been some comfort to them. He also designed his death so that he would be found by strangers. If Ken had had vengeance in mind, he might have arranged for his parents to discover him in a place they could not have avoided seeing in their daily lives. Just to continue living

was hard enough for these two old people who had lost the most important part of their world.

A week after Ken's death, the faculty at Dominican honored him at
a memorial service in the college courtyard. Charlene Stovall, his former
student, recalled that the entire student body was devastated by his death,
especially those who had taken his classes. Not surprisingly for a Catholic
institution, the suicide went unmentioned at the service, but Stovall said
it came as a shock to everyone. Even those few who had complained
about Professor Toole had not foreseen this eventuality. Faculty and students gathered at the service to pray, and the head of Dominican delivered a short eulogy. Although she cried throughout the service, Stovall
was sure no family member was introduced, but Thelma Toole was
indeed present that day.

Thelma's attendance at the service was the last public act of her old
life as Ken's mother. From then on she would begin a new life in a
position that defies description, for there is no word like widow or orphan to name someone who has lost an only child. There is something
unnatural about a child preceding a parent to the grave, and the knowledge that her son had committed suicide only sharpened Thelma's pain.
Perhaps the hurt would diminish with time, but Thelma was sixty-eight,
and her husband three years older. The Tooles had little time and less
strength to recover from such a disaster.

For the rest of 1969 and through the following year, Thelma remained in deep shock and mourning. She no longer taught elocution
and charm to the young ladies of the Garden District. She abandoned
her beloved piano, refusing to allow any music in her life. At this time
there were no bereavement groups that might have helped Thelma
through the grief, but even if there had been, it is doubtful that she
would have joined one. Many mourners find solace in religion, but
Thelma had never been close to the Church, and she did not embrace
what Catholicism offered now. There seemed to be nothing to pray for
since her Kenny had gone where no amount of prayer could recall him.
As the youngest child in her family, Thelma found herself outliving her
siblings. She had been particularly fond of Dollie, and the timing of her
death hit Thelma hard. Confiding in her brothers and unburdening her

grief to them was difficult because, aside from sharing a familial bond, there was a lack of true affection in their relationships.

If Thelma found her husband a comfort she never credited him in later years. Their relationship was the most private of her life, and she never spoke openly of any love that existed between them. Whatever pleasures or disappointments came from their long union were kept firmly stuffed in Thelma's ample bosom. Unlike every golden moment of her son's life, her marriage was never taken out and displayed for the general public.

At the time of Ken's death, his father was already in failing health. John Toole was nearly blind and found it difficult to read and write. Adding to that aggravation was the progressive deafness that followed a terrible bout with the shingles in 1962. Dr. Gorman had treated Mr. Toole for that ailment and for hardening of the arteries, the condition noted on his death certificate. Because Thelma did not request Dr. Gorman's notes upon his retirement, all medical records on her husband were destroyed in 1979. Hardening of the arteries was often used as a catchall phrase for dementia. Dr. Gorman did not refer John Toole to a "specialist" because there was none at the time, and it remains difficult to distinguish Alzheimer's disease from other forms of senility. Sight and hearing problems as well as dementia curtailed John Toole's access to the world outside the house on Hampson Street, and inside there was only unrelieved gloom.

Psychologist Mary Lou Kelly watched several hours of videotape of Thelma Toole and read some of her writings about her famous son. Kelly concluded that Mrs. Toole exhibited traits associated with a narcissistic personality disorder. This sort of psychological postmortem should not be construed as a malicious indictment nor a definitive diagnosis. It is, however, intriguing—and perhaps sheds light on some of Thelma's inexplicable behavior, such as her rudeness to Walker Percy and other people she met during the publication of her son's book. According to the *Diagnostic and Statistical Manual of Mental Disorders* of the American Psychiatric Association, a narcissistic personality is characterized by "a pervasive pattern of grandiosity . . . need for admiration, and lack of empathy, beginning by early adulthood and present in a variety of contexts." Persons with this kind of abnormally high self-esteem are super-

sensitive to criticism because it threatens their sense of superiority, which
they secretly suspect is unjustified. Maintaining healthy interpersonal relationships is difficult for these personalities because they insist on calling
all the shots. The ordinary give and take of family life is not possible
with those who consider conversation to consist of monologues. Narcissistic personalities may be charming and vivacious, but they use these
qualities to dominate the situations and the people around them.

Thelma's distorted self-importance came with a sense of entitlement
and expectation, especially as regarded her son. She demanded that the
world comply with her ambitions and reacted with great defiance when
her plans were thwarted. Idealizing her talents and imagining them to
be mirrored in her offspring, she fantasized of a "genius" son with an
unlimited capacity for success, never admitting that this did not square
with the reality of who Ken was and what he could achieve. If she were
the best, then Ken had to be as well, yet she gave him little credit for it
in private, constantly calling him "stupid." His problems with sexual
identity, substance abuse, and self-esteem went unrecognized and un-
aided by his mother until it was too late.

Robert Gottlieb caught verbal hell for his honest appraisal of Ken's
novel. That Thelma was vindicated by the book's acclaim did not assuage her misplaced sense of outrage, and even after she gained success
and authority, she abused Gottlieb at every opportunity. Devaluing
someone who dares to challenge one's views is another common feature
of a narcissistic personality. Unlike her son, Thelma was never self-
destructive, only unreasonable in her demands of others.

The publication of *A Confederacy of Dunces* was a unique and consid-
erable achievement by Thelma Ducoing Toole, but her pursuit of that
goal was not entirely out of love for her child. Some of her grief at his
death was a rage against the destruction of her plans for him. Refusing
to mourn in private, Thelma spent hours on the telephone sobbing out
her sadness and confusion to her family, friends, and anyone who would
listen. One of the first questions asked after a suicide is Why did he do
it? Twisting the question to reflect her importance, Thelma asked why
had Ken done this to her. Discovering the reason for his pain was sec-
ondary to finding a way to ameliorate her own. This lack of empathy,

consistent with the pattern of narcissistic behavior, was something Thelma displayed throughout her life.

Ken's decision to die shattered the mirror of his mother's reflected glory and made it necessary to find a substitute fantasy. Considering her age and reduced circumstances, it was not easy for Thelma to regain the superior attitude that had sustained her for so long. In her own words, she became "a robot woman" following Ken's death, doing only what was necessary to stay alive. The haughty, often arrogant, behavior that she had previously displayed was absent, and her life had no direction. At the same time John Toole had become little more than a ghost. Indeed, some of Ken's school friends had not known of Mr. Toole's existence and thought his mother a widow long before the fact. In his last years, John slipped farther away from the world, seldom leaving the house, living inside what was left of a once keen and witty mind.

John Dewey Toole's death on December 28, 1974, was as much a relief as a blow to his wife. No matter how she felt about her husband, she could not have wished to have him back in the sad state of health that marked his final months. Thelma was now truly alone in the Hampson Street house that Ken had fixed up for his parents in happier times. She changed the listing in the New Orleans phone directory from "Toole, John (Thelma D) retired," to "Toole, Thelma D (wid John)." This listing hints at a solitude that Thelma refused to accept. Having recovered from the numbing shock of Ken's suicide, Thelma regained the desire to direct the events in her life. Although she did not reopen the drama school, she began to teach charm classes to teenage girls in the neighborhood. In an attempt to recover a social life, she took sheet music to parties and would play with little coaxing. These forays into society marked a turning point, but they were not enough to give Thelma's fragile self-esteem the validation she had found in her son. Thelma had been clinging to his loss because she thought it was all she had left of him. Then she found Ken's abandoned manuscript. This forgotten legacy offered his mother a substitute for her long-harbored aspirations, and the renewed connection to her son brought the old fantasies back to life.

Had it not been for Thelma's emotional neediness, the book may have just become a family relic gathering dust on the top of the chifforobe in what was now the spare bedroom. Instead it became a bridge to Ken, and the final mission of her life was to get the book accepted, published, and admired. Dragging out Ken's old Underwood, Thelma began sending the manuscript to different publishing houses around the country, with the obvious exception of Simon and Schuster. She left several of her cover letters to the Tulane Library. The one to the Third Press in New York reads:

Gentlemen:

The enclosed manuscript titled "A Confederacy of Dunces" was written by my late son, John Kennedy Toole. He was a 1958 graduate of Tulane University. His graduation carried with it honors in English, a Woodrow Wilson Fellowship, and a Phi Beta Kappa key. Additionally, a Master of Arts degree, with high honors, was bestowed upon him by Columbia University in 1959.

I believe this presentation warrants your serious consideration for a possible publication of same.

A favorable response from you will be deeply appreciated.

Yours very truly,

Thelma D. (Mrs. John) Toole

Over a five-year period Mrs. Toole sent the manuscript, accompanied by her imploring letters, to seven publishing houses around the United States. None of them replied with a personal note but rather returned the book each time with a form rejection letter. Some answered more quickly than others, but no form held out any hope or offered helpful advice. Each rejection was a little death for the author's mother. A less tenacious person would have despaired and quit, but in this case Thelma's inflexibility and persistence proved beneficial. Although she was stunned and hurt each time the manuscript came back, she continued to offer her son's work to the world of literature.

In 1975 Thelma Toole was still living in the house on Hampson Street, clinging to what had been the better part of her life. Old, alone, and short of funds, her position in the polite society of New Orleans was in jeopardy. Southern to the core, New Orleans has always prided itself on displaying good manners to visitors, but as in all cities, life can be hard for its vulnerable residents. When Thelma fell and broke her arm, she also tumbled out of sight and into her worst nightmare.

For months she was in and out of hospitals, leaving each time weaker than when she arrived. Although she had suffered from high blood sugar over the years, the diabetes now took a more aggressive hold. Her arm was slow to heal, and she began to have trouble with her hip. She learned to use a metal walker, but her mental state was not so easy to rehabilitate. Thelma was emotionally drained, overmedicated, and absolutely on her own. The depression she suffered after Ken's death returned, but this time she was too ill to call anyone to listen to her problems. Her doctors decided that Thelma was too feeble to care for herself, and she was dispatched to a rest home at the edge of Orleans Parish. It was a dismal place on the fringe of an industrial waste site—quite a come down for a woman who had struggled upward all her life.

The time she spent confined to the nursing home was by Thelma's account the worst in her life, and it is a testament to her stamina that she extricated herself from that appalling situation. Finding an inner strength, Thelma called her brother Arthur to come and get her out of what could have been her final residence. She soon found herself on Elysian Fields Avenue next to the funeral home and only two doors from the house she had left almost fifty years before. She had learned to her sorrow that though it might take twenty years to become "uptown" New Orleans, the move back down could be made in one afternoon. The tiny unairconditioned house with its sheet paneling and cheap linoleum floors looked like a small sweatbox landscaped with concrete. Thelma despised the cramped, austere surroundings, but she was too grateful to be back in the world to complain. She brought with her what bits and pieces she could salvage from her uptown life. Most important was finding room for the baby grand piano in Arthur's crowded quarters. Her little bedroom in the house was crammed with memorabilia. All she had left of husband, son, and former self was stored in boxes under the bed. Among all this stuff was Ken's manuscript, which, like its champion, refused to die quietly. Although she still believed it a masterpiece, Thelma wasn't eager to risk another rejection via the postal service. After the disappointing results of her previous efforts, a new approach was needed, and she was sure one would present itself.

When Thelma was seventy-five, she started teaching Catechism classes at the church across the street. With the priest's blessing she also opened a finishing school of sorts, teaching etiquette, elocution, and Garden District charm to the older, working-class girls at the parish school. Staying in touch with her old friends, Thelma enticed them downtown with offers of dainty chicken sandwiches, chicory coffee, and good gossip. It took courage to straddle the two worlds, but Thelma proved up to the task.

Thelma's bounce back from the edge of the grave was assisted by her older brother. Because his sister could no longer live alone, Arthur provided a home in which she shared living expenses. He drove her where she wanted to go, and Thelma was secure in the knowledge that if she fell again, someone would be near to summon help. Father Arthur Hauth, then pastor of the Church of Saints Peter and Paul, came to the parish in 1970 upon the death of Father Cunningham and became well acquainted with the Ducoing household. By the time Thelma Toole moved in with her brother, Arthur Ducoing had retired from his job as a clerk with Standard Fruit Company, but that didn't stop him from working. Unofficially he was employed as a day laborer on the French Quarter wharves. Each morning Arthur walked to the docks at the end of Esplanade Avenue and unloaded bananas from ships out of South America and the Caribbean. Besides their first names, the priest and Arthur Ducoing also shared an affinity for tropical fruit. Several times a week Arthur would give the priest bananas torn from the large bunch he carried home with him every day. Arthur seldom wore his dentures, and bananas were easy for him to eat. He was short, weighed less than 125 pounds, and was well past retirement age, but he thrived on the hard work. His small, hard body stayed deeply tanned all year long from constant exposure to the Delta sun.

Father Hauth was fond of Arthur and saw him every morning at early mass wearing a T-shirt, work pants, and tennis shoes. Often Arthur requested that masses be offered for his nephew, but he did not talk about Ken with the priest. A comical man who spoke in a broad New Orleans accent, Arthur did like to talk about other things. Father Hauth remembered that Arthur was "always telling jokes or stories. He was a real card, a very funny man, and the most devout member of the family."

In his sister's presence Arthur became silent and shrank into the wood-work. When Father Hauth visited at the Ducoing home, Thelma directed the entertainment and monopolized the conversation. She would sing and play, allowing Arthur to serve refreshments before retiring to his room. Thelma talked quite a bit about Ken, telling the priest about his problems and the brilliant but unpublished work in her possession. Father Hauth could see that her life still revolved around her son. She stubbornly refused to abandon her dream of showing the world what her son had accomplished in his brief life, but there was more at stake than Ken's unrecognized genius. For her it was also a matter of pride and self-image. She needed validation of her judgment of Ken's abilities to show that she had not wasted her own life. It was a serious dilemma for a sick and elderly lady.

The routine at the Ducoing-Toole household seldom varied. Before Arthur left for church and work, he would put on fresh makings for café au lait and lay out the *Times-Picayune* for his sister, who would consume both at the small kitchen table. One summer morning Thelma read an article about a conference of Louisiana authors presenting their latest works at the Royal Sonesta Hotel in the French Quarter. The star of the show was National Book Award winner Walker Percy.

It is doubtful that before July 1976 Thelma was familiar with Percy's complex novels, rich in philosophical and religious subtleties. She preferred poetry and fiction of an earlier age. In later years she never discussed Percy's work or his place in literature. She became and remained a fan of Percy the man and not Percy the writer. And at this point, with Ken's book languishing in a box, all Thelma needed to know about Percy was contained in the newspaper article that gave her new hope of finding an audience for *Confederacy*.

The piece by staff writer Millie Ball portrayed Percy as a kind and courtly man who spent the long day chatting with fans and other authors. Ball remarked on his smiling blue eyes, love of New Orleans, and desire to help his daughter's bookstore business. She made it clear that Percy was a celebrity as well as a great talent, but these attributes were not what caught Thelma's interest. The answer to Thelma's prayers was in column two, where Ball reported a conversation between Percy and an admirer.

Ball wrote, "The two then got into a discussion about a French Quarter apartment Percy might want to rent when he teaches a novel course at Loyola University in the fall. . . . The author said he teaches such courses periodically. 'It's a change of pace for me—a chance to rejoin the human race.' He's received more than 100 manuscripts from hopefuls who want to enroll in the 10 to 12 student course."

Using this information, Thelma Toole devised a simple, straightforward plan to get the author's attention. She would pester Dr. Percy all semester until he agreed to read her son's manuscript. Years before, when Thelma sent Ken to meet Hodding Carter, the latter's polite brush-off caused disastrous results in the Toole household. Thelma wanted no repeat of that mistake, and she was determined that Percy would not only read the book, but be made aware of its literary importance. She began with a letter to Percy's office at Loyola. This was the same kind of letter she had been writing for years—with one important difference. Thelma did not mention the reason she was writing instead of her son. She preferred Percy to see her as the pushy mother of a shy talent rather than a grieving mother clinging to the past.

Walker Percy and his wife, Bunt, had moved from their large house in Covington, Louisiana, to a small place in New Orleans while Percy taught at Loyola. It was a wonderful, exciting experience for both of them, and they enjoyed being in the city. Because he was so busy, Percy filed Thelma's letter with the rest of its kind. He often received such requests and laid them aside, meaning to reply when he could, but he did not reckon on Thelma's plan. She began to call Percy's office and send more letters requesting an interview. By midterm he had begun complaining to his wife about a strange little lady and her persistent attempts at communication.

Past Thanksgiving, Percy was still successfully dodging Thelma. With time running short and the holidays approaching, she kicked her campaign into high gear. Learning Percy's schedule from his secretary, Thelma left a message giving the time she would meet him at his office. On that day, under orders from his sister, Arthur stayed home from the banana boats. Rigged up in a dark suit and wearing a cap, he climbed behind the wheel of his old sedan to drive Thelma and a woman friend uptown. Near three o'clock in the afternoon, Arthur dropped them off at Loyola. He waited in the car as the two ladies carefully made their way to Percy's office. Like all old buildings on campus, Bobet Hall had not been designed with the handicapped in mind. Thelma's age and infirmities made for slow going, and it was all she could do to get herself upstairs. Out of necessity, Thelma's friend came along to tote the heavy box containing Ken's manuscript.

Professor of English Marcus Smith was at work in his office around the corner from Percy's when the pair came to his door asking for the author. Thelma explained to Smith that she had an appointment with Percy to deliver her son's manuscript to him. Since the great man had not yet arrived, Thelma presented her story to the hapless professor. As he later recalled, she thrust the hefty box into his hands and insisted he take a look inside. Lifting the pasteboard lid, Smith saw a few loose items lying on the smudged carbon pages. Two things he remembered were a photo of the woman's dead son and a small crucifix. The memento mori made Smith feel strongly that to Mrs. Toole the manuscript was a "sacred text."

At a loss as to what to do with these ladies, Smith seated them in the waiting area. The only refreshments handy were water and stale coffee in cracked mugs, so he generously offered the women a choice of coffee or tea. Nothing was going right for Smith. The ladies rejected the coffee, and he was forced to abandon his paperwork to play teaboy. He grabbed a passing student, and the two of them rounded up cups with saucers and spoons. When Thelma spurned the proffered powdered creamer, Smith dispatched the student to the cafeteria with instructions to "steal a lemon."

The professor stalled for ninety minutes, making various excuses for Percy, but at 4:30 Smith had to leave. Collecting his things from the office, he took the stairs down to the front door and met Percy coming up. Irritated, Smith gave him a curt synopsis of the situation on the second floor. Used to having people wait for him, Percy responded with a vague apologetic shrug. Not a bit mollified by Percy's unsympathetic response, Smith delivered this prophetic parting shot, "Walker, there's an old lady waiting up there who's going to give you a lot of trouble. I've had my turn, and now it's yours."

By the time Percy strolled up to his office, the cast of characters had changed. Her duty done, Thelma's friend had gone home. Arthur had come from the car to see what was taking so long and remained to keep his sister company. Now that Percy had arrived, Thelma left Arthur standing in the hallway and preceded the writer into his office. Relieved that her chance had come at last, Thelma launched into the speech she had been saving for the past hour and a half. Amazed by the entire performance, Percy caught the words "genius" and "masterpiece" several times. When it became clear that he had no other choice, the writer assured Thelma that he would indeed read her son's book and give his honest opinion. After shaking her gloved hand, Percy showed the old lady out of his office and into the care of the skinny, silent man waiting for her. She did not introduce Arthur to Percy, who thought the old man was a hired driver. Years later while visiting Thelma, Percy looked out of the window during one of her music recitals and saw a man puttering around the yard. Percy knew that Thelma lived with her brother, who kept out of the way when she entertained. After leaving, Percy told his wife that he recognized Arthur as the shabby chauffeur.

On December 17, 1976, Percy sent the following letter to the late author's mother.

Dear Mrs. Toole,

I have finished reading John Toole's *A CONFEDERACY OF DUNCES* and I find it an astonishingly original and talented novel.

No doubt there are many things wrong with it—too much dialogue here, not enough action there—but on the whole I find it an extraordinary display of a mordant humor, wild satire, and an uncanny ear for New Orleans speech and a sharp eye for place (I don't know any novel which has captured the peculiar flavor of New Orleans neighborhoods nearly as well).

Ignatius Reilly is an original—a cross between Don Quixote and W. C. Fields.

I don't know whether this novel will interest a publisher in its present form, but it should certainly be printed one way or another. More of this later. Meanwhile I should like to pass it on, with your permission, to Prof. Marcus Smith of Loyola, editor of the New Orleans Review, for his response. I shall wait to hear from you whether this is acceptable.

Sincerely,

Walker Percy

Included on the back of this letter were Percy's home and office phone numbers. Bunt Percy said it was the "true voice" of the book that so delighted her and her husband. Growing up Percy had listened to the soft southern accents of Alabama, Georgia, and Mississippi. Bunt Percy said that the "speech in New Orleans was such a change from that," and they loved to listen to the people talk. To find this unique speech pattern portrayed so accurately in this unknown book amazed them.

The meeting at Loyola marked the beginning of an often exasperating relationship between the Percys and Thelma Toole. Bunt Percy allowed that Thelma Toole "was as nutty as a fruitcake, but she did get that book published." As soon as she received Percy's letter, Mrs. Toole phoned him, and Marcus Smith became the next person on a growing list to read and admire the work of John Kennedy Toole.

In the spring of 1977 Percy was very excited about the book and sent it to his own publisher, Farrar, Straus & Giroux. Percy's editor, Roger Straus, read Toole's novel right away, but sent it back just as quickly. Although the publishing firm admired Percy and trusted his judgment, the book had a big drawback for any commercial house. Bunt Percy remembered the reason given was that since "the book was a one-off by a dead writer, there was no real future for them in publishing it." Mrs. Percy also felt that perhaps they did not "get the joke" because "New Orleans was not the famous city it is now" and "a Boston editor might not have thought the book was very funny."

In the novel, Ignatius J. Reilly, self-absorbed scholar and consummate slob, lives in a doll-sized cottage in the Irish Channel. His only life goal is to write a magnum opus which would restyle the modern world according to his goofy version of Medieval philosophy. When dire financial circumstances force Ignatius to seek employment, he takes revenge on the New Orleans business community. He manages to start a race riot at the Levy Pants Company, devour the profits of Paradise Hot Dogs, and break up a strip club before nearly getting run over by a bus on Bourbon

Street. Along the way he meets exotic dancers, B drinkers, matchmakers, cops, crooks, and Burma Jones, the coolest black jive cat in the French Quarter. When Ignatius's long-suffering mother Irene has had enough of such shenanigans, she threatens to commit him to the state asylum. Rescue comes in the form of his Bronx minx, the pigtailed socialist firebrand Myrna Minkoff. The two are last seen cruising across the gulf marshes headed for the bright lights of New York, where Myrna plans to continue working for the masses and Ignatius plans no work at all.

Noted for the wordplay in his own novels, Percy enjoyed the humor of *Confederacy,* but according to Bunt Percy, her husband "also felt that it was a fine book"—one that could stand on its own merit and was worthy of publication. It was just a matter of attracting the notice of the right people. Marcus Smith agreed to print an excerpt from *Confederacy* in the May 1978 *New Orleans Review,* giving the public its first look at Ignatius Reilly. An introduction contributed by Percy praised the work and told a little of the manuscript's history. Before the issue came out, Percy sent an advance copy to his friend Les Phillabaum, director of LSU Press in Baton Rouge. Percy included a hand-scrawled note recommending the book.

Louisiana State University Press had been publishing scholarly books since 1935, but like most university presses, it did not set out to publish novels. Changes in the marketplace in the sixties, seventies, and eighties, however, made the idea feasible. As more publishing houses merged and the resulting conglomerates began to concentrate on "blockbuster" books—those that would fly off the shelves and sell thousands, even millions, of copies—it became more difficult for works of poetry and literary fiction, of higher quality but slower to sell, to find places with the commercial houses. A few university presses, with their missions to support serious scholarship and literature, began to take on these finer works, along with the marketing challenges that accompanied such ventures. In 1964 the Press branched out into publishing collections of poetry, and four years later followed with short fiction collections, which were well received but not financially successful. Despite the risk, the Press decided in 1978 to add novels to their list. The first of these was Madison Jones's *Passage Through Gehenna.* Two full-length works of serious fiction were to be put out yearly.

When Phillabaum sat down to read Percy's offering, he was intrigued by the story of Ignatius and his mother. On March 1, 1978, he replied to Percy's note, writing:

I've read the excerpt from *"A Confederacy of Dunces"* and am most intrigued. The writing is unique but at the same time reminiscent of several contemporaries I've admired. You allude to Heller; I think too of Pynchon and Barth. I'll refrain from mentioning Percy. So, in spite of your own ominous comment about the weight of the box, I would like to see the whole manuscript and, if possible, get a bit more information about Toole.

A week later the complete manuscript arrived at LSU Press, where it would be read by Phillabaum and managing editor Martha Hall. Although it had been retyped by a secretary in Percy's office, there were numerous errors as well as blanks where undecipherable words in the manuscript had been omitted by the typist. Its size was equally intimidating, yet Hall loved the work as much as the Press director, and they discussed who might be the most appropriate outside reader for the novel. Phillabaum chose John Barth, who was a friend and a "zany funny crazy sad serious writer" who might like this "zany crazy funny sad serious book." On October 3, 1978, Phillabaum approached him in a letter that withheld information about the book and its author.

As you may have heard, during the past year we committed the ultimate insanity and began publishing novels. It is, however, necessary for us to process them through the same drill that we do our regular books, which means we have to secure outside readings from authorities. Since you are, in my judgment, an authority par excellence, I hope you will be willing to read a manuscript for us and give us your opinion of its worth.

I'll be happy to provide you with more information about the manuscript and the author if you wish, but I suspect it might be best to take it on cold if you have the time. I truly hope you do because I would very much like to have your opinion of the work.

From his desk at the Johns Hopkins English department, Barth replied by return mail on October 9. He dodged Phillabaum's request with what reads like a practiced response.

I wish Mr. Toole, his novel, and yourself well. But my writing students here are so staggeringly productive that I scarcely have time to read anything in print between September and May—by when I am too busy catching up on old reading to take on anything new.
Sorry,
Jack

Perhaps if Barth had known something of the history of the novel and its author, he would have been curious enough to take on the project despite the "staggering" productivity of his students. Yet the Press agreed with Percy that the book must stand on its own, and as Phillabaum noted, a cold reading would be the best test. With this refusal and an estimate of high production costs, the forward momentum stalled again. By the end of the year, LSU still had not decided whether to publish the novel, but the decision had to be made soon. If John Kennedy Toole had written a funny, fine, and *short* book, there would have been no question of it appearing on the Press's 1980 list. At four-hundred-plus pages, the production of *Confederacy* would make quite a dent in LSU's budget, but there was also Walker Percy to be considered. It was a rare thing for him to put a work forward, though his personal virtues were as notable as his stature in the world of American literature. If he believed in the book, the people at LSU Press trusted his judgment.

The business of publishing is not quite as slow as evolution, but sometimes it seems that way. More than two years had gone by since Thelma Toole had finagled that meeting at Loyola with Walker Percy. She was seventy-eight years old now, and her health had not been good in the decade since her son had died. Thelma was vain and stubborn, but she had never been stupid. Knowing it was now or never, she took her best shot. It had the desired result.

From February 22, 1979
Dear Les,
Can you tell me what the Press intends to do about John Toole's novel, *A Confederacy of Dunces?* His mother wants to know and I said I would ask you.
Sincerely,
Walker

The reply from Phillabaum came on February 26, and reads, in part:

> We have completed our readings . . . and I'm completely stunned
> by the whole situation. The book is absolutely marvelous, but why is
> it still a manuscript? Hasn't anyone else seen it? It's wild, wacky, and
> brilliant—fantastic characterization, dialogue that keeps surprising
> from beginning to end. Obviously I need not tell you these things, but
> I have to wonder who this guy was, what else did he do, and why
> haven't I heard about him before. In other words, yes, we want to do
> the book, and the only potential problem is financial. Unless the book
> catches on in a very substantial way, I don't think we will be able to
> break even on the cloth edition alone, but the thing is just too darn
> good not to be published.
>
> Would you be willing to give us your evaluation of the manuscript
> to present to the [press] Committee? Otherwise I will have to send it
> out to someone else, and while I'm sure I can secure a favorable re-
> view, it will just slow things down further.

A few days later Percy replied, agreeing to provide an evaluation of
the novel to the faculty press committee. He closed the letter with the
comment that "as far as revisions I'd leave it alone. I've spoken to Mrs.
Toole (who is delighted also) and she says she might be able to shed light
on individual words which may have been mis-transcribed in the last
typing."

On March 5, Phillabaum gave Percy the go-ahead to write the evaluation. In this letter he also presented Percy with the bottom-line proof of
LSU's dedication to the project.

> It should run to some 450 pages and will cost upwards of $10,000
> for manufacturing alone for a 2000 copy first printing. At a $15.00 list,
> that means we stand to lose between $3000 and $4000 if we sell out
> the printing.
>
> We will however proceed with the book regardless of the some-
> what unfavorable financial picture. We will apply for a grant from
> the National Endowment for the Arts, though I think that a bit of a

long shot. As soon as we have committee approval I would look for publication about a year from now.

At their meeting on the first Friday in April, the review board gave the Press a thumbs up for production of the novel. In a letter dated April 11, Percy congratulates Phillabaum on the wise decision and wishes that they "even make money on it—as you should. For a fact, I think it has a chance of becoming a sort of eccentric minor classic."

From the beginning of his acquaintance with the novel, Percy had known that once *Confederacy* was accepted for publication, editors would volunteer gladly to prune and tidy the long, rambling tale. A colleague of Marcus Smith's had already offered to do this, as well as a friend of Percy's, whom he referenced in the same letter.

> Garic Barranger, a local attorney, friend, actor, writer, critic, culti-
> vated Yale man, who is an admirer of Toole's novel, has spent consid-
> erable time studying it, suggesting changes, corrections, etc. Some of
> his suggestions are no doubt of value. He has struck up a friendship
> with Mrs. Toole, a rather remarkable lady as you will discover. My
> general advice to him, you, and Mrs. Toole is by and large to leave
> the book alone, though a few minor changes might be good.

In 1978, after the novel had been rejected by Farrar, Percy had lent his copy to Garic (Nikki) Barranger, who found that "under all that ver-bal clowning something a good deal more serious is in awesome prog-ress." While the book's fate was being debated at the Press, Barranger wrote Thelma a long letter containing suggestions for editing the novel. With her blessing he sent these thoughts along to Phillabaum on station-ery bearing his firm's letterhead. Because of his interest in the work and friendship with the author's mother, Phillabaum assumed that Barranger was Mrs. Toole's legal representative, and he sent the Covington lawyer a copy of the publishing contract. He could not know that Thelma was loath to accept advice or control from anyone.

In a May 8, 1979, letter to Phillabaum, Thelma wrote: "I learned today that Mr. Barranger contacted you about the contract with permis-sion of Walker and me. The only association I have had with him was his vital interest in my son's novel which pleased me very much. There never was any mention of my engaging his legal services. That was farthest from my mind."

No matter what state Thelma's mind was in, lawyers would occupy a good portion of it for the rest of her life. As soon as Barranger saw the contract, he knew that Thelma would have to prove that she was sole inheritor of the artistic property known as *A Confederacy of Dunces*.

In a long letter dated April 19, Phillabaum sent Mrs. Toole the glad news and enclosed two copies of the publishing contract, writing, "It is my understanding that you hold literary rights to the work, which should empower you to sign as author. If this is incorrect, please let me know with whom we should contract. Assuming that you do have the authority to sign the agreement, I hope you will review it carefully and not hesitate to raise any questions you may have."

In her reply, Thelma ducked the issue and responded with a flowery thank-you.

From May 8, 1979
Dear Mr. Phillabaum,

Your warm, earnest, keen evaluation of my son's literary ability gladdened my heart! The contract, which Walker Percy read and approved, will be returned with my signature at the meeting.

When it is convenient for you to grant an interview, please send a postcard with the day, time and your office address. The anticipatory delight of meeting you will enliven my days during the interim.

Deep appreciation for the "surge forward" you are giving this brilliant novel.

Sincerely,

Thelma D. (Mrs. John) Toole

Fifteen

For this to come out of the worst heartache, the worst tragedy, is overwhelming. But my life is ashes and sawdust.

—Thelma Toole

KNOWING THAT MRS. TOOLE was handicapped, Phillabaum and Martha Hall decided to hold the meeting at the old woman's home. It was to be a working meeting as well as an introduction to the amazing mother who refused to abandon her son's dream. Hall had finished editing the book and wanted Thelma to know exactly what had been done to the manuscript. Neither visitor had ever been so deep into downtown New Orleans. It was a hot spring day, and coming up the concrete steps, Hall and Phillabaum could see through the screen door into the living room. Leaning on her walker, Thelma welcomed them into the warm, stuffy house wearing a pink snap-front cotton coffee coat, a veiled straw hat, and white gloves. Her greeting to them was carefully enunciated: "I have been waiting for you on tender hooks."

As the twosome from LSU sat on the couch, Thelma launched into a forty-five-minute account of her son's life from his precocious infancy to his untimely death. Phillabaum and his editor never said a word as Thelma held forth on all aspects of her son's genius. As Phillabaum later said, "We got the whole chronicle right out of the box." For years later, they would hear these same stories trotted out in polished versions for the interviewers and new acquaintances.

Thelma enumerated her son's accomplishments and attributed them to the outstanding genes inherited from her side of the family. Complaining about her late husband, she told Phillabaum that although he was a mathematical genius, John Toole "squandered his abilities being a car salesman." Not one of the Tooles had ever done a thing for her, she reported, and mentioned Toole relatives who had disparaged her son's memory. Phillabaum said she pointed out "a great distinction between her lace-curtain Irish family" and her husband's "shanty Irish heritage." Throughout this harangue Phillabaum was aware of a little gray man puttering around outside in the yard, but he was never introduced to Arthur Ducoing.

When the monologue ended, Phillabaum and Hall explained the editing to Mrs. Toole, who was very cooperative. After an hour of this, the Press people rose to leave but were summoned by Thelma into the back part of the living room for a performance. Phillabaum remembered being confined to an armless straight-back chair for the next hour as he listened to Thelma's "act." Accompanying herself on the piano, Thelma sang a variety of selections from gay-nineties ragtime to Gershwin, and interspersed the music with vignettes from her life. What had not been covered in the opening monologue was touched upon in this program.

Phillabaum believed at that time—and has remained convinced— that "Thelma Toole was the most bizarre person I have ever met." At the end of the recital, Phillabaum and Hall left Mrs. Toole waving good-bye to them from the stoop of the little house on Elysian Fields. The pair drove in silence through New Orleans and onto the interstate, west to Baton Rouge. They were out of the city before they could manage a word. Once Thelma's spell broke, Phillabaum and Hall rehashed their amazing afternoon for the entire ninety-minute trip home.

Having lived in Louisiana a long time, Phillabaum was aware of the state's quirky laws regarding inheritance. Thelma's offhand talk of "cousins" made him uneasy about her position as sole heir of her son's estate. Phillabaum contacted the Press's attorney, Shelby McKenzie of Baton Rouge, to get a clearer picture of the situation. In a May 2, 1979, letter he laid out the problem to McKenzie.

> The question is what assurance we need to be certain that she has the power to enter into a publishing agreement. According to her attorney, Garic Barranger from Covington, the son's succession was never opened (I believe that's the terminology used) because there was little of value in the estate. How much value there is in the manuscript now remains to be seen, but I don't believe we should proceed without full knowledge that she has the power to enter into the agreement.

In his response, McKenzie was likewise concerned about publication rights because there was no legal paperwork showing clear title to the work. Seeing no problem in obtaining this, McKenzie explained that there is a simple procedure for small successions which permits use of an affidavit to identify the heirs. The attorney could not know that nothing was ever simple where Thelma was concerned, and a legal hassle over the rights began in the summer of 1979. Although Thelma still denied that there was any dispute about sole ownership, Phillabaum gently prodded her to take up the matter with Barranger, who "has acted before now in the role of friendly advisor, and you may want to consult him on the matter of the documents in the succession."

Les Phillabaum did not know that Thelma had met another "friendly advisor" who had more fun and attention to offer than Barranger. Rhoda Faust owned a small chain of independent bookstores and wanted to publish works of regional interest. In 1977 she had asked Percy if he knew of any properties that might be available. Percy said that he would take a look at his own unpublished first novel and see if there was a chance to rework it for Faust's purposes. He suggested that in the meantime she get a copy of the *New Orleans Review* and read the excerpt of *Confederacy*. Faust was bowled over by the brilliance of Toole's work and immediately contacted Thelma to obtain a copy of the manuscript.

At this time LSU Press had not yet come to a decision on the novel, and Thelma offered it to Faust, who began to look harder for funding to begin her business. Rhoda Faust talked with Thelma every day or two in order to, as she said, "Get Thelma off Walker's back." When Phillabaum's team decided to take up the project, Faust stayed close to Mrs. Toole because, she said, "I liked Walker, I liked *Dunces,* and I wanted to be a part" of the whole experience. To celebrate the signing of the contract with LSU, Faust and a friend, author Christine Wiltz, gave a party for Thelma at the New Orleans Lawn Tennis Club. Although she was disappointed not to be bringing out the book herself, Faust was delighted when Thelma mentioned that Ken had left another earlier work, and she offered it to Faust for her new company. Faust jumped at the opportunity, which turned out to be a leap into a nest of legal snakes.

Although Faust was not a lawyer, she knew that getting clear rights to both novels was necessary, but she had trouble convincing Mrs. Toole that this was so. At first Thelma tried to stonewall the questions about rights to *Confederacy.* Seeking to put an end to the issue, she told Barranger and Phillabaum that no succession for her son had been opened and she had lost all papers relating to his death—but only one of those stories was true. When Phillabaum refused to let the subject drop, Mrs. Toole admitted that after Ken's death she had indeed sought legal advice from a former student.

John L. Hantel was a childhood friend of Ken's who had also taken lessons at the Lakeside School of Dramatic Arts. A few days after Ken's suicide, the Tooles came to Hantel's office. He remembered Ken's parents and noticed that Mrs. Toole had not changed. They were both quite dazed and grief stricken, but Mr. Toole was in worse shape than his wife. The lawyer saw at once that the man he remembered as "quite robust" was in a "very weakened condition." Hantel drew up the papers that would grant them access to Ken's bank accounts and the title to his car. Although they were asked, the Tooles never mentioned any other property and certainly not a manuscript. Because it was a simple matter and the Tooles needed the money, Hantel completed his task quickly. The value of the estate was less than ten thousand dollars, and a judgment of possession was granted the Tooles less than a month after Ken died. Eleven years later, Hantel sent a copy of this judgment to Bar-

ranger with the information that, as far as he knew, no succession for
John Toole had been opened.

Thelma had assured Barranger that John Dewey Toole Jr. had no living relatives except for herself, but because she had mentioned "cousins,"
Phillabaum remained uneasy about this situation and wrote McKenzie
on July 10:

> Enclosed are copies of correspondence relative to a matter I raised
> with you a few weeks ago, that of a deceased author, John Kennedy
> Toole. Is what we have sufficient to go forward with a contract signed
> by Mrs. Toole? Frankly, she's something of a dingaling and I would
> as soon have as little to do with her as possible, but that may also be
> an argument for being sure we have everything nailed down before
> proceeding.

Amid the threat of these legal tangles, the business of getting John
Kennedy Toole's work in print went forward. Thelma had supplied
some information about missing words and phrases. She sent pictures of
Ken to Martha Hall, the copy editor for the book, so that Hall could feel
a connection to him. Hall's reply contained the gentle caution that because a book takes seven or eight months to produce, Thelma could an-
ticipate a period of waiting. Good news arrived from the National
Endowment for the Arts in the form of a $3,500 grant for production of
the manuscript, an amount that would help cover the anticipated deficit
involved for printing a minimum order of 2,500 books.

In a letter written July 31, Phillabaum spelled out for Mrs. Toole exactly what his position was concerning her son's estate.

> Because your husband inherited one-half of the estate and as I un-
> derstand it his succession has not been opened, I should obtain from
> you an affidavit that identifies the legal heirs to John D. Toole. My
> impression is that you are his only heir . . . however, if your husband
> had living ascendants or collateral heirs, it will be necessary for such
> heirs to be signatories to the contract as well as yourself.

According to Louisiana Civil Code, modeled on *Le Code Napoléon,*
Ken Toole's estate was divided equally between his parents. Because his

father died without a will designating his wife as his heir, his share of Ken's estate (half of the manuscript) did not pass to Thelma. Instead, it reverted to John's siblings or their heirs.

Not wishing to have the Press delay production, Thelma capitulated, telling Barranger that as far as she knew, her husband's only surviving relatives were his brother, Harold M. Toole, and a niece, Mary Margaret Toole McGuire. Thelma was adamant that Barranger not contact these people. In a letter to Phillabaum, Barranger wrote that he was "working on a diplomatic approach to the problem of securing a renunciation of the succession from either or both of the heirs." He shared the view of the other attorneys that until the renunciation was in hand, "Thelma Toole is the owner of a one-half interest in the property and each of the two remaining heirs are the owners of an undivided 25% interest."

When this was made clear to Thelma, she was absolutely furious and wrote Phillabaum on August 22.

> When I received your letter stating that the law decreed that the names of two of my husband's relatives be affixed to my son's contract, I was in a highly emotional state. Since then, I have quieted down, and will comply. These two people are alien to my son's brilliance, refinement, etiquette, elegance, high standards, noble character, erudition (he received a Master's Degree with High Honors in English from Columbia University) and possessor of literary and scholarly genius. Those two people had no connection with his achieving life.
>
> For ten years I strove valiantly, indefatigably, and dauntlessly to reach a publisher. Seven efforts came to naught. Then Walker and you proved to be supreme benefactors.
>
> Just as soon as I received your letter, I phoned Mr. Barranger and didn't reach him until the next morning. At that moment, I engaged him as my legal counsel, and told him when he received your letter to act with alacrity. He is working earnestly.
>
> Please send the contract as soon as possible, and I will return it without delay.

The task of contacting the heirs fell to Barranger, who was being ridden hard by Thelma. She had never gotten along with her husband's family, whom she considered "vulgarians" who had "disparaged her son's memory." The Tooles' interest was represented by Mary McGuire's husband, Ray, an attorney in New Orleans. Barranger, a dignified, professional man, did not find these people at all crude, but Thelma would have none of his opinions. Citing the attorney-client privilege, Barranger has kept her letters to him confidential, but he did say that the unkind comments about her husband's relatives were "Thelma just showing off" and "acting up."

From the beginning, Thelma had not been completely open with her legal advisor, and their working relationship was compromised. Earlier Thelma had found reason to scold him for his lapses, as in a letter dated June 7, 1979.

Dear Nikki,

At the Saturday evening reception, hosted by Rhoda and Christine and honoring my son, I prepared an expression of gratitude to you for the keen interest in *Confederacy of Dunces* and your generosity in making copies. However, I did not know that you were present.

You didn't bid me good evening, not good-night, nor mention what a memorable night it was! Indifference from people with whom I am associated is very hurtful to me because I am very earnest and sincere.

Another point: you addressed mail to Mrs. Thelma *O'Toole* and reinforced it with your personal stationery typing out Mrs. Thelma *O'Toole*.

You have not given me the respect and courtesy I deserve as a woman of intelligence, culture and many gifts.

Thelma D. Toole

P.S. If I have misconstrued your actions, please write and tell me so.

Walker, Rhoda and Christine came into my life when I was beset by utter loneliness, ravaging despair, and illimitable suffering from the loss of my son. They brought goodness, hopefulness and helpfulness to me. I shall be awaiting your reply.

A week later Betty Schermann, the unwitting perpetrator of the latter insult, typed an apology to her boss's client on their best office bond:

> I am Mr. Garic Barranger's secretary, and I wish to apologize to
> you for the misspelling of your name (O'Toole) in recent correspon-
> dence directed to you at the instruction of Mr. Barranger. This was
> an error I failed to realize, but did realize it when I was handling the
> file later, prior to your calling it to our attention. But thank you for
> calling it to our attention.

Now, some months later, Thelma interpreted her attorney's good opinion of the McGuires as a personal attack and responded aggressively. Because he had dared to speak well of her enemies, Barranger was put on
Thelma's suspect list. Unwilling to trust Barranger to negotiate a settle-
ment, Thelma wrote directly to Ray McGuire, pointedly deleting "dear"
from the salutation.

> Mr. McGuire,
>
> Mr. Barranger phoned September first to say that the conference
> was to be held in *your office* September nineteenth, and I told him to
> cancel that conference. My legal counsel has not complied with my
> directions to hold the conference in his office, to state to you that *no*
> *relatives* be present and to inform Harold Toole, Sr., of the case. The
> latter he relegated to your wife that task. That was a bold avoidance
> of his duty.
>
> The procrastination and the leisurely approach to this vital, urgent
> "immediate action" more, lofty matter make me realize that you two
> attorneys do not have the necessary time and firmness of purpose
> which this profound case needs. The lack of consideration for the pa-
> tient, waiting, gentlemanly, erudite publisher, Mr. L. E. Phillabaum,
> shows thoughtlessness.
>
> My late husband, John D. Toole, did not basically, steadily, nor
> honorably support his multi-talented wife and genius son. His inter-
> ests were elsewhere. Then, the law steps in and decrees that two of
> my husband's relatives be included in the contract. What a ghastly

situation. My son and I alone bore the "trials, tribulations" my husband thrust upon us.

The Louisiana Law Napoleonic Code is not applicable to this case. It was adopted to protect children's rights. Where are the children? An aged man and a mature woman?

It is undeniably wrong.

Thelma D. Toole

P.S. If Mr. Barranger still wants to handle the case, he can arrange a night conference or a Sunday afternoon conference, both in *his office*.

Despite this evidence of her spirit, Thelma was frail, and all this wrangling made her ill. Rhoda Faust began to handle more of the negotiations between Thelma and her husband's relatives. This suited Barranger, who had had more than he needed of Thelma and her tantrums. He had involved himself with the manuscript as a favor to Walker Percy, and because he hoped to get a chance to edit the work. After the Press informed him that they would use in-house editors, Barranger remained connected as Thelma's attorney. He had never asked for nor been offered remuneration for his services. This did not sit well with his law partners, who felt that he was wasting their time on what one called "a dumb project." Barranger said Thelma had "moved into his life," but none of his efforts on her behalf was acceptable.

In a letter to LSU Press dated September 19, 1979, Thelma wrote:

Barranger has dismissed himself as my attorney because "he is tired of all this foolishness and the 'chewing-out' I have given him." I thought attorneys had dignity and a better vocabulary than that. He has blundered woefully and said derogatory things to me. It is a relieving riddance.

Wednesday, September nineteenth, there is to be a conference in Ray McGuire's office at 2-3-4 Loyola building at 1:00 p.m. Rhoda is going to present the two supposed heirs with renunciation forms. No doubt, they will refuse to sign them—then I will address the group with my oratorical training and many years of usage.

Please send wave-lengths of good will in my endeavor and it will bolster me.

When interviewed, Barranger laughed off the letter as "pure Thelma" and said it was completely untrue. According to Barranger's files, Thelma fired *him* in a letter dated September 20 and enclosed a few dollars for some Xeroxing he had done for her. On October 8, Barranger returned the money, saying that he did what he did out of respect for her son's work and not for remuneration. This ended their association, and Thelma became someone else's nightmare client. After the book had become famous, one of his former partners stopped him to ask if this was the same book he had been working on and, if so, would they be getting any money out of it. Managing to keep a straight face, Barranger replied with a simple "No."

It was not possible for those at the Press to distance themselves from the problem, and the staff continued to struggle with the contract as more heirs surfaced and one appeared reluctant to renounce his interest in the manuscript. Mrs. Toole's next attorney, Michael Little of New Orleans, counseled patient diplomacy to settle the matter, but as she had done with Barranger, Thelma began bombarding Little with advice, sending dainty handwritten notes on paper dusted with chamomile and bergamot powders. Hoping to have her wit and intelligence admired, she passed out copies of these letters to the Press director and others.

From October 25, 1979
Dear Mr. Little,

The practical thought that follows is relevant to the legal literary case you are now working on: could someone bequeath a Serves vase, Limoges china, Chippendale furniture, a Mallard bedstead, an Oriental rug, an Aubusson tapestry, a Rembrandt painting, a Drysdale water color, a cloisonné case timepiece, a Dolly Madison bedspread, Madeira embroidered linens, Sheffield silverware, a concert grand Steinway piano, etceteras, etceteras, to blokes, boors, country-bumpkins, gawping at the Mt. Parnassus buildings housing intellectuals and literary giants of which my son was one? I shout vociferous, "No"!!!

I am depending on you to bring this sordid matter to a speedy and successful close.

Now you have the complete equipment to wield legal power: your competence, your thorough knowledge of the case, the three signatures of renunciation, and the terrific force of my husband's nonsupport of his multi-talented wife and genius son, also multi-talented.

Mr. and Mrs. Ray McGuire must be routed from their plaster of Paris throne because of their obstinate behavior, gross money-lust, and lack of humanity.

You are the ringmaster! Crack the whip! Demand immediate obedience!

A copy of the following letter was sent to Phillabaum with the note, "When I consider the basic effort I made in gaining the signatures and the exorbitant fees the attorney is charging, I am irate."

Dear Mr. Little,

The enclosed check for $195.00 represents a half payment of your $395.00 second fee. My payments have been made possible because of my brother's insistence of my suspending my monthly contribution toward household expenses during the months of November and December.

When you receive this mail call me to acknowledge it and tell me of your encounter with McGuire and what transpired. I must report to Mr. Phillabaum.

The purpose of the law is the benevolent administration of justice. Clamp down on the malevolent pair because you have the power of three renunciatory signatures and my husband's hideous nonsupport. This must be done during the week of December 17th, so as to avoid the disruption of Christmas. Talking "turkey," Mr. Phillabaum's generous extension of time, November and December, ends on December 31st. After that, I mean before that, I should be established as the sole and rightful heir of my son's contract.

I have worked earnestly to reach the children of Harold Toole, Sr., to impress upon them the honorable course to take. They said they were doing that because they loved me. How touching! Mary

Toole McGuire said "she didn't have time to talk to me." Low-class, coarse ingrate!

My nervous system is drained by this harrowing legal matter.

I will be waiting your call.

In January 1980, despite the vitriol hurled at them, or perhaps because of it, the five collateral heirs of John D. Toole renounced all claim to the property known as *A Confederacy of Dunces.* They did it knowing that Aunt Thelma was poor and believing that it was the only book her son had ever written. John Toole's heirs never dreamed that it would be what Barranger called a *"succés fou"* worth a fortune. Thelma refused to allow Rhoda Faust to bring up the subject of the rights to *The Neon Bible,* and the novel was never mentioned. After Thelma's death, the Toole cousins asserted their succession rights and were successful in retaining their shares of Ken's second profitable property. That was in the future, however, and at this time there was only the question of how to market *Confederacy,* a wonderful but wacky book by a dead author brought out by a press with no track record at publishing novels.

The book had had a rocky journey for seventeen years, and Thelma had been the driving force. Now she had help fighting for the book, and in a grateful letter to Phillabaum wrote,

May favorable winds assist my son's literary ship, with its precious cargo, and guide it to its longed-for successful port. It is reassuring and comforting to know that you are at the helm.

And the presence of Walker Percy hovers over all.

LSU Press announced the novel in its spring 1980 catalog. During the succession argument, the business of readying the book had been ongoing. None of the firms contacted by the Press displayed an interest in obtaining the paperback rights, but Grove Press in New York heard about the novel in a roundabout way. Kent Carroll of Grove had just purchased paperback rights to an LSU Press book about the prizefighter Jack Dempsey. While Carroll was working on this deal, LSU's subsidiary rights manager, Dianne Guidry, mentioned Toole's book and described the unusual road it had traveled to publication. She told him it was the third novel the Press had taken on, and that the book's champion, Walker Percy, had agreed to write an introduction. Because he admired the Dempsey book, Carroll agreed to read the new novel.

The book came to Carroll in the uncorrected-proof stage, before advance reviews appeared. After reading it, Carroll passed it on with high praise to Herman Graf, head of sales and marketing at Grove, who in turn forwarded the book to Barney Rosset. Rosset had made Grove famous by daring to publish the first U.S. editions of D. H. Lawrence's *Lady Chatterley's Lover* and Henry Miller's *Tropic of Cancer*. Although he rarely acquired books from outside his own house, Rosset decided to license world English paperback rights to *Confederacy*, offering LSU an advance of $2,000 against future royalties, which were set at 7.5% of the book's list price. Around this time *Kirkus Reviews* of forthcoming books appeared, and the write-up on *Confederacy* was very positive.

Feeling that they might have a hit, Carroll called the Press and asked if he could help promote the book, hoping to enhance the value of Grove's contract. Phillabaum gave him the go-ahead, and Graf worked the phone to help sell the hardback edition, an action that would later cause trouble.

The staff at LSU Press was delighted by the glowing reviews that quickly appeared. The original printing of 2,500 copies had sold out before publication (the first order was for 200 copies for Rhoda Faust's Maple Street Book Store), and an additional 5,000 copies were printed. The Press was pleased that the novel was "selling through," meaning books were actually being sold to bookstore customers, not just sitting on shelves waiting to be returned. As sales figures climbed, more reprintings were ordered, for higher quantities, and by the end of the first year, 42,000 copies of the hardback edition had sold.

The Press had commission sales representatives in all parts of the country, and the book was being sold to wholesalers and stores using this network. In the South, LSU used George Scheer and Associates to market the book to the wholesale firm of Ingram in Nashville, Tennessee. Kent Carroll had also contacted Ingram and had spoken to two women there who were very enthusiastic about *Confederacy*. Susan Moffett and Kathy Hemmings went out of their way to push the book. For its part,

Grove Press sent free copies to Waldenbooks and B Dalton Bookseller to get the word out about *Confederacy*.

Although LSU Press was actively and aggressively selling the book themselves, Phillabaum had no objection to Carroll using Grove's contacts to draw attention to the book, since those actions would be to the advantage of all. This informal agreement was jeopardized when some reviewing venues mistakenly listed Grove as the novel's publisher. The success of *Confederacy* was an opportunity to bring LSU Press wide national attention, and Grove's involvement, rather than helping, was obscuring the Press's role. Phillabaum insisted that Grove Press withdraw from promoting the book, which it did. By that time, however, the whole endeavor had taken on a natural momentum.

Once the book caught fire, the only question was how large a success it would be. By May 1980, the Press was on its third reprinting, with 20,000 copies out in the world—and demand only increased as the mythology around the book grew. Toole's novel had become a big story, one that was feeding itself. Phillabaum traveled to New Orleans to meet Mary Vespa, a journalist from *People* magazine, to discuss the book and its history at length for an article she was writing on the late author and his eccentric mother. The tale of Toole and his "masterpiece" had great appeal, piquing human as well as literary interest, and soon Phillabaum and Thelma Toole were deluged with requests for interviews.

From the time the excerpt appeared in the *New Orleans Review,* Thelma had been something of a local celebrity. Her son's work struck an exciting chord with the city's literati, who queued up to entertain the mother of the novelist. Thelma had experienced the most exciting months of her life, but the fulfillment of her dream had a downside as a new void opened in her life. Thelma's obsession with her son had become an obsession with getting his book published, and now that work was complete. All that remained for Thelma was her lifelong obsession with herself, and now she had the influence and the audience to gratify her need to be admired. It would have been easier for a lot of people if she could have celebrated Ken's achievement, as well as her own triumph, quietly—but this would not have been Thelma.

Putting herself firmly in the driver's seat, Thelma was not easily dislodged. From her first acquaintance with the Percys, Thelma had sent the couple gifts that were neither welcome nor appropriate. Percy was amazed to open a package from Thelma containing a pair of pajamas for him and a set of dime-store juice glasses for his wife. In return for these tokens, the Percys were expected to phone and write formal notes of thanks. Small boxes of Russell Stover candies sent to LSU required the same response, and a failure to comply met with severe repercussions in the form of lectures delivered via Ma Bell and the U.S. Postal Service.

Bunt Percy said that at first her husband felt an obligation to be nice to Mrs. Toole. It was difficult to sustain this kindness when she would call Percy and Marcus Smith to come to the parties given by new friends and admirers of *Confederacy*. Thelma would always say "Don't bring your wives," which pleased Bunt, who didn't want to go anyway. Feeling no slight, Mrs. Percy sent her husband, knowing that he hated the piano playing and singing that he called "all that foolishness."

Once the Percys went with her to Lafayette with Joel Fletcher for a visit with his mother. Thelma was determined to be the center of attention and allowed no one a share of the conversation. Bunt Percy said it was an embarrassing experience during a very long afternoon. She remembered Mrs. Fletcher turning off her hearing aid "so that she wouldn't have to put up with Mrs. Toole's antics."

Although they had socialized with Thelma during the first hoopla over the book, the Percys soon noticed that she was willing to cozy up to anyone who would make a fuss over her. Bunt knew Thelma was "completely self-absorbed," but because they felt sorry for her they overlooked it. After the Lafayette visit, the Percys became aware of a group of young men who had begun to hang around Mrs. Toole. The Percys were dismayed at the way these friends encouraged Thelma to behave outrageously at public gatherings. They felt that it took advantage of her age and turned Thelma into a parody.

The last social event the Percys attended with Thelma was the autograph party at the Prytania Street location of the Maple Street Garden District bookstore in May 1980. Owner Rhoda Faust had planned this celebration with Mrs. Toole at the center. All the LSU Press people came from Baton Rouge, and the famous couple from Covington was also in attendance. Mrs. Toole signed books in place of her son and received the lion's share of kudos. Faust had arranged for a piano, and Thelma

brought programs listing the songs she would perform. As she introduced each song, Thelma would dedicate it to a particular person. In a
surprise tribute, she serenaded Walker Percy with a tune from the Dis-
ney version of *Stories of Uncle Remus*. Percy, who had fought a lifelong
battle with depression, grumbled to Rhoda Faust, "Do I seem like a 'Zip-
A-Dee-Doo-Dah' kind of guy to you?"

Bunt Percy remembered the party quite well. She recalled that "many
people had come to the bookstore to meet Walker Percy for his own
sake" and not just as the guardian angel of *Confederacy*. During Thelma's performance, Walker, who had heard her program many times already, retired to a far corner to speak quietly with someone who had
wanted to meet him. Mrs. Toole took great umbrage at being ignored
and berated the author (for "cavorting around with the young folk") in
what Bunt Percy called "a rude, rude letter which just infuriated
Walker." Included with the correspondence was a check in the amount
of $1,000 for Percy's "services" regarding *Confederacy*. Incensed, Percy
returned the check. After that incident the Percys backed off and had
nothing more to do with Thelma. Instead of cooling her ire, their ignor-
ing Thelma made her more furious. She sent long, complaining letters
to friends detailing her wounds.

To Les Phillabaum she wrote: "I haven't received a letter of apology
from Walker for his disrespectful behavior during my performance." Included with this note were copies of a series of letters written to Faust
in late May and early June, which read in part:

> Of my many friends who attended the publication party and you
> and Walker and Marcus, not one said to me: "Thelma, your dual role
> of autographing and performing needs a mark of attention from me.
> You are a very thoughtful person and I want to respond commensura-
> bly. The underlying tragedy of your son's absence I cannot eradicate,
> but I can offer you some assuagement. So I'm taking you to an exclu-
> sive Piano-Bar where you can relax, listen to a gifted pianist play the
> music you love so well and play so beautifully." Not so!!!! When all
> the guests had departed, what I have felt for eleven years came force-
> fully home to me: I am really alone in the world! This paragraph
> could be shouted from the mountain tops and serve as a lesson to

thoughtless, predominance of all "pipples" to mend their ways, and give proper attention to worthy people! About hurts:

Several "pipples" have directed their spleen to me. You know each one. The one I admired, respected, and loved dealt a stinging blow— truly unbelievable!

Extreme ill-health forces me to tolerate the "hell-hole" of my present abode and eschew a "hell-hole" in another location because peace, harmony and love left my life with my son's passing. The elegant furnishings and good taste that marked our apartment no longer is my desire. Nothing material appeals to me anymore.

So as to gain some semblance of composure, I am going to discontinue phone calls and visits for a while. If anyone should inquire about me, simply say Thelma's health hasn't improved.

In truth her health was not good, and these emotional upheavals took their toll. Though much of the turmoil was self-inflicted, it cost Thelma physically and did further damage to her peace of mind. Yet there were good times still to come. In the remaining years of her life, Mrs. Toole traveled, performed, and enjoyed the attentions of many "pipples"—but bright lights and applause could not fill the void that her son's loss only partly explained. If there is a gene that governs contentment, Thelma was born without it.

The staff at LSU Press knew how difficult it was to deal with Mrs. Toole. By the beginning of 1981, she was now on her fourth attorney, and her relationship with Rhoda Faust was floundering. During the tricky negotiations surrounding the rights to the novel, Thelma had called Faust "boss" and let her handle the meetings with the Toole family. One of the heirs refused to sign off on the book without having seen it. Feeling that this was reasonable, Faust lent the woman her own copy of the manuscript, which angered Thelma, who said this "besmirched" her son's work. For Percy's sake, Faust had allowed Thelma to intrude into her life. Faust said at first "I thought she was a sad old woman, but I didn't know that she was vicious." There were months when Thelma would not talk to Faust, only to call again when she wanted something. This intermittent contact allowed Faust to hope Thelma would honor her promise to allow Faust to publish *The Neon Bible*. The final decision concerning Toole's early novel disappointed Faust. In 1987 a New Orleans judge ruled that rights to the novel be split among several heirs. Grove Press was selected to publish the book, which came out in 1989. It remains in print and was made into a film in 1995.

Phillabaum was convinced that there was never "any reason why [Thelma] should fall out with you." He remembered the cause could be as innocuous as having "refilled your teacup before filling hers or not having opened the door properly. Anything could set her off. If she did not get her 'yes' with one person, she would try with another. It had nothing to do with truth or reality. The problem was that unlike Percy or Faust, whom she could just cast aside when she fell out with them and didn't need them anymore, she couldn't do that with us. She had to have contact with us because we paid the royalties." And the sales that provided those royalties kept pouring in, to the delight of everyone concerned.

The fear that *Confederacy* would be only a regional hit subsided when glowing reviews came in from important critics across the country and in Europe. Chosen as a Book-of-the-Month Club alternate selection, the novel was a success with all levels of the reading public. *Confederacy* was also one of four books nominated for the first PEN/Faulkner Award, along with none other than Walker Percy's *Second Coming.* The only place where the book received as many strong negative comments as positive ones was in *Confederacy*'s hometown. Many New Orleanians saw the book as a mirror, and they didn't much like the reflection. In spring of 1981, just as the hardback sales slacked in advance of the paperback publication, the novel received an amazing boost.

On April 13, 1981, John Kennedy Toole was awarded the Pulitzer Prize for fiction for his novel *A Confederacy of Dunces,* marking the first time the prize was given posthumously. LSU Press became the first university press to publish a title that received the fiction honor—and the first southern university press to boast a Pulitzer in any category. When Phillabaum and his colleagues got the news, they did the most appropriate thing and sent out for champagne to celebrate. Phillabaum called Thelma with the news but got no answer. The local paper photographed the happy staff, and the picture was reprinted in the *Times-Picayune.* As soon as Thelma saw the photo, she phoned the Press, piqued that they'd thrown a party and hadn't invited her. No explanation from Phillabaum could mollify her, and Thelma continued to find fault. He said that she had gone from "God bless Les Phillabaum to goddamn Les Phillabaum" in less than two years. The awarding of the Pulitzer must have been a bittersweet moment for Ken's mother, who had lived to see her son's work praised as what Percy called a "minor classic" and yet was unable to share this joy with anyone she loved.

Grove Press in New York was also celebrating LSU's good fortune, because the book was now in their hands. On the strength of the Pulitzer win, Grove changed the proposed trade format to a mass-market edition, kicking up the numbers and the dollars. Kent Carroll said no one goes into the publishing business to make a lot of money, but that "because you love it, when something like the Pulitzer happens, the satisfaction and the reward of doing it are enormous." The day that the prize was awarded, Carroll left work, went to the corner bar, and ordered champagne all around. In the party that followed, the bartender became confused and began to circulate the story that Carroll had won the Nobel Prize for literature.

In the years since the book's first blush of success, it has continued to gain fans worldwide. As of this writing, over 1.5 million copies of the novel are in print, and translation rights have been sold in twenty countries, for languages ranging from Turkish to Finnish, Serbian to Dutch. There are also large-print and Braille editions, as well as both abridged and unabridged audio versions, and loyal followers of *Confederacy* have set up unofficial websites to discuss Ignatius and his cohorts.

At LSU Press, hardback sales remain constant at about 2,000 per year, spiking to nearly 10,000 on the twentieth anniversary of publication, the year 2000. To mark the occasion, the Press issued a special edition of *Confederacy,* with an introduction by Andrei Codrescu. First printings of first editions of Toole's "masterwork" now fetch as much as $4,500.

Although it no longer publishes original fiction, LSU Press has garnered two additional Pulitzers and a National Book Award in poetry. It continues to judiciously—and profitably—license rights to *Confederacy,* in 1990 renewing Grove's soft-cover contract for a $400,000 advance against an unprecedented royalty rate of 12½ percent of the book's list price. And Les Phillabaum is as proud as ever of the big novel with the improbable past.

The year before the Pulitzer, Thelma had started an exciting new project, and a new relationship that held out Hollywood's brand of immortality to the ever-starstruck Thelma. In 1980, twenty-three-year-old Scott Kramer was already a Twentieth Century Fox executive in Los Angeles and assistant to director Paul Mazursky. An avid reader, Kramer heard about *Confederacy* in a circuitous manner. He had contacted LSU Press, which had just published *Flora of Louisiana* by Margaret Stones, thinking he could get a copy to pass along to his gardener mother. He was disappointed to learn from Dianne Guidry that the book of watercolor drawings was sold out, but Guidry offered to send him a copy of their newest novel about New Orleans, which she hoped he would enjoy.

A Confederacy of Dunces arrived at his door in Los Angeles a few days later, and Kramer had read only sixty pages of the novel when he knew he had stumbled across a great piece of literature. He viewed the book as a modern-day Dickens tale whose characters walked a tightwire that could be tied into a neat cinematic knot at the end. Kramer believed good books as they were written could make good movies, and he set out to make a deal. He began making phone calls and by mid-August had purchased a twelve-month option for the movie rights.

Although the rights have since passed through other hands, such as those of Johnny Carson, Scott Rudin of Paramount, John Langdon of Bumbershoot Productions, and back to Kramer, only Kramer dealt directly with Thelma Toole. In January 1981, as negotiations were beginning with Fox, Kramer received a call from Les Phillabaum, who told him in a hesitant manner that "the mother of the book" wanted his phone number. Being a major fan not only of the book but also of the story of Thelma's dedication to her son's memory, Kramer felt no reluctance about talking with her and wondered at Phillabaum's apologetic attitude. Young, confident, and passionate about the project, Kramer hoped to gain insight into Ken, and into the author's mother, from whom he had already received the first of many handwritten letters.

From January 19, 1981
Dear Mr. Kramer,

The writer, mother of John Kennedy Toole, whose novel has gained wide acclaim, has experienced a strong urge to communicate with you about the forthcoming movie. This is based upon my sixteen years of Dramatic Art Training, and a successful career as performer, teacher, and director.

When you formulate plans for the movie, would you please give me an opportunity to speak with the director? I am hoping to be of substantial assistance to him because I have a keen insight into the characters, which my son drew so brilliantly.

My observation would be quiet and not intrusive.

May the movie bring rich financial rewards for your astute judgment in securing the movie rights.

Looking forward!
Thelma Ducoing Toole

After the first phone call, Kramer understood completely Les Phillabaum's caution. Right off the bat Thelma told her man in Hollywood that she had already purchased a wonderful gown for Oscar night she couldn't wait to wear. It was clear she didn't understand how the business of moviemaking was conducted, and Kramer felt an explanation of the nuances of film funding would be wasted even if she would listen to him. In the months that followed, Kramer would fight for his vision of the project, as well as contend with an eager Thelma. One point she made repeatedly was her complete confidence in Kramer's ability to get the film made and shown at the Prytania Theatre in New Orleans. However, her confidence would have been seriously compromised had she been able to take a good look at her Hollywood producer.

Arriving at one meeting with Carson Films, Kramer found executive Marcia Nassiter deep in phone conversation, spelling out his name to the other person on the line, "K not C." She then told him that it had taken "an act of Congress and many favors," but she had located a hair stylist who would see him that very day. Kramer protested that he had put a lot of time and effort into developing his personal style, but she was adamant. He might be allowed to keep a stud in one earlobe, but his bright blue mohawk would not win him points in the boardroom. He was, Nassiter told him, "in a serious fashion crisis."

Trimmed and polished, a handsome Kramer presented himself and Ignatius Reilly to Jeff Berg at International Creative Management (ICM). Berg gave him a quick how do you do, not even bothering to divert his glance from the second hand on his watch. He said, "Tell me what this book is about in one sentence." Kramer knew it wasn't possible to explain the rambling story about an obese, flatulent man and how it could profitably translate to the screen in one sentence or even ten. On impulse, he told Berg, "Forget it. I can't do that. This is a really great book." Berg made a decision to hear Kramer out. The two men sat down, and Berg listened to the story of Ignatius Reilly, then told Kramer to negotiate the deal and Berg would bank it.

Although Thelma had a lot to say, she rarely listened and could not afford many long-distance calls. Consequently she would have her monologue ready when Kramer answered the phone. Often hello and good-bye were as much conversation as he was allowed. Thelma had plans to come to Los Angeles and help with the casting to ensure that the actors enunciated properly. She told him how she had often taken the bus to New York City, stayed at the YWCA, and camped out in publishers' offices while trying to get the book accepted. She offered her ideas and advice to Kramer, who listened respectfully. She would tell him about the fat people she had seen on the streetcars or at D. H. Holmes who would be right or wrong for the part. Thelma reported to him how a local New Orleans actor knocked on her door and announced he wanted to play Ignatius. She thought the incident was divine destiny and hustled him into her house for elocution lessons.

Often during the phone calls, Kramer would be in the middle of a complicated explanation to one of Thelma's incessant questions when, out of the blue, she would burst into a dramatic reading from some theatrical scene pulled from the far reaches of her mind. He would cease speaking and listen in amazement as Thelma performed a soliloquy over the phone. Kramer also heard from Grove's Kent Carroll, who assured Kramer that the book would win the Pulitzer, but Kramer felt that was wishful thinking.

Thelma, on the other hand, knew it was a sure thing, and Kramer remembers that her calls increased during that time. She sounded like a twenty-year-old as she read each review to him. If there was a turn of phrase in an article that she thought particularly amazing, Thelma would take her time and read it dramatically. The conversations grew longer, and she called Kramer each time the book was picked up in a different country to let him know it was being read in Japan, in France, and in Spain. During this period, Thelma's letters to Kramer had a buzz of ecstasy about them. She called Kramer several times a week at all hours, but it was not so easy for him to contact her. Although Thelma and her brother shared the same house, they refused to speak to each other. If Arthur heard the phone first, he would answer it, but if someone asked for his sister, he would put down the receiver without calling her to the phone. In such cases, Kramer would wait several minutes listening to empty air. After a while he understood that Thelma would have to hear the phone ring or see the receiver off its cradle to realize that the phone call was for her. It was certainly an unhappy situation, and a difficult one in which to conduct business. On Thelma's bad days, Kramer had to listen to her complaints about her "enemies," meaning anyone she was unhappy with at any given moment. Les Phillabaum, the former "precious angel on earth," rose to the top of her hit list on the matter of royalty checks. She began referring to him as "Les Philistine," and he took his place just one notch above Robert Gottlieb, who would never be forgiven for his part in Ken's life.

Kramer was always delighted to talk to Thelma, though he wondered at times if he had made her "list." Having no knowledge of the film industry, Thelma refused to understand that making the deal was the precursor to making the movie. She would phone demanding to know what was taking so long. She thought Kramer was withholding information from her, even though there was nothing new to tell. If a week passed, Thelma believed a mountain of progress surely had been made and movie stars were waiting for her elocution lessons. Any explanation Kramer offered concerning the challenges of filmmaking fell on deaf ears. And he surely did not want to tell her that one potential director wanted to shift the focus of the film from Ignatius Reilly to Burma Jones.

One example of the difficulties Kramer was encountering concerned actor John Belushi. Kramer received a call from Bernie Brillstein, Belushi's manager, who said the actor wanted to do the *Confederacy* project. Kramer, along with others who had read the book, thought the popular, overweight comedian would make the perfect Ignatius. Brillstein invited Kramer to meet in New York City, where the actor was filming the movie *Neighbors.* Each night after the day's shoot, Belushi and a dozen or so others gathered for dinner at the Odeon restaurant. Kramer arrived at the appointed hour and took a seat. Belushi came in with his wife, looked straight at Kramer, and asked: "What the hell are you doing at my table?" Kramer explained that he had been invited by Brillstein to discuss a project, so Belushi *allowed* Kramer to stay.

After dinner, when Belushi asked about the project, it was evident that there had been a miscommunication. Belushi had not read the book and knew nothing about the proposed film. Kramer headed back to the West Coast, worrying, among other things, how he would explain this to Thelma. Two weeks later Kramer received another call from Brillstein. The actor had now read the book and wanted to sign up for the project. At Brillstein's insistence, Kramer hopped another plane back to New York.

Again he waited at the big, round table in the Odeon until Belushi and his group arrived. Again the actor demanded to know who Kramer was and why he was sitting at Belushi's table. Upon reminding him, Kramer was astonished to learn that Belushi still had not read the book, but Judy Belushi had. She thought it was a film her husband should do. A hopeful Kramer returned to Los Angeles, where he soon heard from Belushi that, after finally reading the book, the actor wanted to discuss the project. Belushi called Kramer to say that he was returning to California and wanted to set a date to meet at the Chateau Marmont. On March 5, 1982, only a few days before the meeting was to take place, John Belushi was found in a room at the Marmont, dead from a drug overdose.

Belushi's death left the movie deal in limbo. The project had been fraught with problems from the beginning, and with a bankable star gone, the studio looked for an easier film to make. Kramer and others with an interest in the film were very disappointed, but only Kramer had to break the news to Thelma. She put him on the spot, saying, "I've only got a certain amount of time, and that's your clock." Helplessly, Kramer listened to her plead for him to grant her "last wish" and "make a movie of my son's book." In a letter to Kramer, Thelma wrote of her wish to get on the Johnny Carson show, where she would make her pitch to him in person.

During her last three years, Thelma never gave up on Kramer's project. Her phone calls to him continued, but became unctuous in tone, with none of the impatient rancor she had often shown. Kramer felt that perhaps Thelma was keeping herself alive to see the book succeed, to prove that she had not been mistaken when she saw in her son's eyes at his birth that quality of a genius who would make his mark on the world. It is possible that each new success of the book lessened the guilt she may have felt at being a survivor of her son's suicide. Thelma endured and held out hope. Clipped to one set of book reviews that she sent Kramer was the following note: "Dear Friend, Fantasy Sweetheart and Secret Ally: May the future loom brilliantly for the illimitable far reaching epic motion picture. Love, Thelma."

Kramer thought a movie based on *A Confederacy of Dunces* was just around the corner, but despite the great piece of literature he had to work with, he found there was more than one corner to turn and that the block was growing longer. He was not able to meet the deadline of Thelma's clock, though his clock is still running twenty years later, and he remains dedicated to fulfilling her last wish. Kramer's approach has been to persuade potential directors simply to read the book and "see the movie they want to make." But screenplays are often the best vehicle for selling ideas to directors, and a screenplay/director package is more likely to find studio financing. Kramer's search for the right screenplay—one true to Ken's work—and the right director continues.

In one of Kramer's last conversations with Thelma, she asked him, "When are you going to start shooting?" He had no idea the answer to that question would carry over into the twenty-first century, and with the same perseverance as Thelma, Kramer believes a deal that is uncompromising to Ken's work can and will be made.

The other men in Thelma's life did not get the same flattering attention that she bestowed on Kramer. Despite her poor health, she always found enough energy to start a fuss. Kent Carroll remembered that "she drove me crazy," and "when she would call, my heart would sink." Phillabaum continued to get his share of the Thelma treatment. She complained constantly that her royalties were late, despite the Press accommodating the elderly women with quarterly payments instead of the usual annual sum. Although he told her the same thing every time she called, Phillabaum sometimes attempted to spell it out for her, as in this letter of October 1980:

> The implication of your remark . . . that we are improperly or dishonestly withholding monies due you . . . is not the case. It is not an implication that I appreciate.
>
> I am sorry I did not return your telephone call the other day, but never before have you wanted a call returned and you left no such instructions. You have always preferred to call back yourself, and it was my assumption that that was what you planned to do on Wednesday. It was not "a breach of etiquette," as you claim, and I appreciate neither the accusation nor being lectured on courtesy. Our dealings with you have always been scrupulously fair and respectful, and we deserve no less from you.

Of course, the letter had none of the desired results. Once, Phillabaum was at the end of his rope listening to a harangue about late royalties. Saying, "Thelma, I'm not paid to be scolded by you," he was preparing to hang up the phone when he heard a "click." She had hung up on him, and Phillabaum had to laugh at Thelma beating him to the punch.

She retained enough energy to promote the book anywhere she was invited. Accompanied by some of her new friends from New Orleans, Thelma traveled to New York City to be on the Tom Snyder talk show, where she appeared in her trademark hat and gloves. The host was quite stunned at the sight, but Thelma was smug and sanguine during the interview. It was on that same trip that Grove Press gave a party at the Warwick Hotel ballroom. Barney Rosset remembered her performance at the piano being "a lot of fun." He also said that "Of course she was crazy, but we weren't all that sane, so she met the right people." She talked at length to him about her miseries and difficulties, but he didn't pay much attention to what she said, overwhelmed as he was by the overall picture she presented. Seeing her, Rosset formed "a better connection with the author." She brought the Gottlieb letters with her to New York and insisted Rosset and the other Grove people read them. Everyone had their own opinion of the correspondence, but Thelma was interested only in hearing negative comments about the man she called "my son's killer." She didn't hear anything close to that, but still she persisted in making anti-Semitic comments about Gottlieb to Jew and Gentile alike.

During the 1982 Carnival season, Thelma was honored by the New Orleans Contemporary Arts Center Krewe of Clones. She rode in the Clones parade and was crowned at the ball. Bunt Percy remembered a letter from Thelma requesting that Percy attend in costume to be knighted by her as the book's champion. The dignified author was "aghast at the notion," but then the Percys were from upriver, where Mardi Gras antics don't make front-page news. No feeble old lady in the Greenville, Mississippi, Delta would be caught dead wearing a crown of rhinestones and a gold-spangled ball gown, but in New Orleans even the nursing homes have Carnival courts. Bunt Percy said the newspaper picture of Thelma "dressed so foolishly" was just pitiful and "saddened us." No one native to the Crescent City felt that way, and that night was one of Thelma's happier times.

In spring 1984 the character of Ignatius Reilly was first brought to life in a musical production at LSU in Baton Rouge. The stage adaptation and the lyrics were written by Frank Galati, an actor, screenwriter, and director based at Northwestern University in Illinois. It was thought that a noncommercial production would not infringe on other stage or movie rights, and Galati had the ability to condense Toole's long, rambling story into a tight evening's entertainment. After several months of negotiation the deal was struck, but not before Thelma made her presence known.

Thelma communicated with LSU now only through her attorney, an arrangement that thoroughly pleased Phillabaum. Since the publication of the novel, Thelma had let it be known that because of her lifelong career in the dramatic arts, she was available to take part in any production, stage or film. Through John Hantel she questioned whether LSU Press had the authority to arrange for a stage production. When told that it did, Thelma further complained about being cut out of the production—a deliberate action on the part of all concerned.

Escorted by her attorney and other friends from New Orleans, Thelma came to the premiere in a limousine. Her health was poor, and she had become very frail, but as ever with Thelma, the show must go on. Before the performance she was honored by the university chancellor at a reception. It was the first and only time most people in Baton Rouge and at LSU Press encountered the author's mother.

Although she grumbled about not being given the director's position, the production staff did try to appease her by listing her first among those thanked in the program. At the play's end, Thelma proved the old spark was still there. When the house lights came up, she stood in the audience to be introduced. With a grand, sweeping gesture, she declared in ringing tones that "This is the greatest night in the history of the American theater."

As recounted by playgoer Judge Melvin Shortess, Thelma gripped her walker and began to speak of her son and his life. Recalling her appearance, Shortess said the elaborate outfit of hat, gloves, and orchid corsage was compromised by the fact that she was wearing bedroom slippers. Because she went on so long, the audience began to get restless, and not wishing to embarrass her, people began to sneak to the exits. Shortess's wife pulled on his sleeve and whispered they had better get out or they would be stuck in traffic. Shortess recalled telling her he just couldn't go yet. He said, "I felt in some way it was important" to stay for the end of her speech, and he was also too fascinated to leave. When Thelma finally finished, Shortess said there was a mad rush for the door.

Thelma's appearance at the play was her swan song. Following that evening her health was such that it was obvious she would not live out the year. She was in and out of hospitals in New Orleans until her heart failed on August 17. Her death at St. Charles General brought a quiet end to a life that had been marked by drama. She had requested to be buried in the Ducoing tomb near her beloved son. Arthur, although older, survived her by several years.

Thelma Ducoing Toole's estate was worth a quarter of a million dollars. In her will she divided this legacy and all future royalties between Tulane University and five New Orleans men she had come to trust in her final years. She left nothing to Arthur, who continued to live on his pension, alone in the cottage on Elysian Fields. That Thelma excluded Arthur from her will did not surprise Rhoda Faust. She had often witnessed Thelma "acting ugly to her brother" and making "disparaging remarks" about the man who'd had many masses said for his nephew. All this strife lies buried with them. At Greenwood Cemetery there is often evidence that someone has brought flowers to the Ducoing-Toole vault, but it is hard to tell which family member is being remembered.

In her final years Thelma Toole made many speeches in which she declared that "I walk in the world for my son," and she knew more than anyone how much Ken would have enjoyed success. In her letters to Les Phillabaum, Thelma always referred to "my son's" profits and "my son's" royalties, in an ongoing demonstration of her claim on him, as if she found it impossible to praise Ken without asserting that maternal link. Given his generous spirit, it is likely that Ken would have shared gladly the financial gains and the social triumph with his mother. And perhaps, had she not been so wounded by his death, Thelma would not have been so savage to those around her.

If his mother never got over the shock of Ken Toole's self-destruction, neither did anyone who had been close to him. The people who loved him agreed that his suicide was a great tragedy on a personal, not a literary, level. Pat Rickels told of sharing a taxi with a stranger who had been a student at Dominican. When Rickels asked if she had known Ken, the woman began to cry. She did not speak about the novel and the work that Ken left undone. Instead, many years after Ken's death, this woman tearfully recalled what a wonderful person and teacher he had been.

Over the years Rickels had become aware of Ken's battles with depression and alcoholism, but she believed that he might have overcome them if he had given himself some time. Rickels was certain that "Ken would have loved being famous and lionized" by people who admired his work. Although she saw something of Ken in Ignatius, Rickels cared more for the man than for his creation. She missed and grieved for her friend John Kennedy Toole, but at least she'd had the opportunity to know him, unlike most of the world. In recollections decades after his death Pat Rickels paid tribute to a troubled friend who could create laughter but not enough joy to keep himself alive. She said, "Ken was the best company in the world, a great mimic. Everyone was fair game, and he would play all the parts. He was such a sweetheart, the best and the brightest."

Note on Sources

The authors met some years ago in a journal writing class at Louisiana State University taught by Andrei Codrescu. It was his first semester teaching in the Deep South, and the class was a varied group of both full-time undergraduates and part-timers, including a sheriff's deputy, a bartender, and two women who wanted to write. To his credit Codrescu didn't laugh at this ambition. Because he encouraged our efforts, we signed up for his second course the following semester. We became good friends and then neighbors. Even after the course was over, we continued to critique each other's work, rejoicing when a piece was accepted for publication and commiserating when rejection arrived in the mail.

One afternoon, Deborah dropped by René's house with a short story she had written, and we discussed the importance of timing in placing a piece of writing with a publisher. Deborah knew from her producer husband that the same was true of the film industry, and she recalled how a young filmmaker had come to him with a screenplay that was both interesting and inexpensive to make. The timing of the partnership between John Hardy and Steven Soderbergh on *Sex, Lies, and Videotape* was no less than perfect. Deborah also talked of John's current project, saying that after many false starts, John Kennedy Toole's *A Confederacy of Dunces* was about to be made into a movie with Hardy producing and Soderbergh directing.

A few days later René rang Deborah's doorbell and said that she had been thinking about the idea of timing. She suggested that we seize the moment and write a book about the making of the *Confederacy* movie. As we talked it over we realized that any story about the movie would have to touch on Toole's life and the unusual circumstances surrounding the publication of the novel. Deborah contacted her friend and LSU professor Adelaide Russo to see if she knew anyone at LSU Press to whom we could make a book proposal. Russo wasted no time setting up a lunch with Catherine Fry, then marketing director at the Press. Fry was very keen on the idea, and within a week we were sitting across from Press director Les Phillabaum, pitching the book. Phillabaum was delighted about the forthcoming film, but less excited about the proposal, feeling that there was a larger story to be told. Although many articles had been written about John Kennedy Toole and at least two biographies planned by others, the story of his life had yet to be published in book form. Phillabaum suggested that the work have three parts—Toole's life, the story of the posthumous publication of *A Confederacy of Dunces,* and a third section about the film. Without hesitation (and before he had a chance to change his mind), we agreed to undertake the project, which years later has resulted in this book. Ironically, the impetus for the project—the long-anticipated film—has not yet taken its place in Toole's story, though the road it has traveled toward the big screen is a tale in itself.

Before we began our research, all we knew of John Kennedy Toole came from Walker Percy's introduction to *A Confederacy of Dunces* and a few half-remembered articles written at the time the book was released. Phillabaum agreed that it would take a great deal of digging to uncover much of a life as short and private as Toole's had been, but the Press itself was a good place to begin. Catherine Fry gave us free access to a vast store of records, including memos, correspondence, sales reports, yellowed newspaper articles and reviews, and notes from the writer's mother. From this pile we chose as a starting point Dalt Wonk's article "Odyssey Among the Dunces," which ran in the Dixie magazine section of the *New Orleans Times-Picayune* on October 25, 1981. Wonk had led Mrs. Toole through a review of her life and that of her son. Because the piece contained many names, dates, and places, we were able to construct a rough time line of Ken Toole's life. Later Deborah discovered that Jeanie Blake had interviewed Thelma for the *Times-Picayune* a year earlier than Wonk. That February 24, 1980, article contained comments by Mrs. Toole that were more candid than the rehearsed speeches she began to give later.

To fill out the details of Mrs. Toole's family background, we went to the genealogical division of the Bluebonnet Regional Library in Baton Rouge. From census records and other genealogical resources, it became clear to us that since the family tree was firmly planted in New Orleans, we needed to sketch a social history of the city beginning with its founding in 1718. Of the many books we read on the city and its cultural makeup, we found most useful John Churchill Chase's *Frenchmen, Desire, Good Children,* Elsie Martinez and Margaret Lecorgne's *Uptown/Downtown: Growing Up in New Orleans,* Earl F. Niehaus's *The Irish in New Orleans, 1800–1860,* and *Creole New Orleans,* edited by Arnold R. Hirsch and Joseph Logsdon. Deborah contacted scholar Gwendolyn Midlo Hall, who provided additional clarification of terms based on research done for her excellent book *Africans in Colonial Louisiana: The Development of Afro-Creole Culture in the Eighteenth Century.*

Some information in the book came from our own lives spent halfway between Lafayette and New Orleans. General facts about New Orleans and Louisiana come from a vast amount of library research and are not referenced. With their stories, friends like Barry Ancelet at the University of Louisiana at Lafayette and Bonny Bridges Stafford, who had grown up along Bayou St. John in downtown New Orleans, gave life to dry historical data.

Once we felt that the Toole and Ducoing families had been given proper context, we followed the time line of Ken Toole's life, making the first of many trips to the Howard-Tilton Memorial Library at Tulane

University in New Orleans. There, in the Special Collections department, are boxes of memorabilia donated by the writer's mother. In this
archive is a small photograph of Ken Toole and his primary-school
friend John Geiser. Because we were approaching Toole's life chronolog-
ically, Geiser seemed a good choice for a first interview, and happily for
us, he was listed in the phone book.

We could not have begun with a better choice. Geiser spent a morning
showing us Thelma's uptown and speaking of her life. He even allowed
Deborah to play Thelma's beloved piano, which he had purchased from
her estate and keeps as a treasured memento. Through him we met
Imelda Ruhlman, who guided us on a tour of her kindergarten classroom in the old McDonogh #14 school.

After half a century, some of Ken Toole's school friends are scattered
around the world, but many of them remain in Louisiana and the New
Orleans area. The city seems to exert quite a hold on its citizens, who
tend to rhapsodize (and justly so) about its food and joie de vivre. We
found that Ken's classmates and his mother's pupils had interesting tales
to tell and held a variety of opinions about the two. Among those sharing
anecdotes were Patricia Guizerix, John Hantel, Barbara Harris, Judy
Kemp, Jane Kingsmill, Norma Palumbo, and Karen Pickren. Tracking
down these folks led us to others, so we decided to step back and let them
tell Ken's story. Most interviews were recorded, and direct quotes come
from these audiotapes. Some persons declined to be taped, and their
direct quotes come from notes taken during the interviews.

While exploring Toole's early life we learned much about the New
Orleans public school system. Beatrice Owsley, Al Traut, and Daisie
Swanson were valuable sources of information. The library staff at Tulane, including Leon Miller and Director Bill Meneray, were gracious
and accommodating, providing needed support and resources. Ken's college years were recollected by friends like Emilie Griffin, Ruth Kathmann, David Prescott, and Sam Rosamond. Helping us to visualize
Toole's two sojourns in New York were Clayelle Dalferes, Susan Grossman, her brother Kent Taliaferro, and again Griffin and Kathmann.

While examining this part of Toole's life, we discovered that Mrs.
Toole had misremembered the order of some events in her son's life, so
we made adjustments to our time line. In the Wonk article, for example,

she placed her son in Lafayette when he was drafted, when in reality he was teaching in New York. At this same time Deborah's friend Mary Howell, a civil rights attorney, insisted we meet musician Sidney Snow, whose experiences with "Tooley" showed a different side of Ken's character.

Along the way, we discovered news articles in which the same friends told their favorite Ken stories, especially about his time in Lafayette. Robert Byrne had spoken to Dalt Wonk, Liz Scott of *New Orleans* magazine, Lisa Sylvester of the *Lafayette Daily Advertiser,* and Trent Angers of *Acadiana Profile.* Pat Rickels gave many interviews to journalists and continues to share her memories of Ken with audiences statewide.

We located some of the people whose knowledge informs our text through their relatives or from an offhand remark by a stranger. A librarian at the University of Southwestern Louisiana mentioned a graduate student in the English department there who had interviewed Robert Byrne, which was music to our ears since our attempts to contact Byrne had not been successful. We continued to track down leads and received a wealth of information about Ken's life in Lafayette through Maurice duQuesnay, Joel Fletcher, Elemore Morgan Jr., Nicholas Polites, and Pat Rickels. The librarian's offhand remark led us to Carmine Palumbo, who in 1995 had succeeded in getting the first interview Byrne had given in many years as well as the most candid and comprehensive. If we couldn't speak with Byrne ourselves, this was the next best thing. Excerpts from the interviews are quoted in this text with Dr. Palumbo's permission. For those interested in reading more of Byrne's insights, we direct you to the full interview published in *Louisiana Folklore Miscellany,* vol. 10 (1995), edited by Marcia Gaudet.

It was not as easy to find information about Toole's army days. The Tulane library had much to offer in the way of memorabilia, but we received no response to our requests for records from the Veterans Administration. The information officer at Fort Buchanan, José Pagan, undertook a search, but too much time had passed, and he found nothing that added to our understanding of the period Toole spent in Puerto Rico. Toole's own letters were invaluable in reconstructing his years there.

We did locate some of Toole's army friends like Tony Moore and

Fred Mish, who had been interviewed before but again shared their memories with us. Just before the book went to press, René found David Kubach on the Wisconsin Arts Board web site. With Mrs. Kubach's help, René tracked him down in Brule, Wis., where he had gone steelhead fishing. As one of the last non-cellular men in America, he was hard to get in touch with. It took some planning, but after two days of aborted attempts, his interview was conducted using the phone at a Brule gas station when it was found that the pay phone at the quick-stop market wouldn't take incoming calls.

The few years following Toole's release from the army were the most difficult to chronicle. René's first interview in Baton Rouge was with Charlene Stovall, whose impressions of Toole as a teacher remain crisp and were valuable in gaining a perception of his talent in front of a classroom. As a counterpoint, it was interesting to get Dr. Donald Pizer's view of Toole the student.

Events surrounding the publication of *A Confederacy of Dunces* gave rise to all sorts of speculation and misinformation, some provided by Mrs. Toole, who wanted to tell the story her way. One summer we met in New York City, where we had an opportunity to meet or speak with people involved in the consideration of Ken's manuscript by Simon and Schuster. A friend of the Hardys, artistic agent Deborah Mathews, put us in touch with Robert Gottlieb. We also located Jean Jollett Marks. Conversations with them and with Candida Donadio provided an important look behind the scenes.

In New Orleans, Dr. Gorman remembered facts about Toole's health that gave clues to his mental state. Finding Dave Kubach was fortunate because he witnessed Toole's emotional decline during his last years. An acquaintance of René's mentioned a man who said he had known Ken during this time and volunteered to introduce her to Chuck Layton, who was sincere and candid in his taped interview. During the years that this book was taking shape, other men were mentioned as possibly having been intimate with Toole. In making inquiries about three of these men, we found that one had died, the second denied knowing him, and another never responded to our request for an interview.

It took over two years to do the groundwork for this biography, and our research continued even as the book was being typeset. Occasionally we met with dead ends and stone walls. Most people openly related their thoughts about Ken Toole, and our thanks to them are heartfelt. Before the internet made locating individuals easier, we spent hours calling wrong numbers and driving to empty houses.

After calling various state agencies, we located Ralph Diaz and met him at a Burger King in Gulfport, Mississippi. He gave up his day off from work to take us around the county and recount crucial details of Ken's death. Fr. Peterson directed us to a retired priest's home where Fr. Hauth lived. Just weeks after this, we were shocked and saddened by the news that Fr. Peterson had been murdered near the church of St. Peter and Paul.

We spoke to many who had never met John Kennedy Toole but were acquainted with his mother. Gene Winick, Kent Carroll, Herman Graf, Barney Rosset, Rhoda Faust, Catherine Fry, Les Phillabaum, and Marna and Melvin Shortess told stories about the redoubtable Thelma. One of the most charming people we spoke with was Mrs. Walker Percy, who had tea with us in a café near her daughter's book shop in Covington. She has been a supporter of this endeavor and added much to the story. Marcus Smith and Garic Barranger, who knew the Percys and Mrs. Toole, were a great help. In Los Angeles, Scott Kramer took time out during production of *The Limey* to offer letters and impart information about his relationship with Thelma. His respect for her has not wavered. Others who offered information or advice were Shelby McKenzie, Ronnie Brink, George Deaux, Myrna Deaux, Mary Lou Kelly, and Owen Scott.

Many people we talked with told similar stories and could not say if they had heard or had read what they were telling us. For this reason it is impossible to track down the origins of all the anecdotes and information in order to give credit where credit is due. When we knew a story had come from a particular source, we gave it proper attribution. Throughout the book real names are used, with the exception of two men we were unable to locate and whose identities have no bearing on the narrative. In order to preserve the privacy of those individuals, we refer to them by pseudonyms.

Some stories we heard corroborated others, with the threads of information tangled among them. We did not attribute these overlapping stories to the people who told them, because after two decades of repetition, we consider them general knowledge. If anyone interviewed or consulted in the course of our research feels they have not been given due acknowledgment, we do apologize.

Letters included in this book have been edited for spelling or grammar and in some instances condensed for the sake of brevity or to avoid repetition. An exception to this is the correspondence between Robert Gottlieb and John Kennedy Toole. Those letters are transcribed complete and unaltered.

In the final analysis a biography is only the author's reconstruction of a life. No biography can be perfectly accurate because memory is not videotape. Human beings remember the same things differently, and recollections of events often change over the years. It must be noted as well that interpretation of those same happenings may vary from person to person, author to author. The conclusions we have drawn may not be shared by everyone who reads this book, and we encourage readers to make their own determinations concerning Toole's life. It is our hope that in the years to come more of Toole's story will come to light and other books will be published that plumb the mysteries of his life and his death. For our part, we went from not knowing much about John Kennedy Toole to knowing regret at never having made his acquaintance. By the time this book was finished we loved him, admired his genius, and grieved over his death. Although we can do nothing to change that sad finale, we feel that we owe his memory as much of the truth as we can find and invite the reader to close these pages with affection for John Kennedy Toole, child prodigy, son, novelist, and friend.